# PRACTICING
# WHOLENESS

. . . . . . . . . . .

# MURRAY STEIN

# PRACTICING WHOLENESS

## ANALYTICAL PSYCHOLOGY AND JUNGIAN THOUGHT

*A Chiron Publication*

CONTINUUM • NEW YORK

1996

The Continuum Publishing Company
370 Lexington Avenue
New York, NY 10017

Printed in the United States of America

*Library of Congress Cataloging-in-Publication Data*

Stein, Murray, 1943–
  Practicing wholeness : analytical psychology and Jungian thought /
Murray Stein.
    p.    cm.
  "A Chiron publication."
  Includes bibliographical references and index.
  ISBN 0-8264-0905-9 (hardcover : alk. paper)
  1. Whole and parts (Psychology)  2.  Jungian psychology.
  3. Psychoanalysis.  4. Jung, C. G. (Carl Gustav), 1875–1961.
  5. Psychoanalytic counseling.  I. Title.
  BF175.S662  1996
  150.19′54—dc20                                          96-1870
                                                          CIP

Acknowledgments will be found on page 224,
which constitutes an extension of this page.

*For my students and patients,*
*who have also been my teachers*

[T]he underlying idea of the psyche proves it to be a half bodily, half spiritual substance, an *anima media natura*, as the alchemists call it, an hermaphroditic being capable of uniting the opposites, but who is never complete in the individual unless related to another individual. The unrelated human being lacks wholeness, for he can achieve wholeness only through the soul, and the soul cannot exist without its other side, which is always found in a "You." Wholeness is a combination of I and You, and these show themselves to be parts of a transcendent unity whose nature can only be grasped symbolically. . . .

C. G. Jung, *Collected Works* 16, par. 454

# Contents

# Introduction

Wholeness is a difficult concept to work with in any field, and psychology and its practical application in psychotherapy are no exception. As a concept it extends to all-inclusiveness and therefore threatens to scatter its force in vagueness and the nebulous wonders of cosmic speculation. As I use it in this book I have in mind the general human urge to want to fulfill all potentials given by our organism, by our times and the society we live in, and by our imagination. Wholeness is what we desire most deeply even if we do not know what it is we are striving after and cannot put a name to it.

If wholeness is the goal of our deepest human desire, it is also something that encompasses our entire lifetime and all our efforts at self-expression. It is not something we achieve once and for all. It is not static, a state of being that can be arrived at. To use the metaphor of art making, we can say that living well is an art but it is an art that is never perfected or completed. The painting that we create by living is a work always in progress, and even death is not necessarily the final brush stroke to the canvas. How we live and how we die are certainly the keys to our individual styles. One person paints an austere picture in shades of white, black, brown, and gray. Another paints in exuberant splashes of primary color. Abstract or representational, impressionistic or surreal, classic or romantic, each style is a way to embrace wholeness and to reveal its extensions. There are many paths to wholeness, many ways to express it concretely in life, and many modes of exploring and revealing its endless possibilities.

To *practice* wholeness is to engage in this endeavor intentionally. Like practicing the piano, it is a daily activity. One practices to deepen the art, to increase the range of expression, to discover nuance. Wholeness is no more achieved than piano artistry is finally attained. It is won anew every day. Perhaps one day builds on another and the present is the result of the past, and yet as any concert performer will confess, each day is a brand new struggle to attain the pleasures of fluency and the delicate fingering required by genuine artistry. No day may pass without conscious, deliberate effort. Put aside the cliché that practice makes perfect. It does not. Practice overcomes resistance for the moment, but that resistance reappears and must be conquered afresh. Perfection is out of the question.

To practice wholeness in the psychological sense is to practice living on several levels at the same time. There can be no wholeness without the practical and concrete expression of a life lived in reality, in society, in the time frame of chronological life possibilities. There is a time to have children, for instance, and if this is ignored one cannot make up for it with imaginary children. Not that every life lived toward wholeness must include having children—but if children are to be a part of it they must appear at a particular time, concretely and actually. There is a time to make a career, and again if this time is missed a price is exacted. So, life lived concretely and practically in an everyday sense is one dimension of practicing wholeness. Another dimension is the symbolic. Imagination and dreams belong to one's wholeness, and practicing wholeness includes holding consciousness of them as they appear in life. These factors often add a sense of meaning and psychic depth to periods of life that otherwise would be two-dimensional. They also lure us forward into a future of possibility. There is also the dimension of emotion and feeling, which adds color and music to wholeness. There is the dimension of intellect and understanding, which clarifies who and what we are and perhaps suggests what is going on. Differentiation and discrimination are essential products of practicing wholeness. Moving in and through these several dimensions and linking them to one another is what practicing wholeness is all about.

Finally, practicing wholeness is active. This does not exclude reflection. The verb "to reflect" indicates that this is also an activity. Reflecting upon events and the recent and far past is as important a factor in practicing wholeness as is creating new futures, new plans, new objects. The accent, however, is on the dynamic element. Wholeness is not a thing, a substance, a state of being to be achieved or held on to or enjoyed; it is in fact nothing in and of itself. It is a concept that keeps us moving along a spiral of consciousness. We practice wholeness by staying close to our true selves, by using our energy to act in the world with integrity. Only in the final analysis can one say what the pattern woven into the tapestry of an individual life has been. In retrospect, looking back over one's youth and middle years and late years from the vantage point of old age, one might be lucky enough to glimpse the overall pattern and perceive the meaning of the whole. Along the way one also has moments of insight, glimpses of the whole as it is unfolding. But one is never absolutely sure, for the ultimate

pattern and its meaning are a mystery, perhaps known onl
At best we interpret and study the details for a hint. And in t
time we go on practicing, daily, faithfully.

A brief word about how this book came into being. My othe
have been conceived of and written as single whole works. Tnis one
arrived in pieces. After some fifteen years of writing lectures, chapters
for anthologies, and professional papers I realized that I had been cir-
cling around a single theme, which I have now named "practicing
wholeness." To put these pieces together and make a single volume
of them, I had to add some transitional material and to arrange the
parts in a sequence that I hope shows a coherent flow from beginning
through middle to end. The coherency that is there is due more to an
unconscious ground plan that extended over these years rather than
to a conscious decision made by the author at the outset. It seems to
me that this is especially fitting given the theme of this work, for as
I conceive of it practicing wholeness is similarly a matter of working
on pieces of the whole as they present themselves in life.

In the first part of the book I set out the general concept of wholeness and attempt to detail what it is made up of by using Jung's theory
of instincts and archetypes. As Jung conceptualized the psyche, it is
formed out of the union of body and spirit, instinct and archetype. He
listed five instincts and an indefinite number of archetypes. The object, from the point of wholeness, is to unite instinct and archetype
in a field of activity that is not severely restricted by the pathological
structures incurred in one's personal life history. In this part of the
book, too, I point out some methods for increasing the range and effectiveness of practicing wholeness and extend the discussion into one
of the most common and mundane areas of life, the workplace.

In the second part of the book, which makes up the majority of its
pages, my focus is the clinical practice of psychotherapy. Here I set
out a general philosophical statement about the practice of analytical
psychotherapy by examining the relation of psychotherapeutic treatment to human nature. From there I move on to several aspects of
treatment as these confront the practicing therapist and the practiced-
upon patient: the reconstruction of personal history and its meaning,
the nature of the relationship between therapist and patient and the
role this plays in the healing process, and some psychopathological
problems that stand in the way of practicing wholeness. Certainly I
cannot claim that this section is exhaustive of the kinds of things that
happen in the course of long-term psychotherapy, which in Jungian
circles we call analysis, but I do believe it is representative. Throughout all of these chapters, the central concern is the practice of wholeness as this takes place within the context of psychotherapy.

It should be clear to the reader from even this brief introduction that I regard the practice of wholeness as an essentially nonclinical activity. By no stretch of the imagination can it be considered as a unique product of the therapeutic industry. It is a human activity that reaches across cultures and across historical eras to include human beings, women and men, adults and children, throughout human history who have seriously struggled to understand themselves and to extend the scope of their consciousness and self-actualization. Practicing wholeness is what the more adventuresome and expansive, and/or intensive among the general human population have done in all times and all places. This book is a witness to that universal human phenomenon and an attempt to give it greater definition and precision as well as to promote its usefulness in all areas of the contemporary world.

*Wilmette, September 1995*

. . . . . . . . . . .

# PART 1

# Psychological Wholeness In Theory and Practice

· · · · · · · · · · · · · · · · · · ·

# The Dream of Wholenes.

anning through the gravel-like assortment of texts, ideas, images, stories, and doctrines that make up the world's religious and folk traditions, one can quickly and without much effort identify many golden nuggets that speak of the archetypal human dream of wholeness. There is, for example, Plato's famous myth, which depicts human beings as originally round and whole. Later they became divided into halves and consequently spend their lives searching for their other severed, lost part. This accounts for the mating urge in all its varieties, hetero- and homosexual. Our longing for the "other," for the soul mate, is, according to Plato, identical to our longing for our own lost original wholeness. We want to put ourselves back together again. So the sexual drive aims for wholeness, for restoration of what was once one unified and complete human being.

There are many other symbols and images that likewise depict and reach for wholeness. Ezekiel's vision of four living creatures, each with four faces and represented by a wheel within a wheel (Ezekiel 1); the Chinese Taoist symbol of Yin-Yang bound in a circle; the Gnostic images of Adam as Anthropos and of God as Mother-Father; Leonardo's drawing of the naked human being outstretched within a circle; the Tibetan mandalas; Nietzsche's poetic rendition of Zarathustra's return and his new doctrine of the "higher person"—these are but a tiny sample of the important nuggets of gold to be found in even a cursory survey of the materials available.

In our century the most powerful statement concerning the issue of human wholeness has been made, I believe, by Carl Jung. Not only was his vision of human wholeness the most central experience of his inner work, as he reveals it throughout his autobiographical *Memories, Dreams, Reflections*, but Jung's entire psychological theory is founded on the presupposition of the human potential for wholeness and is an elaboration and detailed explication of that primary datum. His theoretical model of the Self, as presented in his late work *Aion*, is an

historical and cultural, as well as psychological, detailing of
.ept of wholeness. His notion of individuation, which guides
.n psychological and spiritual development, is oriented by the
.upposition that its aim is wholeness. His theory of psychic parts—
.he archetypal figures, such as the shadow, the persona, the anima and
animus, as well as the personal complexes—depends implicitly on the
notion that they are parts of a whole, the Self, which coordinates and
contains them. Jung's central guiding myth is the myth of wholeness.

Looking now at our Western religious traditions, the Biblical traditions, which include the three religions, Judaism, Christianity, and
Islam, we can immediately see a significant departure from the ground
plan of wholeness in them. All of them emphasize one aspect or another of wholeness at the expense of the others. If wholeness is inclu-
sive, they are exclusive; if wholeness requires a balance among the
various typical polarities such as masculine-feminine and good-evil,
the Biblical traditions are one-sided. The Biblical God image is defined
as purely masculine and paternal. He is a Father God. And He is a
jealous God: "Thou shalt have no other gods before me" (Exodus 20:3)
is not only *one* of the Ten Commandments, but the first one. And
it means, in reality, that there are to be no other gods, period. This
commandment requires the absolute, exclusive claim of one particular
god image upon one particular group of people. Their covenant with
Him is a quasi-legal contract of mutual obligation, and the chief requirement on the human side is faithfulness to this one, sole Diety
and to His will. There will be little tolerance among this people and
its descendants, among which all of us who have grown up in the
Biblical cultural and religious traditions are included, for any other
possibilities that wholeness might allow or even demand.

Chief among those features of wholeness suppressed by and within
this tradition was the Great Goddess in all her forms. This act of
suppression is stated symbolically in the story of the Fall of Adam and
Eve, where Eve's affinity for the serpent (an animal representative of
the Goddess) leads her to pay attention to her feminine instinct and
to lead Adam astray. This is decisively punished by God. He places
enmity between Eve and the serpent, thereby erecting a psychological
barrier between woman and her own unconscious depths and blocking
her connection to the Self, as represented by the images of the Goddess.
This also protects Adam, of course, from the power of the Goddess.
This is further cemented by driving Adam and Eve out of the Garden
of Eden, which is an image of the Great Mother as container. The Fall
from Paradise has often been given a positive interpretation, being
seen as a necessary early separation of the individuating ego from
its state of fusion with the mother. This makes ego autonomy and

independence possible. Only in recent times has the ultimate outcome of this development begun to be seriously questioned by many therapists and cultural commentators. Perhaps *this kind* of separation/individuation does not lead to the best results, if the end product turns out to be a heavily defended ego that has difficulty with the modes of interdependence and cooperation because of an excessive and one-sided emphasis on individualism and egocentrism.

With its strong bias toward patriarchal culture and its exclusive worship of a male Father God, the Biblical tradition produced a particular type of conscious human attitude. It is an attitude that tends toward rigid perfectionism at the cost of compassion and toward one-sided valuation of the abstract and "spiritual" at the expense of the physical and material. It denigrates the material world as "nothing but" material, and it seeks to dominate the natural world and other "natural" peoples instead of cooperating and communicating with and understanding them. It assumes a superior and exclusionist attitude toward other religions, whose Gods are generally taken to be mere figments of the untutored pagan imagination. It denies the value of feminine elements in both men and women and tends to place women in second-class positions of power and leadership. The doctrine of "no other gods" has split the wholeness of the human psyche, and while it has stimulated the growth and development of masculine ego development it has undermined the human urge toward wholeness.

This is itself of course a one-sided and highly selective interpretation of the Biblical traditions and their psychological implications. It lifts up certain salient features, which I believe to be the most significant highlights in those traditions, but it neglects to mention many other features that would contradict it. These other features can modify the view just put forward in significant ways, but they do not erase it or cancel its primacy. On the contrary, they confirm it. For the point to be made is that the one-sided favoritism given to the Father God, Yahweh, at the expense of the "Others," was subtly undermined and subverted in the Bible itself. These other elements, while played down in favor of the patriarchal Yahweh and His strenuous adherents, left traces in the Bible itself as they began to return in various forms and figures and themes in the course of the centuries during which these traditions were consolidated in written form. There is, for example, the figure of Sophia in the Hebrew Wisdom literature, who, according to Jung, represents Yahweh's forgotten and repressed feminine side, His wisdom and compassion. There are also the great Prophets who preach the value of servanthood and emphasize compassion as well as justice. At times they bargain with Jahweh in favor of a wayward and obstinate people. Later, in the Christian Scriptures, the figure of Jesus presents a less one-sidedly patriarchal, masculine image of God: there are women in his circle; he has some distinctly feminine qualities ("suffer the little children to come unto me"); and the hallmark of his ministry is compassion ("forgive them for they know not what they do") rather than strenuous righteousness. In fact, the emphasis on love in the New Testament, and on God as Love, leads strongly in the direction of recovering the wholeness that was lost earlier in the militant phase of development when the Promised Land was conquered under the leadership of a savage warrior God and the enemies were obliterated under the force of His mighty hand, without mercy. Later in the development of the Biblical tradition, the formulation of the Christian doctrine of the Trinity and the appearance of mystical elements in Judaism took this movement of recovery of original wholeness yet a step further, recognizing in the Godhead elements that would be identified as feminine (in Christianity it is the Holy Spirit, in Judaism the Shekinah). According to St. Augustine, this feature is the bond of love that joins God the Father and God the Son and binds the Divine to the Human.

These elements, then—Sophia, the Prophetic voices, Jesus, the Holy Spirit, the Shekinah—modify the one-sidedness of a purely masculine Father God, Yahweh, and also serve to complement, possibly also to undermine and subvert, the purely patriarchal values espoused by the older and classical Biblical tradition. This movement was carried perhaps to its furthest point in the Catholic tradition in the devotion to female saints and to the Virgin, all of whom in effect become "other Gods" (or Goddesses rather) in a surreptitious manner. And yet all of these only represent adjustments and modifications of the fundamental masculine archetypal pattern that governs the Biblical traditions; they do not carry the change all the way to transformation.

There have been attempts to transform the tradition radically and to recover original wholeness much more completely and fundamentally, but these were eventually rejected as heresy. One of these was Gnosticism. The Biblical Gnostics, so called because of their reliance on esoteric teaching and belief in private revelation that led to direct *knowledge* of God (*gnosis*), radically relativized the figure of Yahweh, the Creator God. Over against Him they placed the Pleroma, the ultimate source of all being, of which Yahweh was but one, and not the greatest, emanation. Him they named Yaldabaoth. The Gnostic critique of Yahweh and of the Biblical version of creation and history radically upended the Biblical account and cast it into the position of at best a partial truth. The truth of the matter, the Gnostics would say, is that Yahweh is only one small piece of the Whole. There are many other equally important or more important figures. To begin with, Yahweh has a mother, Sophia. There are others as well. And all of these transcendent beings have their source and are anchored in the primordial Pleroma, which is the origin of all the Gods and Goddesses. When the Gnostics prayed to this Primordial Ground of Being, they would speak to a Mother-Father, the Ultimate Deity, a figure who contains the opposites and represents total wholeness rather than only one piece of it.

What was emerging in the theology and experienced revelations of the Gnostics was an image of God that recovered original wholeness more completely than had been expressed in the Biblical tradition. But from an historical, rather than a psychological and spiritual, point of view, the Gnostic vision of God was premature. So it was suppressed and violently denigrated for some seventeen or eighteen centuries, until its rediscovery and recovery in our own time. Gnosis was a powerful intuitive spiritual impulse that emerged among a small group of religious geniuses and visionaries, but it reached ahead too far for its times and so was lost to history until the twentieth century. Perhaps we are in a position to integrate its methods and vision today.

Even in his early work on psychology and religion, Jung recognized the importance of the Gnostics. Already in early works such as the ground-breaking study, *The Psychology of the Unconscious* (published originally in German in 1912/13), Jung makes references to Gnostic writings. Available at that time mostly only in the writings of the Church Fathers, he read them for their insights into the workings of the psyche. Throughout his later career, Jung continued to read the Gnostic writers and to feel the deepest affinity for them. He traced his own depth psychology back through the alchemists to the more ancient sources of intuitive knowledge in the Gnostic writings. In fact, so identified with the spirit of Gnosis was Jung that he composed a sort of Gnostic text—"The Seven Sermons to the Dead" (1916)—in the voice of a famous Gnostic from Alexandria, Basilides. Modern depth psychology, Jung would argue, has its roots back in the Gnostic visions and speculations of the early centuries of the Christian era. When Jung was accused of being a modern Gnostic by Martin Buber, he attempted to deny the charge by claiming to be an empirical scientist, but in other contexts he would have been proud to accept this designation.

It is regrettable that Jung died before the magnificent treasure trove of Gnostic texts discovered in 1946 at Nag Hammadi in Egypt had been edited and translated into modern languages. One of the most famous and significant of these codices was actually named for Jung— the Jung Codex—and was given to the Jung Institute in Zurich, which returned it to its proper home in Egypt in the mid-1950s. But Jung had long since prepared the intellectual and spiritual ground for the recovery and positive appreciation of the message of these Gnostic texts. His numerous writings on alchemy, on the heresies of the Christian tradition, on the Biblical tradition and its one-sided patriarchal attitude, and his studies of symbols and archetypal images from historical materials and modern dreams had all added up to a solid foundation upon which an edifice of understanding of these strange ancient texts could be constructed. It is this understanding that is so valuable and essential for our times if we are to advance the cause of recovering psychological wholeness in our day and for the future.

The accidental discovery of these texts at Nag Hammadi in 1946 by a group of Egyptian shepherds was synchronistic. Coming at moment in Western religious history when they could be received without prejudice and when those who study them can so greatly benefit from the recovery of this ancient intuitive wisdom, this find makes it possible for us to see exactly how the Biblical traditions can be further developed and transformed.

We stand at a moment in Western spiritual history when the Mother-Father God image has a chance of becoming integrated into the heart of our spiritual traditions, into the doctrines of God. The Judeo-Christian visions of God are now going through deep internal change. This is a transformation process that has its roots within the collective unconscious of the Western spiritual attitude and that is surfacing now in many areas. It shows its effects in the dreams of individuals and in their spiritual malaise and groping, in theological developments such as feminist theology, in doctrinal developments like the promulgation of the dogma of the Assumption of the Virgin, and in practical theology that has paved the way for the widespread ordination of women and gay men and women into the clergy. It can be seen too in the general restlessness of a pluralistic culture that will not be contained within the narrow limits of a one-sided image of God anymore and in the uncompromising demand for individual spiritual freedom to explore and to experience the mystery of God for oneself. The strictly patriarchal vision of God is dead. What is emerging is a concept of wholeness, perhaps personified as a Man-Woman Deity, a unified Pair, which promises the recovery of the ancient, primordial, archetypal dream of wholeness.

It can be argued with great persuasive power that we live in a post-mythological age and that in this age "God is dead," as Nietzsche proclaimed at the turn of the last century. The myth of a God "out there" in space somewhere, of a personified parent figure who cares for us and looks after us as His children and sometimes punishes us for our bad ways, is an image that may give comfort to some but is hard to reconcile with our other cognitive maps. Such images, we now know or believe we know, are the by-products of archetypal structures that govern the psyche. They are projections of these psychic structures into the heavens. That is to say: they are fantasies. We now read these images for their psychological meanings—what do they tell us about the state of the psyche of the person who is doing the thinking or imagining or believing?—and not for their potential ontological truths. The Gods are not things; they are images, thoughts, fantasies. Visions no longer give us information about the "beyond" out there but about the psyche in here.

While images and visions are only psychological, however, they also do create personal meaning, orientation, and interpretive frameworks. They become the metaphors we live by. Images eventually become concepts and lead to reflection and to abstract notions that we use to educate, to condition, and to create social policy and physical reality. As Jung so often pointed out, every human artifact began with an image, with a fantasy. So images have great power and effect, and we must not underrate them just because we assume something about their origins. And besides that, we may not know as much as we sometimes think we do about the source of archetypal images, for, as Jung also cautioned more than once, we do not know much about what lies beyond the psyche and conditions it. "Out there," the structures of reality may reveal themselves to us by similarly structuring our psyches archetypally and transforming our fundamental attitudes. We may all be evolving, psychologically, spiritually, historically according to a transpersonal pattern of development.

One question today is, what does it mean for us in the Western religious Biblical traditions that the image of God is changing from a patriarchal one of God the Father, and even from the modified patriarchal one of God the Father, Son, and Holy Spirit, to one that could be named God the Mother-Father, or God the Quaternity? Both of these— God the Mother-Father, and God the Quaternity (Four in One)—advance the recovery of the primordial dream of wholeness, but they do so with different nuances and emphases. And these are important.

The movement toward the perception of God as Mother-Father leads the way to the recovery of the maternal, feminine elements within the Pleromatic Wholeness that is God, elements that were dramatically displayed and fully articulated in the Great Goddess religions and mythologies of antiquity. This movement reaches back to the Garden of Eden where it all began, mythologically speaking, and recovers Eve and the Serpent, who represents the chthonic energy of the Goddess and Her worship. Now the Serpent will again have a place in the home, as it had in antiquity, and the painful enmity between spirit and matter, mind and body, heaven and earth, man and woman may be healed and overcome. This is the movement of holistic health and of proper concern for the natural environment in our time. The watchwords here are Balance and Harmony. This complex of values, whose icon is God the Mother-Father, must be and will be integrated into the core of the religious life and thought of the Biblical traditions. What it promises is healing the split between spirit and matter that has been so endemic and central in Western spiritual traditions and religions. This is truly transformative. Perhaps it is revolutionary. Certainly the fires that burn in the energy sources of this drive toward transformation are hot and occasionally erupt into volcanic proportions. This change in the perception of God's singularity of gender is perhaps the hottest spot in the entire spiritual landscape today, and its implications are multitudinous and still quite unmapped. Much work, practical and theoretical, needs to be done in this area. Studies, books, discussions, experiments of all kinds are necessary and are under way. More will come.

The other great theme in the transformation process now at work in Western religions is more subtle, less well-known, but certainly as far-reaching. It is the movement toward conceiving of God as Four rather Three (in One). The development of the God image from One to Three was an important differentiation within the archetype, but it did not reach beyond the patriarchal archetype very far or in very great depth. It produced a psychological trend within consciousness of great energy and dynamism. Three is a number of masculine dynamism unfolding and expanding, and it was this energy that converted the minor sect (Christianity) of a minor Near Eastern religion (Judaism) into a global force. Christianity enlisted politics, economics, and military force and harnessed them all to its ends of converting the entire world. It produced an energetic and restless religion, not a peaceful one, and the latter day representatives of this tradition—the explorers, the inventors, the empire builders—exemplify this kind of expansive energy.

The movement from Three to Four transforms this restless expansiveness into quiet emptiness, and repose, features that are more characteristic of Eastern, Oriental religions. While Three is a number of dynamic change, Four is a number of stability and peace. The movement of change in the God image from Three to Four, from Trinity to Quaternity, is represented today by the widespread integration taking place in Western religions of Eastern spirituality and its methods of meditation and contemplation. These have not been absent in the Biblical traditions, but they have been recessive and relatively underdeveloped. Now they are becoming more prominent and will continue to grow in power and centrality. The centrality of the Quest image will give way to images of the Quiet Center, the Place of Peace, the Self in Repose. Centeredness and repose are the watchwords of this movement.

So, Balance and Harmony from the one side of this massive transformative process; Centeredness and Repose from the other. God the Mother-Father and God the Four in One. Both of these trends are the hallmarks of the postmodern search for wholeness. The ancient dream of wholeness is alive and well and in our time is taking these forms. It is a powerful and indeed irresistible historical movement, and we would do well to understand it and to become aware of its implications. It should be taken up most particularly into the center of our Western religious theologies and traditions of spiritual practice and be allowed to transform them. This will give them new life and relevance for the coming centuries, and it will also provide our evolving culture with some measure of continuity with its own historical heritage. But it will also demand great change in orientation in the religious traditions. The Age of Conquest and Evangelization is over; the Age of Depth and Wholeness is just beginning. After the age of Jahweh and Yahweh-Sophia, and after the Age of the Father-Son-and-Holy-Spirit, we will have the Age of the Centered, Whole Human Being.

Let me conclude with an image for this new era. It comes from a dream of an ordinary man. He dreamed that he entered an empty room. The boundaries of the room were not visible, although this was a contained space. On the floor of the empty room sat an adult figure whose gender was indeterminate but a bit more feminine than masculine. This figure sat in the empty room in the lotus position. It was a Western person, and her/his gaze was fixed on the distance just over the dreamer's shoulder. End of dream.

This is a dream for the future, a dream for the new age we are entering. It presents an image of Balance and Repose, of human Harmony and Centeredness. This image is the successor of the Biblical tradition and its images of a mighty Father in the Heavens and His son hanging in agony upon a cross. It is an icon for our present and foreseeable future. Behold the image.

### REFERENCES

Jung, C. G. 1961. *Memories, Dreams, Reflections.* New York: Random House.
———. 1991. *The Psychology of the Unconscious.* Princeton: Princeton University Press.

# *t w o*

. . . . . . . . . . . . . . . . . . . . . . . . . . . .

# Practicing Wholeness
# with Dreams and Imagination

It is not particularly novel or especially modern to try to understand oneself and one's purpose in life by consulting dreams, myths, and images. In fact, this is probably one of the most ancient ways to seek self-understanding. To listen to dreams or to consult an oracle, to orient oneself in life by means of religious belief and story, to go on a vision quest—all of these are familiar to us from our study of history and anthropology. The ancient Delphic "Know Thyself" meant that as human beings we should learn to know our place in the larger scheme of things: We are not gods, we are mere mortals. This also meant that in order to get the true measure of oneself, one needed to know about the gods, the immortals. Understanding yourself as a human depended on knowing yourself in relation to myth.

In contemporary times, however, the search for self-understanding and meaning has generally been conducted in a more personal and individualistic way. By introspecting and reflecting on one's own particular history and relationships, modern people have tried to fashion a sense of meaning. This has often ended in failure because there has been no point of reference outside of the ego. Existentialism came to the inescapable conclusion that meaning, if it is to exist in any fashion, must be more or less arbitrary and created by the individual. In our time, self-understanding has been pursued predominantly without reference to dream or myth. As Nietzsche declared over a hundred years ago, "God is dead." Yet unborn at Nietzsche's time was the notion that the unconscious could provide a resource.

Another modern strategy for seeking self-understanding has followed the path of scientific method. If we do some studies and find out what human beings are like "objectively," then we can craft some kind of self-understanding out of that. So sociological studies and surveys, as well as genetic and neurological studies may provide some generalizations that, with caution, we can apply to ourselves and come up with some partial understandings of how we operate. We become objects of study to ourselves and treat ourselves like scientific problems to investigate and solve. In this scientific paradigm, self-understanding is controlled by studies and evidence.

Modern psychology has provided some additional tools for approaching the question of self-understanding in a so-called objective way. We can learn about psychodynamics and psychopathology and personality structure, and then by applying this theoretical material we can hope to figure out what is going on in ourselves. What is my DSM diagnosis? What does the MMPI show? Am I projecting? If so, which complex, which archetype? Am I in a state of transference? If so, which type? Do I suffer from the father complex, or is it from the patriarchy? Am I an INTJ or an ESFP? To the uninitiated these questions may sound arcane if not absurd, but to those in the inner circle of psychological language games, these questions are familiar. It is not at all uncommon these days for someone to come into therapy and offer a quite complete self-analysis in the first sessions. What is left to do in therapy?

There is another way to approach the question of self-understanding and meaning, however, and still remain a modern person. This other way, which approaches self-understanding through dreams and active imagination, picks up on the ancient and traditional way of consulting dreams and mythic stories, but it does so with the difference that dreams and myths are not interpreted as traditional people usually do. Nor are they viewed as fascinating curiosities and amusing pastimes suitable for breakfast conversation or parlor games, as most moderns have looked on them. Rather this method uses dreams and a mythic imagination to create the psychological portrait of a specific life and a current situation by using the theoretical understandings of modern depth psychology. This method takes the dream, the myth, and the image as psychological data from which to fashion meaning.

Here is an example. A woman's mother-in-law is dying in the hospital. On her deathbed, she can no longer speak clearly, but her eyes indicate some consciousness of what is happening. During the night after a visit, the daughter-in-law dreams that she is in a room and faces a large empty cage. The animals that had been in the cage are fighting on the floor in the darkness at her feet. To one side she sees a large white peacock sitting on a telephone. The peacock is facing away from her, toward an open window that looks out to the mountains. The dreamer simply observes this scene for some time, and when she awakes she knows that the dream refers to her mother-in-law's condition.

What does the dream tell her? The mother-in-law's body is struggling for a few more moments of life (the animals fighting on the
floor), but her soul, a beautiful and serene white peacock, is waiting
to take flight. The cage is empty, and release is at hand.

To understand this dream in this way does not reflect a relapse to
premodern attitudes and a naive belief in gods and miracles or in messages from God in our dreams. When we find such impressive symbolic images in dreams and use them as important reference points
for reflecting upon life's meaning, we may speak of the "god(s) within"
but continue to understand that dreams issue from the unconscious.
They give us important information and offer viewpoints that consciousness needs. In other words, dreams and myths are messages from
the psyche rather than messages from God. The psyche gives us food
for thought and for reflection in the form of dream and image, and out
of these we make meaning.

And yet. . . . A hesitation. We may, if we're careful, also hear in
some dream images and mythic symbols occasional "signals of transcendence," and in these signals discern something that, even given
our lingering modern attitudes and spiritual inhibitions, approaches a
personal revelation of a transcendent spirit. About this, of which I will
speak quite often in the following chapters, caution is appropriate but
not fear.

## Jung's Ur-Experience

I turn now to Jung's autobiography, *Memories, Dreams, Reflections,*
as a point of reference for this reflection on the theme of practicing
wholeness with dreams and imagination. In doing this, however, I am
not proposing to use Jung's autobiographical account as a kind of modern gospel, the stories and patterns of which become idolized as
models to imitate. I turn to this account as a case study of what it
means to understand oneself through using dreams and imagination.
It is an example of what I am trying to describe in this chapter. First
I will recount Jung's Ur-Experience (Ur-meaning original, basic, formative) that is recorded in *Memories, Dreams, Reflections,* and then I
will go on to draw some conclusions from it and try to show how one
can make use of Jung's methods.

The background for Jung's Ur-Experience lies in the years before
1913 and the outbreak of World War I in Europe. In 1913, Jung turned
thirty eight years old. Since the age of twenty five he had lived and
practiced psychiatry in Zurich, first at the Burgholzli Klinik under
Eugen Bleuler and then in his own private practice. He was on the
psychiatry faculty at the University, but, most importantly, he was

the President of the International Psychoanalytic Association and had been for several years the confidant and chosen heir of Sigmund Freud. In general attitude, he was a man of science, committed to the method of empirical research though not greatly convinced by the standard scientific worldview of the day. He was a modern man, having read quite widely in philosophy and having adopted the critiques of Immanuel Kant, who argued against the possibility of pure, objective knowledge of reality as such. He was also postNietschean in the sense of having accepted the impossibility of conventional belief in God or myth. William James was an important figure as well, and Jung adopted the pragmatic test for clinical theory ("What is its cash value?" "Does it work, does it heal?") and was importantly influenced by James's radical empiricism. Beyond all of that he was also a Freudian to a large extent, which meant that he had partially at least accepted a "hermeneutic of suspicion" (Ricoeur) as the best approach to the products of the human mind, such as dreams, beliefs, convictions, fantasies, and unproven assumptions. In other words, he was thoroughly a modern man, posttraditional, postreligious, skeptical. For Jung it was unthinkable to seek refuge or self-understanding within the confines of his family's religious tradition, Christianity. That would have been immediately interpreted, by himself first and foremost, as a regression and a defense against the demands of modernity and a departure from scientific method.

This was Jung, then, in 1913, when the important story, for our purposes, begins. In January of that year he and Freud agreed to end their correspondence, which had flowed back and forth between Zurich and Vienna continuously since their dramatic first encounter on March 3, 1907. While breaking with Freud, a man who had been his guide and mentor for some six years and whom he had admired and respected immensely, Jung was also publishing his big book, *Symbole und Wandlung der Libido* (translated into English in 1916 as *Psychology of the Unconscious*), in which he openly stated disagreements with some major aspects of Freud's theories. That book represented his most recent research and thinking and contained a trove of material on myths and world religions, as well as symbols and stories from Europe to the far corners of the earth. It was ostensibly aimed at elucidating the fantasies of Miss Frank Miller, a former patient of the Geneva psychiatrist Theodore Flournoy. For Jung the final chapter, "The Sacrifice," signified also the sacrifice of his privileged relationship with Freud, and with it came the loss of fatherly guidance and intellectual orientation afforded by this older genius and mentor. Little did Jung know at the time how profoundly this loss would affect him.

Having declared his differences and independence from Freud and launched himself into uncharted territory, Jung stood before a personal abyss. Without a guide for the first time in his professional life, thirty seven years old and approaching the onset of midlife and a looming midlife crisis, Jung stood poised to plunge into the maelstrom of psychic confusion, a "creative illness" as Ellenberger has called it. It was a period of deep introspection and soul-searching, also a period of mourning.

Here is how he later expresses his thoughts and feelings at the beginning of this period:

> After the parting of the ways with Freud, a period of inner uncertainty began for me. It would be no exaggeration to call it a state of disorientation. I felt totally suspended in mid-air, for I had not yet found my own footing. . . .
>
> About this time I experienced a moment of unusual clarity. I looked back over the way I had traveled so far. I thought, "Now you possess a key to mythology and are free to unlock all the gates of the unconscious psyche." But then something whispered within me, "Why open all gates?" And promptly the question arose of what, after all, I had accomplished. I had explained the myths of peoples of the past; I had written a book about the hero, the myth in which man has always lived. But in what myth does man live nowadays? In the Christian myth, the answer might be, "Do *you* live in it?" I asked myself. To be honest, the answer was no. "For me, it is not what I live by." "Then do we no longer have any myth?" "No, evidently we no longer have any myth." "But then what is your myth— the myth in which you do live?" At this point the dialogue with myself became uncomfortable, and I stopped thinking. I had reached a dead end.
>
> (*MDR*, pp. 170–71)

Here Jung is recalling an inner dialogue that occurred just as he was beginning a time of internal turmoil that would continue intensely for four or five years and really not conclude until he understood a dream that he had in 1928, some fifteen years later. In this dialogue, there are two voices: one asks questions, the other answers them. Why open all the gates? What have you accomplished? What is your myth? In what myth do you live now? These are questions Jung must have been asking himself often and anxiously. These puzzlements of an alienated soul have a familiar, modern ring to them. The answering voice, also Jung's modern ego, walks him into a cul de sac where he has to admit defeat and confess that he is without an orienting myth. He has fallen away from his religious tradition long since, and now he experiences the *Angst* of modern man.

This is fundamentally a crisis of meaning. Here we see a modern person who understands a lot of material objectively, a scientific ego that is fairly bursting with knowledge but lacks a point of transcendent reference or a sense of meaning. There is no reference beyond this ego that provides perspective and purpose. This is what Jung himself would later call, in the title of a book, "modern man in search of his soul." Whatever Jung had learned about psychology, myth, and symbol up to this point was of little use to him as a guide to *self-understanding*. It was objective, impersonal knowledge. While he could use this material to understand the inner worlds of other people, he could not find in it much of value to grasp his own. His primary experience of meaning had not happened yet.

What did take place was that he was plunged into the roiling cauldron of his own psychic process. Over the course of the next five years Jung became a Jungian. He discovered that not only patients have a psyche but that he had one too. And he learned that if he attended to the psyche, it produced images and ideas and fantasies that were similar in pattern to the myths and symbols he had studied earlier. But many of these images also were extremely odd and puzzling to Jung. In the midst of this involuntary immersion in the depths of his psychic process, he was worried, as a psychiatrist, because he could see little difference at times between his own mental states and those of his psychotic patients.

The chapter in the autobiography that describes these years is titled "Confrontation with the Unconscious," and in it one finds an account of some of Jung's extremely vivid dreams and fantasies. The fantasies were produced and engaged by a method that he devised and called active imagination. With active imagination he could further explore the depths of his psyche, but in a controlled way.

Here is an example:

> In order of seize hold of the fantasies, I frequently imagined a steep descent. I even made several attempts to get to [the] very bottom. The first time I reached, as it were, a depth of about a thousand feet; the next time I found myself at the edge of a cosmic abyss. . . . The atmosphere was that of the other world. Near the steep slope of a rock I caught sight of two figures, an old man with a white beard and a beautiful young girl. I summoned up my courage and approached them as though they were real people, and listened attentively to what they told me. The old man explained that he was Elijah, and that gave me a shock. But the girl staggered me even more, for she called herself Salome! She was blind. What a strange couple: Salome and Elijah. But Elijah assured me that he and Salome had belonged together from all eternity, which completely astounded me. . . . They had a black serpent living with them which displayed

an unmistakable fondness for me. I stuck close to Elijah because he seemed to be the most reasonable of the three, and to have a clear intelligence. Of Salome I was distinctly suspicious. Elijah and I had a long conversation which, however, I did not understand.

(*MDR*, p. 181)

After he had this experience, he of course reflected on it a good deal. What did it mean? It is clear from his account that, on the one hand, he did not take a Freudian reductive approach to it, which would perhaps have led him to think that he had stumbled upon a screen memory of the primal scene from his parents' bedroom (father, mother, and the phallic snake). Nor does he take this first experience of active imagination as a divine revelation and try to create a new religion out of it. In the text, he makes some amplificatory connections to Gnostic tradition (Simon Magus and Helen), to German mythology (Klingsor and Kundry), to a Chinese fable (Lao-tzu and the dancing girl) and also to the associations between the snake and the hero-myth. He relates Elijah to the principle of Logos and Helen to the principle of Eros, but ultimately, he says, "such a definition would be excessively intellectual. It is more meaningful to let the figures be what they were for me at the time—namely, events and experiences" (p. 182).

Things did not end here. A little while later, he says, another related figure, who took the name Philemon, appeared from the unconscious. "Philemon was a pagan and brought with him an Egypto-Hellenistic atmosphere with a Gnostic coloration" (p. 182). This figure came to Jung in a dream:

There was a blue sky, like the sea, covered not by clouds but by flat brown clods of earth. It looked as if the clods were breaking apart and the blue water of the sea were becoming visible between them. But the water was the blue sky. Suddenly there appeared from the right a winged being sailing across the sky. I saw that it was an old man with the horns of a bull. He held a bunch of four keys, one of which he clutched as if he were about to open a lock. He had the wings of of the kingfisher with its characteristic colors.

(*MDR*, pp. 182–83)

Philemon became for Jung arguably the most important inner figure he ever encountered. From his ensuing dialogues with Philemon, he says, he learned "psychic objectivity, the reality of the psyche. Through him the distinction was clarified between myself and the object of my thought. He confronted me in an objective manner, and I understood that there is something in me which can say things that

I do not know and do not intend, things which may even be directed against me" (p. 183).

It becomes apparent in *Memories, Dreams, Reflections* that Jung's deepest understanding of himself came about through dreams and dialogues with Philemon and other inner figures like him. Philemon replaced Freud as Jung's mentor and gave him lessons about the nature of psychic life. "Psychologically, Philemon represented superior wisdom. He was a mysterious figure to me. At times he seemed to me quite real, as if he were a living personality. I went walking up and down the garden with him, and to me he was what the Indians call a guru" (p. 183). As a guru takes a disciple and teaches him spiritual lessons and guides him in the ways of a spiritual discipline, so Philemon functioned for Jung as a guide to self-understanding. The major lesson Jung learned from Philemon was psychic objectivity, that is, the notion that the ego must not identify with the contents and figures of the psyche. The psyche is objective, while the ego is the seat of subjectivity. He learned to dis-identify himself from his thoughts. He could study them, consult them, dialogue with them and paint pictures of them, but he should not naively believe them or claim them as his own or as himself. He could consult the inner voices, but he was not necessarily obliged to follow their directions. "The essential thing is to differentiate oneself from these unconscious contents by personifying them, and at the same time to bring them into relationship with consciousness" (p. 187). And this attitude would become the hallmark of the Jungian approach to the unconscious. Understanding oneself includes necessarily, after Freud, understanding something about the unconscious, and this was the way Jung found to do it.

It was through his inner teacher and guide, Philemon, that Jung learned how to deal with the products of his unconscious, which had come to him in such an overwhelming fashion during these years. More than that, however, he also learned a great deal from the inner figures themselves, from the dreams and fantasies. He learned that his personal psyche is much larger than he had supposed, that the unconscious reaches deeper and extends much further than he or Freud had ever thought, and that complete self-understanding is an impossibility. There will always be more, and there will always be a mystery. One can never reach a final conclusion on questions about the ultimate meaning of one's life. The unconscious keeps on unscrolling, and the detail and limits are beyond the individual person's grasp.

At the end of his period of intense personal turmoil and conflict, Jung says that he felt he had caught a glimpse of what for him was an ultimate factor. In his general writings he calls this the Self, perhaps following the terminology of the Uphanishads and ancient notions of a higher personality. The dream that convinced him that he had glimpsed this factor is reported at the end of the chapter, "Confrontation with the Unconscious."

In this dream, Jung finds himself in the English port city, Liverpool, on a dark wintry night. He is walking through the streets and climbs some stairs to a place where many streets converge. It is a square, and the streets come into it radially like the spokes of a wheel. In the center of the square he sees a round pool, and in the middle of that there is a small island. On the island stands a single magnolia tree. Everything is dark except the island. Brilliant sunlight streams down on the island and lights the reddish leaves of the radiant magnolia tree. Jung is smitten by the beauty of the sunlit island and the illuminated tree. On this dream he comments: "I had a vision of unearthly beauty, and that was why I was able to live at all. Liverpool is the 'pool of life.'" "This dream," he goes on, "brought with it a sense of finality. I saw that here the goal had been revealed. One could not go beyond that center. The center is the goal, and everything is directed toward that center. Through this dream I understood that the self is the principle and archetype of orientation and meaning. Therein lies its healing function. For me, this insight signified an approach to the center and therefore to the goal. Out of it emerged a first inkling of my personal myth" (*MDR* pp. 198–99).

So the chapter that opens by framing his personal life crisis as the lack of a personal myth ends by affirming the discovery of a new myth. The notion of the Self would become the centerpiece of Jung's psychological theory and practice for the next many decades until his death in 1961 at the age of eighty-six. The Self became his major point of personal and professional orientation, and for him it represented a transcendent reference that lies beyond ego-consciousness, beyond the layers of social and cultural conditioning to which the psyche is subject, and even beyond the limits of the psyche itself. It is "out there" beyond subjectivity, just as is the God of traditional religion. From his dreams and his active imagination dialogues, Jung fashioned a myth that satisfied his soul and offered him a sense of meaning in life.

## Jung's Account as a Model

If one wants to take Jung's account as a model for practicing wholeness through using dreams and through the development of a personal myth using active imagination, one needs to observe several points.

First, it is a personal and an individual approach. One cannot go somewhere—to an analyst, a teacher, or a school—and get a personal myth in a few lessons. One cannot find it in books about collective

myths or other people's personal life stories. It begin
and observing one's own inner life, especially as
dreams and active imagination. The notion that the
there somewhere that fits one perfectly and will l
wholeness and self-understanding is ruled out in this
no substitute for personal work. The answers do not
side but rather from inside.

A second point is that one cannot reach any great degree of wholeness and self-understanding by limiting oneself to one's own or other
people's conscious knowledge. If one tries to understand oneself by
making an inventory of everything one remembers, everything one
has observed, everything one has heard and all the feedback one has
gotten and will ever get—this will certainly go a long way, but it will
not reach far enough into the territory of the unconscious psyche. For
that one needs dreams and active imagination. And one needs not only
one or two dreams, but a long series of them. In the dream series,
there are patterns and developments that individual dreams cannot
show except in a highly abbreviated form. To move beyond the kind
of self-understanding that is mostly just self-consciousness and into
the mystery, one needs dreams and the dialogues of active imagination. These open access to the unconscious.

reincarnation

A third point is that one should not hope ever to achieve complete
wholeness, even if one keeps at this work into one's deep old age.
There is always more. There is always mystery. As many signals of
transcendence as one may receive, there are still more coming that
will alter and modify what one has and what one is. Practicing wholeness is an evolving process. One will continue to dream throughout
life, and one's dreams will continue to surprise. Like education, understanding oneself is a lifelong endeavor, and it is never complete.

And finally, myths have an important role to play. The myths of
traditional peoples and religions provide us with general patterns of
psychic structure and perception and meaning. Myths can act as guides
in understanding one's own patterns of attitude and dream life. It is
much easier to grasp a symbolic dream cognitively if one has a wide
knowledge of myth. For instance, knowing that serpents have been
associated with hero-myths helped Jung relate to the image of the
serpent in the cave with Elijah and Salome. This is very different from
saying that the study of myths will by itself help one to understand
oneself deeply. By itself intellectual study will not take one very far.
When one experiences a serpent in a dream or interacts with one in
active imagination, however, this experience reaches one psychologically and somatically in much deeper ways that can be obtained by
studying myths about them.

## *Conclusion*

The final paragraph in Jung's "Confrontation with the Unconscious" offers a summation for this chapter as well. He is writing this from the vantage point of old age, as the wise old man we all recognize in the famous pictures of him; he is in his mid-eighties. And he is looking back on his entire life and career, so full of creativity and richness. As he sums it all up, he says:

> The years when I was pursuing my inner images were the most important in my life—in them everything essential was decided. It all began then; the later details are only supplements and clarifications of the material that burst forth from the unconscious, and at first swamped me. It was the *prima materia* for a lifetime's work.
>
> (p. 199)

It was these images of the psyche that provided the raw material out of which Jung constructed his myth of meaning. This is a method that he then also applied in his clinical practice with patients, and so it has come down to us Jungian analysts and practitioners as a model for how to go about practicing wholeness and creating personal myths of meaning in these post-modern times.

### REFERENCES

Ellenberger, H. 1970. *The Discovery of the Unconscious.* New York: Basic Books.
Jung, C. G. 1961. *Memories, Dreams, Reflections.* New York: Random House.
Ricoeur, P. 1970. *Freud and Philosophy.* New Haven and London: Yale University Press.

*three*

. . . . . . . . . . . . . . . . . . . . . . . . . . . . . .

# Symbols as Transformers
# of the Psyche

Since its beginnings in Freud's late nineteenth-century clinical workshop, psychoanalysis has been concerned with the dynamics and the contents of repression. The therapeutic concern has been to reduce repression, to bring the light of consciousness into regions where it was previously excluded, and thereby to vivify ego consciousness, to extend its options for choice, and to increase the range and scope of personal freedom. Lifting repression was seen as the key to psychological change, the pivot on which turning points turned.

What gets repressed and remains repressed is still a key issue for psychotherapeutic theory and also, or especially, for practice, even if we now know that simply lifting repressions is not enough. For Freud the chief content of repression was, of course, sexuality in its most basic, original, and instinctual forms as he understood them. Oedipal sexuality and its attached contents of fantasy and thought were the prime targets of the repression mechanism. With their repression went much memory as well. This accounted, in Freud's mind, for childhood amnesia. Moreover, the repression of Oedipal sexuality lay at the heart of culture, and for Freud this explained the civilized person's psychic discontents and miseries.

Umberto Galimberti, a contemporary Italian writer and psychotherapist, suggests that there are other, and perhaps more important and far-reaching repressions than the instinctual/sexual one. Following Jung, he points to the spiritual end of the psychic spectrum:

> Repression takes place not so much at the level of drives as at the level of meanings, which are defined in such a one-sided and rigid way that there is often little possibility for the individual to express meaning in a different way, a way that could also be defining. . . . More than a field for the play of impersonal drives, the human being

> is an opening to meaning, and freedom shows itself much more in
> the extent of this opening than in the release of drives.
>
> (p.91)

It is a task of psychotherapy , therefore, to lift repression on the possibilities for meaning that a client may entertain within the domain of consciousness. We now know that meanings and ideas are also targets of repression, not only impulses and instincts.

Dreams and fantasies are classic subverters of the various collective orthodoxies that are built on and support the continued repression of individual meaning. It is not surprising, therefore, that collective orthodoxies of all kinds seek to discount the value that might be placed upon these products of unconscious process.

In the history of the religions that have developed a strong orthodoxy (i.e., correct teaching and doctrine), one sees clearly a direct attack upon such subversive contents of the unconscious. In the Biblical tradition, for instance, the ancient prohibition on images ("Thou shalt not make unto thee any graven image, or any likeness of any thing that is in the heaven above, or that is in the earth beneath, or that is in the water under the earth"—Exodus 20:4) was extended to include the representation in art of any images at all, including inner images, not to mention mythical figures. Dreams, too, were suspect and subject to tests of correctness. This repression of images and other gods on the part of Yahwistic religion attempted to channel all religious notions, fantasies, and dreams pertaining to meaning (i.e., divine will) into one ironclad formulation, namely the covenant between God and the chosen people. Any other dreams, images, or attempts to formulate meaning were deemed "false"—given by "false prophets" or by "false dreams" or "false teachers." All of these were seen as leading the children of God away from the path of truth and righteousness.

In later centuries, this same rigor was expressed in the Christian consensus and the orthodoxy that took form in the Creeds. The conviction grew that truth and the authority for guarding it resided in the Bishops and in their teaching function. Their authority derived from contact with the original source of the tradition, the Apostles, and before them from Christ himself. That meant that anyone who had a new, "original" vision, a dream or fantasy or intuition that imparted meaning and claimed truth, would be suspect. Eventually this rule came to define heresy. A canon of texts was established, authority and doctrine were consolidated, and heresies were declared.

Among those excluded from doctrinal purity were the Gnostics, whose central method, like that of modern psychotherapy, was introspection and personal inner experience. Their visionary states and unique personal experiences led them, they felt, to "knowledge" *(gnosis)*. The authorities of the Church eventually suppressed their teachings and discouraged their methods. They would reinforce the repression, on a collective and cultural level, of images, dreams, and fantasies that would undermine the position of established doctrine and the role of its enforcers.

In our time, too, we of course have orthodoxies of a collective and often political sort, which dictate correct speaking and thinking, and to step outside of these boundaries invites guilt and sometimes censure. Over against these modernistic monotheisms, psychotherapy has tended to support the individual's continual struggle to discover meaning in a unique fashion based upon personal experience. In this sense, modern psychotherapy is Gnostic.

What these large historical movements have done on a massive cultural scale, tribes and families do on a smaller stage. Within tightly knit family units, the individual's quest for personal meaning is severely held in check by the biases of the group and its rules of communication and expression. The same can be observed of work groups, therapy groups, and professional societies. The individual's attitudes become locked into a particular frame of reference, into a culture, as it is now called in the business world, and this restricts the possibilities for exploring nonorthodox thoughts and fantasies. The same holds true within the various schools of psychotherapy. These too have become monotheisms, with creeds, rituals, and taboos. Modern consciousness is anything but free of groupthink.

At its best, however, psychotherapy aims to gain insight into how and why the repression of the native human tendency to discover and to assign personal meaning to experience (which Jung called the instinct for reflection) takes place. It asks, as Freud did about dreams, about the censorship that occurs deep within the intrapsychic matrix. Such censorship is built on a structure of complexes, imagoes, and developmental outcomes that have foreclosed the openness to meaning wherever and however it may occur. Moreover, psychotherapy seeks to undo this type of repression in order to widen the horizon of possible meaning and activity. In order to do this, it opens the doors to imagination, fantasies, and dreams. It could be said that the goal of psychotherapy is to open up the psyche and to support a psychic center that grows out of experience and is not dependent for meaning primarily on collective sources of approval and validation. Along the way to this result in therapy there are many turning points.

An example: A thirty year old man dreamed repeatedly about the death of his father. In some dreams, he was at the funeral. In others, the father was still alive but ill and about to die. In actuality his father had died some two or three years earlier. These dreams brought up his ties to his father and his unfinished business with him. He had never been able to talk to his father openly or to relate to him fully and honestly. Now, in the relationship with me as his therapist, he could do so, and as we worked together and discussed how he was thinking and feeling about me, he was able to finish his separation with his father. This led to a change in his dreams, to dreaming of me directly. He identified with me and continued to work out his separateness and differences from me at the same time. He then entered training to become a psychotherapist, a direction he affirmed while working with me but one that he had had fantasies about before but would not allow himself to acknowledge and to act on. Now they carry meaning and he can act on these dreams and fantasies, while at the same time recognizing his similarities and differences from me. This is precisely what was not allowed by his father, i.e., to become like him and yet to be himself and to be different. The father had insisted on all-or-none orthodoxy. This had blocked the client's fantasy and his forward movement in life.

Questions of meaning—of finding personal meaning in life generally or in particular life experiences such as loss, death, disappointment—confront the practicing psychotherapist regularly. How does the therapist approach such questions? Certainly it is not to help the client create rationalizations. Nor can one reach to a shelf for a ready-made meaning or pluck one out of a bag of shopworn cliches. This is to say, one's own theories and general life experience or religious convictions are of no help. Offering them will result only in hollow platitudes, in cliche therapy. An approach is to look, with the client, into the possibilities for meaning in the client's own material, which is made up of memories, dreams, fantasies, intuitions, and occasionally full-blown thoughts that appear in the course of the therapeutic process. More useful than any knowledge the therapist may have is the faith that meaning will appear from within the darkness of the client's own psyche.

The relation of the question of meaning to affect and emotion is not the relation of question to answer. Emotion does not answer the question of meaning but rather often motivates the question in the first place. Emotion cries out for the answer, but it cannot offer the so-lution. And yet emotion signals when the solution may be at hand, for an answer to the question of meaning that does not bring a response of emotion, a full and heart-felt "Amen" from the quarter of feeling and affect, is not a convincing answer. And yet this signal of emotion is not by itself a reliable guide to meaning either, for we can surely be mislead and deceived into premature solutions by the intense and often desperate need to have an answer and to bring the question to a close.

A woman in her midforties came to see me for therapy after her only child had died in an accident. She had no connection to formal religion and could not seek refuge or comfort there. Her friends were no help either, and they only added discomfort in their attempts to console her for her terrible loss. When she came to me she had a strong sense that her daughter's soul was still alive, but she could not affirm this rationally and doubted her intuitions about life after death. They might be purely defensive or nothing but wish fulfillments. No one in her circle could convince her about this one way or the other. Nor could I. I felt as helpless as she did in the face of this catastrophic event. We agreed to talk about her feelings as they came up and to look at her dreams. Over a period of three years she had some one hundred dreams in which her daughter appeared, and from these she came to the conviction that her daughter's life did indeed continue "on the other side." I could not validate this for her, I could only support her in her explorations and accept the dreams as having validity of their own. Who was to say, "But they are only dreams"? How can I judge when dreams reflect realities and when they do not? I could only affirm with her that some of these dreams had the feeling of truth about them while others looked and felt like memory images, wish fulfilling stories, and compensations for her loss. For her these dreams were convincing and brought precisely the comfort she needed and could not find elsewhere.

From the viewpoint of the therapist, the answers to the individual's quest for meaning can emerge only through the opening to the unconscious, where images, dreams, and fantasies have their home. Thus the quest for personal meaning quickly brings the therapeutic process up against the repression of unconscious processes and their products, namely dreams and fantasies. The quest for meaning, in most cases, results in sterile ruminations, a circle of obsessive thinking that leads nowhere and remains within the chained sequence of thoughts and possibilities currently available to consciousness, unless material from the unconscious can be included. The precision of a particular and satisfying answer to the question of meaning is impossible to fashion from the offerings of a ruminative process.

Repression of meaning and the meaning-making function may be directed not only at the products of unconscious process such as dreams and fantasies and intuitions, but also at the notion of their potential value. By the culture they are considered to be mere figments of fancy that have little or no bearing upon reality. Stripped of psychic content, however, reality is simply the given, and as such it is without significance for the individual. Reality can be assigned meaning by collective opinion, but this will not satisfy the individual ultimately. The repetitions of stated value and assigned meaning by the agencies of collective life—by church, national figures, various political and social representatives of these monotheisms—creates a collective psychic reality. This is a set of values and notions that adhere to the consensus and have the power to persuade the individual that whatever meaning exists can be discovered only by formal learning and education. Culture holds and contains such assigned meanings, and indeed it forms the starting point for the individual's quest for personal meaning. But culture also turns out to be a fierce guardian of its own formulations and meanings and thus contributes to the repression of personal, individual attempts at meaning.

According to Galimberti, again:

> In our culture the truly repressed is not instinctuality but transcendence, understood as an extension of meaning beyond that which is codified, that is as symbol, which, because of its natural ambivalence, is free from the dictatorship of meaning that governs signs. The real difference between Freud and Jung is a difference in identifying what is repressed. This also results in a difference in therapy, which, instead of attempting to sublimate instincts, brings into play symbols in order to extend the meaning of codified understandings.
>
> (p. 92)

Through the discovery of symbols in the unconscious, an approach to personal meaning becomes possible.

To grasp how a symbol performs the function of releasing and sustaining meaning within consciousness, it is necessary to see how symbols create mental links. It is well known that the word symbol, from the Greek *symbolon,* derives from a concrete practice in antiquity of breaking a coin into two pieces and distributing these pieces between two contracting parties. When the two parties later come together and present the pieces, linking up what had been previously broken in half, their contract is validated. The *symbolon* is the object that, when made whole, links parts and validates an agreement or understanding.

A symbol, then, has a foot in two (or more) areas and links them. Without the symbol they remain divided and apart, incapable of relating to each other. In the psychic realm, the two great areas that need to be connected, in order for meaningful living and "flow" (Csikszentmihalyi) and activity to take place, are instinct (or affect) and image (or thought). Affect and instinctual behavior without image and idea produce meaningless acts such as addictive behaviors; ideas and images without connection to instinct, on the other hand, lead to sterility and schizoid mentation. When connected through a symbol, they generate meaningful activity.

While Freud spoke mainly of one instinct (i.e., sexuality), and then later of a second (death, or aggression), Jung proposed, as I noted in chapter 1, five "instinct groups" (or "dynamic factors"). These instinct groups, which channel energy into the psychic system, are (1) nurturance, (2) sexuality, (3) activity (including "play"), (4) reflection, and (5) creativity (Jung 1936, paras. 237–45). Although one can speak of these instinct groups as drives, they are experienced by the individual as psychic urgencies, not as purely biological necessities. By the time the instincts pass from the physical base to the experiencing subject (the ego), they have been transformed by the process of psychization: "Instinct as an ectopsychic factor would play the role of a stimulus merely, while instinct as a psychic phenomenon would be an assimilation of this stimulus to a preexisting psychic pattern" (ibid., par. 234). This transformation from pure biological, ectopsychic stimulus (instinct) into a psychic phenomenon depends, in my view, upon what Bion called the "alpha function." This is a mental function that converts raw events or stimuli into psychic experiences that can be assimilated and made available for conscious action and knowledge. This type of function is required to link instincts as pure stimuli to the preexisting patterns (archetypes), and when this happens it provides the basis for individual meaning. This is also the precondition for psychological wholeness.

How does this linking take place? We can easily recognize its positive functioning and its misfunctioning: meaningful activity and behavior on the one hand, meaningless or random discharge of physical and mental energy on the other. But the exact nature of the mechanism that links ectopsychic stimuli (instincts) and mental images like concepts and signs and thoughts is still obscure. Bion traced it to the mother's reverie, which stimulates alpha functioning in the infant through the psychic bond created by projective identification.

Projective identification is, in the first place, the means by which the nascent ego invests energy in the world and by which the mother responds by investing herself in the infant. This is the means by which the psyche invests reality (i.e., the object world) with personal significance. Once the alpha function has been established in the child's own psyche as an ongoing psychic function, the child can create meaning intrapsychically and independently. The alpha function links, among other things, ectopsychic stimuli (such as the instincts) to the images and thoughts that can give them meaning in consciousness. This is, I believe, the way Jung understood the function of symbols and what he meant by the term psychization (but never spelled out clearly). It is a process that assimilates the ectopsychic stimuli (instincts) to preexisting psychic patterns (archetypes) and renders them available to the conscious psyche. This process enables the ego to experience meaning and meaningful activity. Thus the ego finds meaning, it does not make meaning. We discover aspects of wholeness, we do not create them.

The preexisting psychic patterns of which Jung speaks in this passage are archetypal images. An archetypal image is a mental content—like a dream image or motif, a fantasy, or an idea or notion—that has a general, more or less universal and impersonal reference. As Jung conceptualized it, it is not a memory trace in the brain, either personal or inherited. The prime reference is not to memory or to objects of memory. Circles, squares, stars, gold, diamonds, heroes, wise old men and women, monsters, the child, the mother are images of high or ultimate value that appear among many peoples at many times. They will have a specific referent for a particular culture, mythic system, or individual, but they also refer beyond that to some vague, unspecified, transcendent, and otherwise unarticulated realm. These are images that float around, so to speak, in the collective psyche and seek specific content in order to receive concrete expression. When a link is created between one or more of the preexisting images and one or more of the instinct groups, then meaningful conscious activity of some kind can and will ensue and wholeness can be approached.

Psychotherapy is incapable of creating either the instincts or the preexistent images. It can only work with what is already available. Its task is to create an open space where archetypal images—in the form of dreams, fantasies, images, and thoughts—can enter and seek links to the vaguely felt ectopsychic stimuli that impinge on the edges of the psychic realm. Therapy's "free and sheltered space," to use the fine phrase of Dora Kalff, is created and protected by therapists who are careful to provide a secure vessel and who are able to enter into a state of reverie and mutual projective processes with analysands. This occurs only in the absence of collective judgment. Therapy's sheltered space ideally receives and accepts whatever comes into it without bias or discrimination. As therapists we observe before we select. We suspend collective and personal value judgments. We entertain the nonrational, the illogical, the unconventional, the frightening and grotesque. We allow for links to form, dissolve, and reform between images and fantasy figures and other mental contents on the one hand and ectopsychic stimuli (i.e., instinctual striving and demands) on the other.

The release of instinctual energy from a state of latency in the unconscious and the transfer of it over into ego consciousness and activity depend upon its linking up with an archetypal image that can give it shape and significance. A turning point in therapy depends upon this happening. The instincts need what I call a "field of operations" in which to function and to discharge their quanta of psychic energy, and the archetypal images define these fields and provide the psychic lenses that make recognition of suitable objects in the world possible. When instinct and archetype connect, "flow" (Csikszentmihalyi) results. This is the experience of meaningful, satisfying activity. Its expression ranges from infants nursing to monks meditating and chanting. Human activities are meaningful when instinct and archetype are joined.

Some years ago an alcoholic man in his early forties came to see me for therapy at the request of his wife. In the fifth or sixth session I asked him to tell me what it was like for him to drink and to get drunk. He closed his eyes and described a scene that I remarked greatly resembled nursing at the breast. His eyes came open with a start and he laughed, both in humor and at recognition of a truth.

After several years of struggle, including active participation in AA, he discovered that meditation on some Buddhist texts in the evening could soothe him as well as alcohol. This also nourished his mind and soul as well. He soon located a teacher, who initiated him and told him that his task in this life was to take care of his family and five children. At the end of our therapy sessions some five years after we began, he had fully replaced his alcoholic, meaningless, and imageless binges with a structure of meaning that satisfied him spiritually and soothed him physically. Meditation allowed him to link his craving for nurturance (mother's breast, the bottle) with concepts and ideas that nurtured his soul and spirit. This was a good marriage, and it created a field of meaningful activity.

Once instinct and image are firmly united, with the result that a field of activity has been created and employed several times, a symbol appears quite spontaneously that serves as an icon for this union. This can be a word, an image, a sound (like the traditional OM). When this symbol is evoked, it suggests the field of activity from which it is derived. The symbol then links image to energy and leads spontaneously to behavior that is meaningful to the individual. The symbol can be used to retrieve memory from this field of activity as it has been employed in the past. The symbol can also be used to communicate meanings that relate to or are derived from that field of activity. It can be traded, like a coin, and used to exchange one thing for another, or to engage other types of related activity and meaning. Symbols link to symbols and become fields of cultural discourse, like the spiritual traditions.

Personal and individual symbols are more difficult to use in this way, because the field of meaningful activity in which they are grounded is often obscure for others or for the collective to see and to appreciate. These kinds of symbols become a sort of personal, individual language that can be shared with one or two intimate friends but not generally. Analysis and psychotherapy tend to produce this type of a limited culture. Two persons engage in the activity of therapy on a regular basis for some years, and in this context they share many psychological experiences. Dreams, images, and fantasies are taken in and digested by both persons within this interactive field. Symbols of therapy itself will come into being, which refer to it as a product of the marriage between the instinct of reflection and the archetype of, for instance, the mother or the healer or another form. Thus a dream or image can become an icon for the analysis itself. Or the icon from analysis may refer to another area of life (to work, family life, or inner space). In all cases, the images and dreams that become icons through therapeutic reflection and reverie create a culture, a universe of discourse, that is shared by therapist and client and joins them together. The meaning and the form of this culture will be as unique and idiosyncratic as the two individuals involved. It is their alchemical product (the *lapis*), the result of their unique interaction with one another.

Each analytic case that shows evidence of being a major turning point for the analysand also marks a turning point for the therapist. In this sense, the culture of analysis is a shared experience of transformation.

## REFERENCES

Bion, W. R. 1977. Learning from Experience. In *Seven Servants*, New York: Jason Aronson.
Csikszentmihalyi, M. 1990. *Flow.* New York: Harper & Row.
Galimberti, U. 1989. Die Analytische Psychologie in Zeitalter der Technik [Analytical Psychology in a Technical Age]. *Zeitschrift fuer Analytische Psychologie und ihre Grenzgebiete* 20:87–120 (author's translations).
Jung, C. G. 1936/37. Psychological Factors Determining Human Behavior. In *Collected Works*, Vol. 8. Princeton: Princeton University Press.
Kalff, D. 1981. *Sandplay.* Los Angeles: Sigo Press.

# *four*
. . . . . . . . . . . . . . . . . . . . . . . . . .

# From Freud to Jung and Beyond, Turning Points in Modern Psychological and Religious Attitudes

In a letter dated May 13, 1912, Carl Jung accepted Smith Ely Jelliffe's invitation to stay in his home in New York while delivering lectures at Fordham University: "I accept your kind invitation to stay in your house during the time of my lectures. I am very grateful for this arrangement because life in hotels in New York is somewhat disagreeable" (Burnham, p. 190). In 1909 Jung had spent some days in New York with Sigmund Freud and had at that time apparently had a bad hotel experience.

Dr. Jelliffe had invited Jung, along with Henry Head and Gordon Holmes of London and William Alanson White of Washington, D.C., to lecture in Fordham's International Extension Course in Medicine. The course was attended by nearly a hundred teachers and psychological practitioners. After the lectures, Jung was awarded an honorary doctorate for "his contributions to psychoanalysis and above all his demonstrations in word associations, time reactions, and the measurement of emotional stress" (ibid).

During his visit to New York in September, too, Jung gave an interview to the *New York Times* in which he revealed his analysis of the collective American psyche, particularly his assessment of the man/woman relationship as he had observed it among Americans. In it he stated that "America is the most tragic country in the world today," and commented that "American wives have thrown themselves into social activity because they are not happy with their husbands. Neither the men nor the women know this." Ending on a more positive note, he said, "Eliminate prudery and America may become the greatest country the world has ever known" (McGuire, p. 14).

Jung was thirty-seven years old and still quite Freudian in his views, as these comments indicate. He and Freud had had numerous exchanges on the subject of prudery in their correspondence, and let it suffice to say that this was not a complimentary term. There were some, like Otto Gross whom Jung had briefly analyzed in 1908 and who had left a strong impression on him, who believed that sexual inhibitions of any kind were at the root of all human misery. Jung was somewhat more guarded in his opinion. The fact is, he was President of the International Psychoanalytic Association in 1912, but he was also in the advanced stages of his break from Freud.

Jung's Fordham lectures, somewhat misleadingly titled "The Theory of Psychoanalysis"—as though he were presenting a consensus view rather than a critical and constructive statement of his own—summarizes his sharpening disagreements with Freud, particularly around the issues of the psychogenesis of neurosis, infantile sexuality, and libido theory. Jung disagrees that sexuality is always the primary causal factor behind neurotic symptoms, and he asserts here that other factors, like a general fear of life and the avoidance of conflict in the present, are often the key ingredients in generating and maintaining neurosis. The patient must come to the point of facing up to the present conflict, rather than retreating into a lengthy and digressive analysis of the past, in order for cure to be effected. Second, Jung challenges Freud on his broad view of sexuality, which includes such infantile behavior as nursing. Jung would prefer to consider a second instinct, nurturance, rather than subsume all gratifications and pleasures under the rubric of sexuality. And this leads him, in turn, to the more basic disagreement regarding the term "libido." Jung opts for an abstraction from particular forms of libido, such as the sexual or the feeding, and prefers instead a more general understanding like "psychic energy." How this energy is channeled, formed, and utilized by a person depends on the complexity of the whole personality, which includes the instincts but also the complexes and last, but not least, the ego itself.

It is crucial to note that "libido" was a basic issue between Jung and Freud. The word is derived from the Latin *libido*, meaning "violent desire, appetite, longing"; also "immoderate; passion, lust" (*Cassell's*). It is a strong word, a word aflame with emotional intensity. What Freud and Jung were debating was the nature of human desire: its goals, its role in psychological and cognitive life, its transformations, disguises, and sublimations. Freud had placed desire, specifically sexual desire and pleasure, at the center of neurotic problems and at the center, too, of normal emotional development. Thwart sexual desire and the result is neurosis. Freud disagreed passionately with Adler, who placed the desire for power and control at the center of human motivation.

From both of these positions Jung sought to stand back. He wanted, he says, a more abstract theory, one not quite so close to emotional experience. Call it energy, he argues, and transform psychology into a kind of emotional physics that can chart and measure the various forms of desire, gauge their transformations, and calculate exchange rates as desire transforms from physical to sexual to spiritual hunger and thirst. For Jung, spiritual lust was as genuine a human potential as sexual lust, spiritual greed as real as an insatiable power drive. The traditional realms of body, soul, and spirit must not be reduced to one; each can become engorged with libido.

If stripping libido of its purely sexual connotations and turning it into neutral "energy" or "psychic interest" was the first turning point in Jung's revolution of psychoanalysis (which Freud himself followed, incidentally, a couple of years later—see Moore and Fine, p. 113), a second turning point came in his theorizing on the ways in which that neutral energy is structured and channeled. This aspect of the Jungian revision of psychoanalysis rests upon the introduction of archetypal theory. According to late Freud, there are basically two instincts—Eros and Thanatos, life and death—and these account for the sources of libido and its most primitive, basic organization. At less primitive levels, these instincts and their energies are deflected, displaced, refracted, sublimated, and deployed by the complexities of the psychic system. Pretty much every human endeavor, other than sex and war, have to be seen, in the final psychoanalysis, as defensive against the main thrust of the instincts. Put another way, Freud's reductionism holds that the Oedipal myth describes the basic human pattern of psychic functioning, and all else is aberration or variation on that theme. There is basically a single nuclear complex. In contrast to this account, Jung proposed an entirely different model of the psyche.

In a letter written in 1913 to the then newly formed *Psychoanalytic Review*, of which Drs. Smith Ely Jelliffe and William Alanson White were coeditors, Jung commends the editors for their breadth of vision. Research should be directed, he writes, to the parallels between the "delusional structures of the insane, the illusions of the neurotic, and the dreams of the normal as well as abnormal individuals" and to

> studying the remarkable analogies with certain ethnological structures. . . . It is beyond the powers of the individual . . . to master the manifold domains of the mental sciences which should throw some light upon the comparative anatomy of the mind. . . . We need not only the work of medical psychologists, but also that of philologists, historians, archaeologists, mythologists, folklore students, ethnolo-

gists, philosophers, theologians, pedagogues and biologists. . . . The collaboration of all these forces points towards the distant goal of a genetic psychology, which will clear our eyes for medical psychology, just as comparative anatomy has already done in regard to the structure and function of the human body.

(Burnham, pp. 192–93)

Jung wrote this ambitious, visionary letter just at the beginning of his study of archetypes.

Archetypes, which are what he would later call the building blocks of the human mind, represent the anatomy of the psyche; they are basic patterns of imagination and thought and are similar to the patterns of behavior studied in ethology. Jung's suggestion to Jelliffe and White was to study archetypal patterns, which can be observed from empirical research and evidence to exist among human beings in all times and places. If these basic patterns could be teased out, identified, and elucidated, Jung believed, we would have a map of the mind's basic structure. And this structure could, in turn, explain the forms taken by libido. Desire would then be linked up to specific structure, to mental image and thought.

If the archetypes account for the anatomy of the mind, the instincts account for its blood supply of desire and energy. Jung never departed from instinct theory. It grounded his theory in body, in matter, and in medical science. Archetypal theory supplements but does not supplant instinct theory for Jung. In his lecture at the Harvard Tercentenary Conference in 1936, Jung lists five instinct groups: hunger, sexuality, the drive to activity (which includes the play instinct), reflection, and creativity (Jung 1936, paras. 237–45). "Among the psychological factors determining human behavior," he writes, "the instincts are the chief motivating forces of psychic events" (ibid. par. 233). Instincts as we experience them, however, are not "ectopsychic," i.e., rooted purely in the biological substrate, but have undergone a process of modification called *psychization:* "Instinct as an ectopsychic factor would play the role of a stimulus merely, while instinct as a psychic phenomenon would be an assimilation of this stimulus to a preexistent psychic pattern [i.e., archetype]. A name is needed for this process. I should term it *psychization*" (ibid. par. 234).

These psychized dynamic factors, the instinct groups, are in turn influenced by six *modalities,* three physiological and three psychological: sex, age, and hereditary disposition on the physiological side; conscious/unconscious degrees and balances, introversion/extroversion degrees and balances, and spirit/matter degrees and balances. From the last of these modalities, the matter/spirit, or downward/upward tension, arise "ethical, aesthetic, intellectual, social and religious systems of value . . . which in the end determine how the dynamic factors in the psyche [i.e., the psychized instinct groups] are to be used. Perhaps it would not be too much to say that the most crucial problems of the individual and of society turn upon the way the psyche functions in regard to spirit and matter" (ibid., par. 251).

Together with the psychized instinct groups, the archetypal image patterns determine the contents of the collective unconscious. They condition one another. According to Jung in 1954, instincts and archetypes lie along a spectrum, with instincts rooted in the infrared, or somatic, base of the psyche and archetypes in the ultraviolet, or spiritual, realm (1954, par. 414).

The theory of archetypes is a key point on which the Jungian revision of psychoanalysis turns. There are many smaller points of difference, but this is an essential one. The nub of it is that instincts are conditioned from within the psyche rather than only, or primarily, from without, and that the nature of this conditioner is spiritual.

This conditioning of instinct by archetype takes place in at least two ways. One is that the archetype provides the instinct with an image that conditions its applications. Another is that an archetype can block or override an instinct and generate an alternative motivational force, a spiritual motive:

> . . . the archetypes have, when they appear, a distinctly numinous character which can only be described as "spiritual," if "magical" is too strong a word. Consequently this phenomenon is of the utmost significance for the psychology of religion. In its effects it is anything but unambiguous. It can be healing or destructive, but never indifferent, provided of course that it has attained a certain degree of clarity. This aspect deserves the epithet "spiritual" above all else. It not infrequently happens that the archetype appears in the form of a *spirit* in dreams or fantasy products, or even comports itself like a ghost. There is a mystical aura about its numinosity, and it has a corresponding effect upon the emotions. It mobilizes philosophical and religious convictions in the very people who deemed themselves miles above any such fits of weakness. Often it drives with unexampled passion and remorseless logic towards its goal and draws the subject under its spell, from which despite the most desperate resistance he is unable, and finally no longer even willing, to break free, because the experience brings with it a depth and fullness of meaning that was unthinkable before.
>
> (Jung, 1954, par. 405)

Archetypes can also, therefore, like instincts, become saturated with libido, with passion and emotional energy, and can take possession of consciousness. Archetypes are like instincts of the spirit, moving toward meaning and ideology and religion by means of idea, image, and ideal. Archetypes allow, or cause, us to idealize.

The Jungian revolution, then, places the religious impulse and spiritual drive on a par, as psychic force and motivator, with sexuality and any of the other instincts and ectopsychic determinants. Like the instinct, too, the "archetype is pure, unvitiated nature, and it is nature that causes man to utter words and perform actions whose meaning is unconscious to him" (1954, par. 411). Both instinct and archetype have their roots outside of the unconscious, but at opposite ends of it so to speak, at the somatic and the spiritual ends of the spectrum. They meet and interact in the middle ground of psyche, and their interplay accounts for the combination of the "higher" and "lower" urges and longings we feel and find ourselves possessed by. And "for anyone acquainted with religious phenomenology it is an open secret that although physical and spiritual passion are deadly enemies, they are nevertheless brothers in arms, for which reason it often needs the merest touch to convert the one into the other. Both are real, and together they form a pair of opposites, which is one of the most fruitful sources of psychic energy" (ibid., par. 414). Instincts and archetypes are never, or rarely, far apart.

While the archetype is "pure unvitiated nature," it is of nature in a sense other than the physical one of matter. Jung's concept of nature here clearly extends out from matter to include the spirit. "Just as in its lower reaches, the psyche loses itself in the organic/material substrate, so in its upper reaches it resolves itself into a 'spiritual' form about which we know as little as we do about the functional basis of instinct" (ibid., par. 380). The linkage of spirit and matter takes place in the region of psyche, where spirit, through archetypal images and ideas, and matter, through instinctual perception, meet up with one another and confront, conflict, harmonize, and mingle their influences.

At this point, we can look back and gauge how far Jung has come from the psychoanalytic reduction of psychic life to one or two instincts. Instead of only two instincts—Eros and Thanatos—he finds five: hunger, sexuality, activity, reflection, and creativity. And beyond these instinct groups, he has discovered a spiritual realm and its manifestations in archetypal image and idea, which, equally with instinct, belongs to "pure unvitiated nature" and impacts the conscious psyche with pressures, demands, and striving. Libido engorges equally instinctual and archetypal factors in the collective unconscious. So the ego's ethical stance now becomes doubly difficult. Not only must the ego manage pressures from the instincts responsibly and appropriately, but it must also, equally responsibly and appropriately, manage the demands of spirit: "Confrontation with an archetype or instinct is an *ethical* problem of the first magnitude, the urgency of which is felt only by people who find themselves faced with the need to assimilate the unconscious and integrate their personalities" (ibid., par. 410).

The message here is that it is not good enough to unleash archetypal energies upon consciousness in the name of developing a spiritual life. That part may be easy enough. In fact, it is so easy, and so natural, that it is practically a universal human experience. Few people, other than the most severe moderns, are without a numinous experience of the spirit or ignorant of the enthusiasm it produces. The resulting inflation is common enough. The real task is to manage one's spiritual infusions in an ethical way.

By ethical Jung does not mean something moralistic or conventional. He means conscious and balanced. "The ego keeps its integrity only if it does not identify with one of the opposites, and if it understands how to hold the balance between them" (ibid., par. 425). To be ethical is to stay conscious of oneself, to remain disidentified from archetypal images and instinctual perceptions, and to stay balanced among the opposites of one's "pure, unvitiated nature."

That said, we must recognize that the Jungian revolution offers an enormous opening, for research and investigation and practice, into regions that have been largely taboo or pathologized in psychoanalysis, namely, religious experience, visionary states of many kinds, parapsychology and so-called magical practices and occult wisdom, and all the forms of human spirituality. Jung himself explored many of these areas in numerous works, describing archetypal patterns and images and concentrating especially on images of the center and the whole (the Self). Numerous other analysts and researchers after him have carried forward this research, notably Erich Neumann, Marie-Louise von Franz, and James Hillman. Jungian thought and its contributions to psychology and culture studies have been largely distinguished by an emphasis on the spiritual, ultraviolet end of the psychic spectrum. Still, much more remains to be done.

## Psychotherapy

I will turn now to the question of how this model of the psyche, as finally elaborated by Jung, has already, and can even more, change our thinking about psychotherapy and what happens in it. Like Freud, Jung was early on impressed with how cut off an individual can become from that vast part of human nature that we call the unconscious. The region of unconsciousness is defined by two factors: on the one side, there are the instincts and archetypes per se, which never have been and never can be conscious; on the other side, there are the contents and areas that once were conscious but have been lost from consciousness and claimed by the unconscious. In other words, there are contents that have never been conscious and that come up (or down) out of the realm of pure unconsciousness, and there are contents that have been repressed or simply forgotten. It was agreed by Freud and Jung that most neuroses result from the fact that consciousness has become too much cut off from the unconscious. One has fallen out of touch with one's nature and become excessively one-sided. Treatment ought therefore to be directed toward rectifying this.

First hypnosis, then dream interpretation and interpretation of free association were the means by which psychoanalysts sought to overcome this illness. Later, in Freudian psychoanalysis, it became the analysis of the defenses and the improvement of ego functioning that were seen as the key features of treatment. Interpretation of transference and reconstruction of childhood experience were also central. All of this was aimed at restoring a kind of psychic balance and facilitating the flow of libido into constructive channels and activities.

As far as psychosis was concerned, Jung viewed it as a state of possession, in which a highly charged unconscious content, a complex or an archetype, overwhelmed the ego and took charge. The archetype's consciousness then became the ego's consciousness, and reality testing became greatly disturbed. "I am Mary, Queen of Scots" might come from the lips of a psychotic housemaid, for example. The ego was, in turn, unable to free itself from this state of psychic possession. It had been unable to defend itself against this massive incursion from the unconscious in the first place; its boundaries were too permeable. Also the ego was usually withdrawn from reality and seeking compensation in fantasy. This state of affairs can be seen either as a problem of the ego—it is too weak to maintain itself and its boundaries—or as the result of an overcharged content of the unconscious that is simply irresistible. In the case of schizophrenia, Jung suspected a "toxin," an organic substance that brings about this condition of severe mental disturbance and freezes it into place.

Neither Freud nor Jung thought that their brands of therapy could cure everyone. Both were fairly careful in defining what kind of person is suitable for analysis. Jung was convinced that he had learned much about the psyche from his experience with many psychotic patients—the archetypes are blatant and clearly visible there as they are not in more normal patients. This experience, on the other hand, greatly tempered his therapeutic enthusiasm, and he recognized the limitations of analysis in the treatment of psychosis, particularly of some forms of schizophrenia. This reserve continues to be the case among Jungian analysts and therapists today. On the one hand, much can be learned about the psyche from florid psychotic states; on the other hand, psychotropic drugs seem far more effective in restoring individuals to normal, or at least quasi-normal, ego states than are other known types of therapy. John Perry, in the 1960s and 1970s, carried out some fairly radical treatment programs with first-time psychotics, without medication, and saw their experience as initiatory and transformative. Some of his results have been questioned, however, and today there are no similar treatment programs available for patients. The efficiency and economic advantage of psychopharmacology has, perhaps to our detriment in other ways, carried the day.

It is another story with borderline patients, however, and many analysts will accept these into analysis and find treating them both enlightening and rewarding. Their access to unconscious material is impressive, and with the support of the containing environment of analysis and the relationship with a therapist, they can make great progress in becoming creative and psychologically aware individuals (see Schwartz-Salant, 1989).

It is outside of these groups of more severely disturbed persons, however, that the large bulk of analytic cases comes today. Most people who come to Jungian analysts are neither psychotic nor borderline. In fact, many would have no DSM diagnosis at all. In everyone one can find traces of narcissism, of course, and certainly everyone has mad moments, gets depressed, or feels anxious. But for most, the problem is more like: "I'm just not very happy," or "I keep making the same mistakes over and over again," or "I'm self-destructive" in some way, like the multitude of addictions that have been uncovered in recent years. People are simply stuck or blocked or "always in conflict," and they want to find out why and what they can do about it.

When therapy with one of these individuals begins, one is usually confronted with large areas of unconsciousness. There is a center of awareness, an ego, and this awareness extends out a ways into personal history. But there is usually little note taken of dream life, and mostly amnesia rules over early childhood, not to mention infancy. Too there is often a kind of cramped conventionality in thinking. The conscious person seems too small to house a whole personality. What is called for is an expansion of consciousness. For these people Jung's model of the psyche is extremely useful. These are often candidates for what he called individuation, which is the practice of wholeness.

Individuation, the Jungian term for growth in consciousness, can be compared to spiritual development. There are certainly important differences, but the thrust is similar: both aim at growth in awareness and an increase in the sense of personal meaning in life. The difference is that individuation attempts to include the dark, instinctual, shadow aspects of the unconscious, while spiritual development is usually aimed at eliminating them. Individuation also poses no program or predetermined or hoped-for outcome. Individuation, at its most basic level, requires wedding instinct and archetype within the domain of psyche and raising this to consciousness. The goal of Jungian analysis is to come to know and experience the full range of the psyche as much as possible and to find healing for its splits and divisions. The goal is wholeness.

The concept of wholeness, which is the Jungian definition of psychological health and wellness, is founded upon the notion of a marriage between the instincts and the archetypes, raised finally to the level of consciousness and ego functioning. The result is that libido flows progressively forward into living with a sense of meaningfulness. In recent times this has been studied by Csikszentmihalyi at the University of Chicago. He names it "flow."

The marriage of instinct and archetype is the fundamental healing event. Unless this union takes place, the instincts and archetypes remain inchoate and undeveloped. They retain primitivity and the ability to fragment and flood the ego. Or, in the absence of this marriage, the ego is simply left stranded, meaningless and empty.

An instinct unwed to an archetype, which is what Bion would probably call a Beta element, is an experience searching for a chance to happen, or a happening that cannot be thought about and is therefore uncontained and meaningless. An archetype unwed to an instinct, on the other hand, is a thought or an image waiting to land and become incarnated into flesh and blood, to be experienced; it is provisional and potential, ungrounded, a *puer aeternus* sort of psychic thing, an impotent mental content.

This state of primal chaos, where instincts are not linked to archetypal images and where ideas float around without connection to body and action, is not unusual at the beginning of psychotherapy. A person eats compulsively, for example, mindlessly and without image or meaning. Or a person lives in a schizoid mental state cut off from life. These states reflect the absence of a union between instinct and archetype. There is malaise, meaningless activity, lack of consistent motivation, and a great deal of unconsciousness.

In the unconscious, meanwhile, there are many unthought thoughts, unknown bits of knowledge, and these need to come into consciousness. When they do, this increases the ego's knowledge base. The ego's knowledge needs to become enriched and expanded, so that more, but never all, of the unthought thoughts lurking in the great dark universe of the psyche can find a resting place within consciousness. The increase of knowledge within the analytic setting is fostered for one thing through recording, reporting, and reflecting upon dreams. The analyst's (sometimes wild) interpretation of dream thoughts and fantasies helps too, and these are gradually confirmed (or disconfirmed) by the analysand through the further unearthing of images and thoughts in the transference. All of this takes place in the transferential field of analysis, where archetypes tend to get fueled with libido by exposure to an open and probing and (one hopes) creative mind.

This enrichment of personal self-knowledge is accompanied simultaneously in analysis by an increase in the experience of the unconscious psyche. Repressed and unfelt instincts gradually emerge in tandem with unthought thoughts; emotions and yearnings seep into consciousness through activation of the transference; the projection-making factor (the anima/animus) becomes engaged, and unconscious motives and strivings are perceived in the other, which can eventually be felt also within oneself. Both archetypal images and instinctual perceptions become experienced through dream states and also through waking states of consciousness.

Healing comes about in therapy through the gradual linking up of thoughts and images (archetypally based) with impulses (instinctually based). When this happens, the result is meaningful action. The analysand makes some changes that are the result of the increase in knowledge and experience in analysis. There is movement with direction, which is not defensive or the product of splitting, repressing, or other fragmenting maneuvers, but rather the result of genuine channeling of libido through the union of archetype and instinct. Instinctual energies, in tandem with the ideas and images from the archetypal, spiritual end of the psychic spectrum, now move in a spiral upward toward a point of personal and impersonal meaning. This meaning is grounded in impersonal necessity, in Fate, in God's will.

In Western religious life, it is the unwed instincts that continue to cause psychological problems. In modern secular life, it is the unwed archetypes that cause the malaise. Jungian therapy tries to do better. It holds out for wholeness.

### REFERENCES

Burnham, J. S. and McGuire, W., eds. 1983. *Jeliffe: American Psychoanalyst and Physician.* Chicago and London: University of Chicago Press.
*Cassell's New Latin Dictionary.* 1969. New York: Funk and Wagnall's.
Csikszentmihalyi, M. 1990. *Flow.* New York: Harper & Row.

Jung, C. G. 1936. Psychological Factors Determining Human Behavior. In *Collected Works*, vol. 8. Princeton: Princeton University Press, 1969.

———. 1954. On the Nature of the Psyche. In *Collected Works*, vol. 8. Princeton: Princeton University Press, 1969.

McGuire, W. and Hull, R.F.C., eds. 1977. *Jung Speaking*. Princeton: Princeton University Press.

Moore, B. E. and Fine, B. D. 1991. *Psychoanalytic Terms and Concepts*. New Haven and London: Yale University Press.

Perry, J. 1976. *Roots of Renewal in Myth and Madness*. San Francisco: Jossey-Bass.

Schwartz-Salant, N. 1989. *The Borderline Personality: Vision and Healing*. Wilmette, IL.: Chiron Publications.

# five

# Practicing Wholeness
# in Organizations

Organizations can be murder. Is there anyone who has not been badly mauled by one? Almost everyone has a horror story to tell about wounds inflicted by group process. In an age when establishing victimhood is the entry into collective acceptance, almost everyone can qualify if one just thinks hard enough about one's experiences with groups.

We begin dealing with organizations in our original families. In fact, our earliest experience with mother in infancy is a form of organizational life, the dyad. After that we enter families, and families we know for sure can be murder. Think too of all the other organizations that have to be dealt with in the course of growing up: schools, scouts, fraternities and sororities, the army, corporations, government. If one of these does not get you, the IRS will. Groups of all sizes and dimensions affect us and must be considered: families, tribes, ethnic and racial groups, nations, the international network of national and business organizations, on and on.

So pervasive and psychologically deep-reaching are the effects and influences of all these organizations on our inner lives that we may well ask if there is such a thing as the individual. If one removes all the layers of identification, introjection, and projective identification, is there anything left? Or are we made up of a conglomeration of all the pieces we have swallowed? or just a piece of something gigantic that has swallowed us? Where does deconstruction come to a halt? Is wholeness simply a patched up network of learned associations?

As one committed to the way of understanding the human psyche as described by Jung and later by his followers and collaborators, I have to affirm that what is still left after all else is peeled away is the Self. This makes up the core of the ego, a potential center of individuality and the source of wholeness and authentic personhood. We do possess a unique signature, a fingerprint, a still, small voice of a personal, nonrational conscience, and our integrity stems from this center, which has physical, psychological, and spiritual dimensions. But to get to this essence and to stay with it is demanding and requires a great effort. This is what I mean by practicing wholeness.

It is precisely this kernel of irreducible individuality that organizations often key on and seek to destroy, for it poses a critical threat to their dominance and authority. Perhaps it is unfortunate that we need collective extension, being social animals as we most decidedly are, for that is the point at which organizations make their entry into our psychological worlds. This is not only a narcissistic need, for in seeking to practice wholeness we find out soon and often enough that we need relationships. We need involvement with organizations precisely in order to come to greater consciousness. And it is this need that makes organizations so dangerous and so alluring to the individual. Precisely because we need them in order to become ourselves and to become whole, human organizations are fraught with danger and have the power to overwhelm and destroy us. Yet, we have no choice. We must enter and deal with organizations. The alternative is primary narcissism or autism.

In dealing with organizations, the individual is also dealing with the unconscious, both personal and collective. Organizations are not only out there, and separate from us, i.e., "other"; they are also the screens upon which we project our inner world. Inner and outer rapidly blend and become fused when we truly enter into organizational life. My notion is that the more intense this interaction becomes and the more it turns into a conscious relationship, the more fruitful this engagement can be for individuation, for the practice of wholeness and for spiritual development. Still it must be recognized that this interaction with organizations can also injure and sometimes even destroy a person's wholeness. How to turn the corner from experiencing the organization as a threat to individuality and as a potential destroyer of wholeness to finding in this relationship an opportunity for elaborating the Self and making this a more conscious and dynamic relationship? This is the problem I am setting out to explore in this chapter.

A fairy tale that Jung used to open his masterful paper, "The Spirit Mercurius" (1948), suggests an approach.

> Once upon a time there was a poor woodcutter. He had an only son, whom he wished to send to a high school. However, since he could give him only a little money to take with him, it was used up long before the time for the examinations. So the son went home and helped his father with the work in the forest. Once, during the mid-day rest, he roamed the woods and came to an immense old oak.

There he heard a voice calling from the ground, "Let me out, let me out!" He dug down among the roots of the tree and found a well-sealed glass bottle from which, clearly, the voice had come. He opened it and instantly a spirit rushed out and soon became half as high as the tree. The spirit cried in an awful voice: "I have had my punishment and I will be revenged! I am the great and mighty spirit Mercurius, and now you shall have your reward. Whoso releases me him I must strangle." This made the boy uneasy and, quickly thinking up a trick, he said, "First, I must be sure that you are the same spirit that was shut up in that little bottle." To prove this, the spirit crept back into the bottle. Then the boy made haste to seal it and the spirit was caught again. But now the spirit promised to reward him richly if the boy would let him out. So he let him out and received as a reward a small piece of rag. Quoth the spirit: "If you spread one end of this over a wound it will heal, and if you rub steel or iron with the other end it will turn into silver." Thereupon the boy rubbed his damaged axe with the rag, and the axe turned to silver and he was able to sell it for four hundred thaler. Thus father and son were freed from all worries. The young man could return to his studies, and later, thanks to his rag, he became a famous doctor.

(Jung 1948, par. 239)

Like the spirit sprung loose from long captivity in the bottle, the unconscious side of organizations can be overwhelming. Jung felt that the fierce Germanic god of thunder and martial fury, Wotan, had been released in Nazi Germany, for example (see Jung 1936). On lesser level, a similar spirit of destructiveness was released in my patient Ruth's relationship with her corporation. "It" had her by the throat.

Ruth was an attractive woman in her late thirties, single, well-placed at the executive level of a large corporation. When she had been offered the job a couple of years earlier, it had seemed like a dream come true. She would get to work at the top levels of a large company, report to the president, and make a lot of money. But the best part was that this company was about to embark on a major transformation of its culture. It was committed to a program for excellence and had hired a topflight consultant to come in and shake things up. There would be change! Creativity and new ideas were highly prized by the president, and this consultant had a sterling reputation. The company was an old one, entrenched in outmoded ways, and it badly needed to change its systems, to introduce new technology, to reeducate all of its managers, and generally to prepare for the twenty-first century.

All of this was intensely exciting for Ruth and promised a high level of job satisfaction. But what had actually happened as she got into the position was that the demands of the job and the rapidity of the changes initiated by the consultant, and the consequent pileup of responsibilities, were overwhelming. She worked through weekends, she stayed late into the wee hours during the week, and she lost every shred of a personal life. It was reduced to nil. She had not dated for a year, she felt no sexual desire, and she suffered from sleeplessness and anxiety. Meanwhile the demonic consultant felt free to call her up at any time of the day or night with more suggestions. When I first saw her, she was near collapse physically and emotionally. Truly the spirit was out of the bottle and had her by the throat, and it presented itself in the form of the dynamic consultant, the demon of creative change and transformation.

How to trick the spirit back into the bottle and contain it? Cleverness and ingenuity are clearly needed. When the unconscious is released, it often sweeps us up in a gust of enthusiasm. We may become inspired with creative ideas, so many that it would take an army to accomplish them. We are pumped up with energy, "beside ourselves" with emotional intensity, fervor, and belief. Jung called this ego inflation. The ego gets inflated when the plug is pulled on the bottled-up unconscious, and it becomes inundated with a flood of ideas, fantasies, wishes, and ideas for projects that come pouring out of the unconscious. When the ego identifies with them and begins to believe they are its own, it creates a problem. If the ego could let them go, observe them, consider and sift and discern which are the better ones, the degree of inflation would not be as severe. But to the ego it seems that each idea and fantasy is a jewel, and so the responsibilities become enormous. Ruth felt an urgent need to be a part of this corporate change, to be at the center of the team that was transforming this company; this was why she had been brought in, after all, and she could not let them down. She could not let herself down. She was identified with the spirit of transformation, and it was killing her.

In Ruth's own history, her mother had been excessively controlling and intrusive. It had been all Ruth could do to get away from home, so strong was the glue. It almost killed her mother when she moved away, and she had to move far in order to get away at all. Now she could not get away from the job, and the only solution seemed to be to quit and to move away again. Like the mother, the job had taken over everything, had intruded into every aspect of life, and had destroyed any chance for a personal life outside its boundaries. The job had become the devouring mother, and the corporate organization was allowing this to happen. Indeed the organization was applauding her dedication and expenditure of energy. She was giving her all, indeed her wholeness, to the organization.

Naturally business organizations love highly motivated employees. Employees who are willing to give themselves fully and without reserve to the aims and needs of the corporate body enrich the organization even as they destroy themselves. But this is like the dysfunctional family that is feeding off of its young rather than preparing them for independent life. One of the essential functions of a good organization, as of a good family, is to contain the spirit of its unconscious and to keep it from devouring its members. The Great Mother archetype, which is projected upon all large organizations that claim to take care of their members—paying them, giving them benefits like medical insurance and pension plans and the perks that make life comfortable—has a double aspect. Erich Neumann's classic work on this subject, *The Great Mother*, reveals how images of the Great Mother archetype show her as nourishing and containing on the one hand but smothering and devouring on the other. A well-run, consciously managed organization would attempt to ameliorate the negative side of this archetype by setting limits on employees' involvement, which would protect its members from becoming overinvested and devoured. There *is* such a thing as too much overtime! And sometimes this means fighting the employees themselves, who want more overtime and who become addicted to the workplace. Because members of these organizations project the Great Mother upon the corporate body and then become deeply dependent upon it and look to it for the basics of material life and sustenance, the power held by the corporate body is enormous. This is especially true in a materialistic, non- or antispiritual culture such as ours is. Far beyond rational considerations, it is felt that the organization controls life and death. To be banished from it is to starve and collapse, to suffer loss of soul. This means a severe abandonment depression. The base of support for the ego's existence in the world is threatened. So tied into organizational life can the individual become that the Self seems at stake, the core of the personality at risk. Promotion comes to define selfhood completely and the very meaning of life itself; demotion leads to abandonment and death. Reversing the birth process, the Self disappears into the body of the Great Mother organization.

When individual and organization come together, one can observe the intermeshing of the spirit of the organization's unconscious and the unconscious of the individual. As in Ruth's case, this is not necessarily a bad thing to have happen. The fairy tale can teach us that the release of the spirit Mercurius is bad, but only temporarily. It would have been worse had it not ever been released at all, for then there would be no chance to have an encounter with the unconscious, which is essential for personal growth and the search for wholeness.

Are there people for whom the genie never springs from the bottle and threatens to destroy? Some years ago I wrote *In MidLife*, where I describe the transformation process that typically occurs at this stage of the life cycle. Often it begins with a feeling of failure or loss, then deepens into crisis and a deathlike experience, followed by a period of psychological floating or drifting that I call liminality. In this period of extended crisis, reevaluation, inner struggle for renewal and for identity at a deep level, there often occur major dreams and visions that lead the way ahead. The release of the spirit of the unconscious, which must then be contained and brought into relation with the ego, is typical of the midlife period. In the end, persons emerge from this transformational experience with a broader and more complex sense of the Self, a deeper feeling for who they are, a clarified personal voice, a more individualized signature. They have courage to stand up for their convictions and feelings. They have what Ruth so badly needed at her stage of life. Often this midlife transitional period of life is full of strong emotion and turmoil, with divorces, vocational changes, alterations of lifestyle, and other inner upheavals not being uncommon.

This was the picture I presented to a church group one Sunday morning. While I explained all this, I noticed that many heads nodded knowingly and eyes twinkled in recognition of the struggles. Afterwards the period of questions and responses was lively and affirming, but then as I was packing up to leave a well-dressed gentleman of about seventy and his wife came up to me and told me that they could not remember anything like that ever having happened to them. They simply could not even remotely relate to what I was talking about! To myself I thought: This is what William James meant when he wrote about the once-born and the twice-born souls, and these were among the once-born. Perhaps, I mused still silently, these are the lucky ones. Yet it also seems clear that they miss out on something essential, at least from the point of view of practicing wholeness.

Jung himself went through a troubling and difficult midlife crisis, full of bloody dreams, horrifying images, fears of psychosis, inner upheavals so severe he says he thought he was losing his sanity and had to practice yoga to calm himself. This struggle with Mercurius went on for about five years. Day after day he recorded his dreams, worked with his inner images, drew pictures of his visions, struggled to understand this material, and was finally able to contain it and make it yield up its treasures for life. It transformed him, and at the end of his life in old age, he wrote about this period of "creative illness" (Ellenberger) as follows:

> The years when I was pursuing my inner images were the most important in my life—in them everything essential was decided. It all began then; the later details are only supplements and clarifications

of the material that burst forth from the unconscious, and at first swamped me. It was the *prima materia* for a lifetime's work.

(Jung 1961, p. 199)

*Prima materia* is a phrase from alchemy, and I would like to turn to some alchemical notions now to discuss the problem of containing the unconscious and relating to it, in an organizational structure or generally in life, in such a way as to promote individuation and the search for wholeness.

I think of individuation in the second half of life, the practice of wholeness, and spiritual growth as synonymous. Spiritual practices of whatever religious tradition have as a common goal the increase of awareness about God, the divine, or the ultimate principle that is, or should be, at the center of one's conscious being. Jung's spiritual practice, as outlined in his works and autobiography, involved dealing with the unconscious in such a way that the Self becomes more and more clearly articulated (see chapter 2). The Self is, for Jung, the God term, and the methods used for pursuing this goal of wholeness may be broadly useful, while the content is always unique and different in each case. It is about some of the methods that I wish to comment.

Jung found alchemy to provide useful models for discussing the individuation process, which corresponded in many ways to his own practices of active imagination, dream interpretation, and working with the unconscious in any and every form in which it appears, including projections and transference. What the alchemists did was to project the unconscious and its processes onto their work. By studying their reports, Jung felt he could see how the unconscious reveals itself to the psychologically naive consciousness, and this same unconscious matrix and set of structures can be found and worked with in the modern psyche, of himself and his patients. In the course of studying the works of the alchemists, Jung learned some methods for working with the unconscious.

We face the situation that the unconscious is powerfully projected into organizational life, and that what we meet in the organization is the spirit of the unconscious. Is this one's own unconscious only, or is it the organization's unconscious? Both are to be found in this mixture, and often they are uncontained and therefore potentially exceedingly dangerous for the individual's emotional stability (witness Ruth). But this very fact, that organizational life constellates the spirit of the unconscious and releases the genie from the bottle, also offers the opportunity for greater expanded practice of wholeness and for the transformation of both individual and organization. Through an intense engagement with organizational life, the individual may discover an opportunity to become twice-born, and the organization may also grow and change. The reward for doing this kind of psychological work of differentiation and transformation is what the alchemists called "philosophical gold," which Jung speaks of as the Self. It is the *medicina catholica*, the universal ·medicine; it is further a magical transformer of lead into gold; it provides access to creative life. But how is one to capture this prize of the spirit?

First the genie must be tricked back into the bottle, and only then can one enter into a more conscious dialogue with it. This is the first step of the process, after the initial release has taken place. When the spirit is released, the *prima materia* becomes available, but this is an extremely volatile and even toxic spirit and needs containment. When Mercurius is freed in a real-life situation—in a relationship, in the workplace, in a family, in the streets—one is confronted with a lot of affect and with intense pressures to discharge impulses, and one's self-protective defenses naturally come into play. This is when one puts up resistance, and these defenses—such as denial, repression, splitting, projection—are an instinctive attempt at containment. If these defenses work, the situation will cool off and calm down, but unfortunately the potential for transformation will be lost, too. The unruly spirit may be driven back into hiding, but it will only reappear again later and perhaps more destructively; or, worse yet, it will stay away, in which case the fizz goes out of the bottle and the system becomes lifeless and flat. On the other hand, if these defenses do not work, something else must be done to contain the unconscious. It was Jung's genius to discover a way to contain the spirit of the unconscious without losing track of it or repressing it.

The alchemists called their container the *vas bene clausum* ("the well-sealed vessel"). Into it they placed the *prima materia,* a highly ambiguous substance often made up of seemingly disgusting ingredients. Yet the *prima materia* was a precise material, not just any old rotten thing. Many puzzling recipes for this material can be found in the arcane texts of the alchemists. It had to contain the potential for development and hold within it the disguised essence of the gold to come. Jung would speak of this as the shadow. The shadow is the first appearance of the unconscious, and it contains the germ of future developments.

In organizational life, shadow projections abound and can be found, for instance, in envy reactions and rivalries. One envies someone who has some sort of perceived access to the Self (see chapter 13), perhaps in the form of a creative spirit or a privileged position vis-a-vis the power throttle in the organization. You may pity someone whom you genuinely perceive to be inferior to yourself, but you will not envy such a person. Envy tells you that you have hit upon some of the nasty but valuable pay dirt, the *prima materia*. Where envy is, the Self cannot be far away. Only it is hidden.

Systemically, too, if one organization envies another, it is projecting the collective, or organizational, Self onto the other organization. Somehow they have got "it"—i.e., special access to markets, more creative people, stronger charismatic leadership—and that is what you hate them for and why you want to destroy them. It also indicates precisely what the organization needs to work on.

Envy reactions, though, are often covered up and disguised as contempt. You can fool yourself into thinking the envied one is actually inferior and yet find yourself continuing to compete just the same. Once you actually see the issue, however, and recognize the envy, you can focus on overcoming it by aiming your efforts in the direction of accomplishing what the other has and is envied for. Emotional truth increases the accuracy of response and enhances development.

Analysis is a *vas bene clausum* where such emotional material can be contained and considered. This is the great value of the analytic vessel. Every sort of psychic substance can be poured into it with the assurance of safety and confidentiality. The analytic vessel is a free and sheltered space where the shadow can be acknowledged, the *prima materia* collected and the transformations of the *lapis* observed. Within the setting of organizational life this is somewhat problematic. How safe is it to reveal shadow reactions within an organization? Does the organization provide a safe place for expression of such feelings? Power issues and complex interpersonal relationships may make it extremely dangerous to be too open about one's thinking and feeling. Better to keep these private, one's reality testing function quickly interposes. And yet, by doing so, one stands in the way of potential transformation in the organization. When repression prevails, creativity falls. Feelings of envy and bitterness grow and feed off the silence. If members of an organization do not feel free to share themselves openly and spontaneously, the spirit of the unconscious gets bottled up in a way that yields no benefits. You end up with an uptight, stagnant organization.

If an organization is well put together, it will have the capacity to contain the shadow and to work with this unsavory material as it arises. Organizational containers need to be provided where personal confrontation and working through of conflicts are allowed to take place safely. This requires consciousness and safeguards. Perhaps it means including experts in managing such matters on the staff, and a third more or less neutral party is sometimes indispensable for hearing, reflecting, and balancing such emotionally charged and potentially explosive exchanges. Providing this within organizations is more than good human relations management; it facilitates releasing and utilizing the creative fizz that sparks an organization and keeps it vital and alive. Competition and rivalry, and especially envy, are deadly and corrosive but only if they are rampant and unmanaged. Contained and worked with in the *vas bene clausum*, they can actually yield great benefits. For shadow is the form in which the unconscious makes its initial appearance. Its appearance means that the unconscious is present, that the process is alive and working, and that potential for growth and dynamic movement is available.

In alchemy, this was called the *nigredo* state, the stage of fertile blackness, and the alchemists rejoiced when they arrived at it because it meant that the transformational process was under way and working. The *prima materia* is in the vessel, and it is cooking. There is a spark of life, which inevitably creates imbalance and conflict and draws the psyche into the work. Wherever people are involved in their work, their psyches are powerfully engaged, and with this comes the energy for the organization to become creative and to grow and differentiate as a collective.

For the individual, however, containment may well mean backing away from the organization for a time, in order to make conscious what had been projected onto the institution or onto some of its members. When we enter an organization and our unconscious becomes activated by our relationship to its other members and structures and to its collective unconscious, we typically drop into a state of relative unconsciousness and assume identity with some part of it, with a role, a function, or a position. This identification is most likely based on an archetype that the group psyche needs to have represented and enacted, and the individual's unconscious is ready to identify with the needed archetype and to participate in it. Jung called this state of unconscious identification *participation mystique* (1948, par. 253). This refers to a state of nondifferentiation between subject and object, in this case between oneself and an aspect of the organization. As psyches mingle and merge, the person begins enacting an archetypal role offered, or even demanded, by the group unconscious. This may be the role of savior/hero, for instance, the one who comes in to save a company, to transform it through charismatic leadership. Or it may be the role of the Great Mother, in the guise of the head of the personnel department, for instance, who takes up the job of looking out for the interests of all the employees and making sure that no one gets hurt or neglected, that all are nurtured and cared for. It may be the sacred role of the scapegoat, not explicitly hired for this purpose but ending up acting as the receptacle into which the group shadow is poured, then attacked and driven away in order to relieve the shadow burden for the whole group. In all these cases—and many more that one could mention, like the trickster, the lover, the king, the femme fatale, the *soror mystica*, the wise old man or woman—the hallmark of psychological identification with role is *participation mystique*. The organization uses its individual members to assume roles as the need for them becomes activated in the group.

The complex constellation and enactment of these many archetypal roles creates the psychological underpinning for what is called an organization's culture. A group's culture is created by the interplay of archetypally determined roles and enactments, the wider cultural and social habits of the matrix in which it exists, and the personality traits and characteristics of its members, most importantly of its leaders. One, or a combination of several, archetypal images will dominate and come to characterize an organization's culture. It may be an Ares war culture that girds for battle when its sales force meets and plans the future campaigns. Or it may be a Great Mother family culture whose mission is to nurture the young and provide for their futures. The hero culture of start-up companies is obvious to even a casual observer. The senex culture of old established *Fortune* 500 companies was legendary until the urgency for transformation of these cultures swelled to tidal wave proportions and swept away the established attitudes. Culture shifts in organizations follow archetypal pathways, too, and characteristically they move in death and rebirth cycles.

It is the rare individual or organization that has much insight into the archetypal underpinnings of organizational culture and transformation. The psychological factors of corporate life and change have been largely ignored until recently. How cultures are created and how and why they change from one type to another are still enigmas. Generally speaking, individuals and groups are not motivated to become conscious of what is going on with such unconscious identifications and archetypal enactments until there is significant pain and anguish in the organization. Without pain, there is little desire or demand for consciousness. When the pain becomes intense, as it did for Ruth, then the demand for consciousness reaches the threshold of becoming a matter of psychic life or death. Ruth could not afford to remain unconscious much longer or she would utterly burn out.

The alchemists spoke of a death that took place in the early phases of their work. In a set of operations outlined by Gerard Dorn and elucidated by Jung in his late magnum opus on alchemy, *Mysterium Coniunctionis* (1955–56), a stage in which the soul separates from the body and joins the spirit occurs early in the work. This is actually a second union, since the first union produced the original entity and was a union between soul and body. This second union Dorn called *unio mentalis*, the mental union. Physically what has happened is that the moisture (the "soul") in the *prima materia* has been driven out of the lump of material in the flask by the intense heat applied to it and has risen to the top of the vessel in the form of steam. There it has condensed and formed droplets. The alchemist's notion was that the soul (water) had been united with the spirit (air) to form a new combination, leaving the body (earth) dead and inert in the bottom of the vessel. This was compared to the death of Christ whose soul departed from his body for three days. Jung interprets this psychologically to mean the dissolution of *participation mystique* and the dawning awareness of that with which one had been unconsciously identified and of how the identification had come about in the first place. The soul has been unconsciously fused with an object (another person, an organization, a role) without awareness of this. Now, in the stage of *unio mentalis*, there is insight into what has been going on.

This also means death, since the identification is destroyed and the object that was identified with is now much less animated. When a projection drops away from persons or organizations, they become much less important, fascinating, repugnant, or emotionally engaging. The emotional situation is neutralized, and one realizes what was going on. The projection can now be contained mentally, in conscious understanding.

Psychological theories and constructs can be extremely useful for the purpose of containing unconscious, projected contents and holding them in consciousness while they are examined and analyzed. For this reason, a psychological education is to be recommended for everyone. Good psychological concepts increase the possibility of containment. But organizations and individuals resist this movement toward consciousness, and for good reason, since it results in a symbolic death. Consciousness is threatening. Becoming conscious of projections sounds appealing in the abstract, but when one actually gets down to particulars it is extremely upsetting and disturbing. Why is this? To break off *participation mystique* is to risk loss of meaning and a tumble into depression. One's unconscious identifications give one a sense of place, of purpose, of attachment, and as long as they do not seem to threaten life itself, one is loath to give them up. Even painful identifications are clung to far beyond what is rational. Battered wives and children continue to believe that husbands and fathers and mothers really do love them but somehow cannot demonstrate this love. They only need another chance, a little more time. It turns out usually that even a lifetime is not long enough. It is known all too well among psychotherapists that unproductive and harmful attitudes and thoughts are clung to with great tenacity, because they are familiar and comforting and because projections are able to override reality perceptions and induce delusions. The projections stand in for the lost or abandoning mother or father, and to risk giving them up provokes deep anxieties about isolation.

It is not at all unusual that a person will repeat, in a work situation or an organization, the role played in childhood within the family. The group becomes the family, and the archetypal roles adopted by the individual reflect childhood roles. As the original family meant original security, even if delusional, the organization is imagined to provide the same. If the father was an alcoholic and the mother was hysterical and intrusive, a crazy company is ideal: goalless and uncontained, it feels just like home! There is a sense of security in this.

But the Self presses for something else. It wants conscious wholeness. Individuation is driven by the Self, by a necessity other than the repetition compulsion. The Self presses for consciousness even against the resistances of one's neurotic attachments. Development, in Jung's understanding, moves like a snake, spiraling over the same ground again and again, but at increasingly higher levels of consciousness. There is purpose in repeating. The unconscious will choose an organization where one can repeat, so that in repeating one can also spiral into further consciousness. A Jungian view of the unconscious includes this teleological tendency. It is driven by the Self. The spirit of the unconscious, while it can and does overwhelm the ego sometimes, also wants to be released for a purpose. So the drive toward consciousness, towards greater and more precise articulation of the Self within the realm of actual life experience, is fueled by this teleological pressure forward and upward. The human being demands to know, to understand, to become aware of what is going on. This curiosity is inspired by the Self.

Following the alchemical image, an initial result of the work is death of the body, the loss of a psychological identification and *participation mystique* with the organization. When this occurs, the individual's quality of participation in the organization changes. There is less of the knee-jerk reaction, less routine predictability, less room for the organization to coerce a person psychologically without some conscious reflection and independent judgment. Now the secretary does not smile automatically when the boss comes huffing and puffing by her desk; the CEO takes a day off to be with his wife or child; the chief accountant takes an interest in organizing the office picnic. People step out of stereotypical roles a bit more. They come across as more whole persons. A sense of their greater individual complexity is felt and communicated. The individual feels less compulsively in-

volved in the organization. There is some personal freedom, some
room for personality, some privacy and space in the area around the
person. For a time there may also be flatness, depression, emotional
absence, a dead period. There is a corpse at the bottom of the vessel.
Some energy disappears from the organization, too. It is a time of
stepping back and evaluating: Is this what you really want to do with
your life? Is this role, this position, this activity how you want to
spend your life energy? Do you really need the organization as desper-
ately as you thought, now that you know it is not the Great Mother?
At this time, people may lose interest and drop out of the organization.

The *unio mentalis* offers one a position of strength, a standpoint
over against that with which one has identified in *participation mystique*. Here marriages break up, families dissolve, business partner-
ships change, and individuals make important life decisions.

In Dorn's description of the alchemical opus, the stage of *unio mentalis* is followed by a reunion between the soul-spirit substance and
the body. The body becomes reanimated. This is compared to the res-
urrection of Christ, and the new body to his glorified, symbolic body.
Jung speaks of this as the birth of the symbolic attitude, the second
birth if you will, in which the concrete tasks of life are taken up again
but now in a more conscious way. One may play the same role again,
but now with consciousness, not identified with it or driven by an
archetypal imperative, but by conscious choice and with insight. This
is the spiritual attitude par excellence, in which spirit and matter are
united, so that concrete activities are undertaken with the kind of
conscious seriousness ordinarily reserved for sacramental acts.

Without an archetypal connection, work is sheer labor. The archetypal connection transforms labor into meaningful work. One's role
in organizational life similarly must be infused with archetypal energy
in order to carry personal value and meaning. This relation of activity
to archetype can be entirely unconscious and acted out in a state of
*participation mystique.* When one returns to the task after achieving
*unio mentalis*, however, there is an awareness of the symbolic dimension of doing it right. The archetype gives the activity meaning, but
consciousness is required if that activity is to become symbolic for
the performer of it.

The Protestant Reformation affirmed the possibility of a vocation
for all persons no matter what particular activity or work they engaged
in. Vocation was not reserved only for the religious. What this said,
psychologically, is that archetypes are connected to many human activities besides the officially sacramental ones. Pluralism of vocation,
rather than exclusivity and elitism, was at the center of the Protestant
theological perception. This means that all human activities and roles

are potentially meaningful if there is an archetypal connection, and all can be rendered symbolic for the performer of them if consciousness is brought to bear. In the ancient world, this was commonplace; the gods and goddesses were plural and each presided over a particular set of activities and over specific areas of life. Homemaking (Hestia), love-making (Aphrodite), warring (Ares), blacksmithing (Hephaestus), and other activities were divinely ordained and guided. In the East, too, this notion is familiar, and the most humble service tasks and roles in organizations take on significant symbolic meaning:

> From ancient times, in communities practicing the Buddha's Way, there have been six offices established to oversee the affairs of the community. The monks holding each office were all disciples of the Buddha and all carry out the activities of a Buddha through their respective offices. Among these officers is the tenzo, who carries the responsibility of preparing the community's meals. . . .
>
> This work has always been carried out by teachers settled in the Way and by others who have aroused the bodhisattva spirit within themselves. Such a practice requires exerting all your energies. If a man entrusted with this work lacks such a spirit, then he will only endure unnecessary hardships and suffering that will have no value in his pursuit of the Way. . . .
>
> Down through the ages, many great teachers and patriarchs, such as Guishan Lingyou and Dongshan Shouchu, have served as tenzo. Although the work is just that of preparing meals, it is in spirit different from the work of an ordinary cook or kitchen helper. . . .
>
> Renyong of Baoneug said, "Use the property and possessions of the community as carefully as if they were your own eyes."
>
> (Dogen and Uchiyama 1983, pp. 3–4)

In treating organizational life as spiritual practice, one holds a conscious attitude toward the nature and symbolic significance of the role one is playing in the organization. In the case of the tenzo it is the role of nurturer, food preparer, a positive Great Mother archetypal function performed for the community. The same would be done with other roles as well, be they Father, Guide . . . or Scapegoat.

The scapegoat in a group is usually regarded as an unfortunate and innocent victim of group process. This is true enough if the role has not been consciously adopted and symbolically understood. Most of us do not fully understand the role of the scapegoat in organizational life, especially when the dynamics are swirling around us, but it does seem to be the case that the scapegoat makes it possible for the rest of the group to feel freed from shadow contamination. The scapegoat bears the shadow projections of the group and, if successful in carrying them, manages to dispose of them, at least temporarily. The scapegoat performs a cleansing function. To take on this role consciously and to do it well is perhaps the most difficult task anyone can perform in an organization. It is a therapist function. It should be reserved for the wisest and most spiritually developed, though of course it usually is not. Usually it is assigned to someone who is easy to despise, to consider vulgar or beneath contempt, who shows no competency and whom one can imagine offers little positive value to the organization. But if by chance the scapegoat role should fall upon a spiritually gifted individual who knows how to bear its weight and to work with the shadow creatively, the entire organization will grow in consciousness. The scapegoat becomes the central figure around which the most critical conflicts will constellate, and through these conflicts and clashes between the warring opposites the light of new consciousness and a higher synthesis of organizational energy will take place. The scapegoat functions as a sort of lightning rod, and this person must be extremely tough, spiritually, to take the hits.

In our collective cultural history, the scapegoat archetype was played out consciously and with full symbolic understanding by Jesus Christ. The symbol of the cross is the lightning rod that by taking the full charge of the clash between the opposites good and evil became the moral center of Western consciousness for two thousand years. As told by scriptural texts, Jesus consciously accepted the role of suffering servant and scapegoat, carrying the sins of the world as projected upon him willingly as a mission from the Father. He assumed this role for the collective of which he was a part. The Apocalypse of Peter, a Gnostic text (Robinson 1977), speaks of the laughing Savior, indicating his spiritual attitude of being in the role but not identified with it. Out of this drama came the birth of a new consciousness.

The return to archetypal role, after due conscious consideration and acceptance, is the second stage of our alchemical opus.

In the third and final stage, Dorn says, there is another union. The integrated substance, made up of spirit, soul, and body, unites with the *anima mundi* (the world soul). Jung interprets this to mean a still wider conscious connection with the world and a broadening of interest and meaning beyond the individual and even beyond the immediate organizational collective. In our terms, it would mean extending the horizon beyond a particular organization or time period to a more universal perspective. Few individuals, much less organizations, reach this stage of development. Religious aspire to it, joining the unique particularity of their originating figures and specific beliefs and practices to the Universal, the Godhead. The continuous awareness of this connection is maintained through rite and ritual, where the temporal and the eternal meet in a sacred space and time, which recapitulates what happened *in illo tempore*, as Eliade (1959) terms it. Our more secular organizations stop short of this stage, perhaps for modesty's sake, and limit their concerns to self-interest. Indeed, it would be hard to say with conviction that the interests of General Motors or Exxon Corporation coincide with those of humankind throughout all of human history. This, however, is precisely what religions do say: The Law is eternally valid and divinely given; Christ is for all the ages; Mohammad is the one true Prophet of the one true God; Buddha and Buddha consciousness are timeless. As repeated and reinforced through rite and ritual, this kind of consciousness is carried through the generations of the religious organization's life. It is the role of the sacramental specialists, the priests and priestesses, to remind the members of a religious tradition of this connection of the individual and the universal. This priestly role is quite different from that of the CEO-type Protestant minister, who sets goals and leads the organization forward; it is also different from the scapegoat who provokes new consciousness. The priest is the ritual master who, through symbolic actions and gestures, points the organization beyond itself to the source of its being, to the spiritual light from which all of history descends and to which it returns. The function of this role is to remind organizations and individuals of their finitude, of temporality, and of the eternal backdrop against which all of human life is played out. The priest, by gesture and symbolic action, by dress and symbol, rather than by intellect or creative thinking, grounds time in eternity.

Most of the organizations to which we belong and in which we play roles, consciously and unconsciously, do not (and cannot) provide a context for this third level of consciousness. It would be false to their identities to try. Yet perhaps some lesser degree of this level could be attempted. To have someone in a company who considers wider and longer range ramifications than the quarterly bottom line; who considers the impact of an organization's activities upon the environment not only for this generation but for the coming ones; who reflects upon and brings consciousness of the impact of certain products and sales practices upon the quality of life of the wider population—such a person in an organization would move it in the direction of the third level of consciousness.

Individuals can, to some extent, bring this level of consciousness into their organizations, if they have reached it themselves. If they do, they may begin to play the role of scapegoat, the bringer of new consciousness, through the conflicts they provoke in the group. They may also find themselves playing the archetypal role of the wise old man or woman, who can see further than one generation and can look intuitively into the ageless depths.

To maintain this kind of consciousness in the midst of the dynamic forces of organizational life, which place tremendous pressure on the ego to cope and manage, it is helpful to practice some private daily rituals and to keep at hand some symbolic objects. Keeping a journal of dreams, reading a Scripture, praying, meditating, practicing active imagination are essential and generally available practices. Beyond that, individually meaningful rites and rituals consciously practiced and symbolically understood, can be of immense value, and this value will carry over into the life of the organization as well.

I have deliberately used the words organization and organizational life rather than community, which is a much warmer and emotionally appealing word. Organization has a sort of harsh impersonal edge to it. I did this deliberately, because to speak of community, it seems to me, is often deceitful, since community most likely does not exist in the organizations to which we belong. It is a highly seductive word, because we want community so much, precisely because it is so infrequently experienced. But even more important, the notion of community sets up a polarity, community being the positive side of a tension that reaches across the divide into the opposite sort of murderous organizational experiences that many people witness and feel personally. I hope, in this chapter, to indicate some possibilities for positive development, individual and collective, without constellating the opposite devolutionary process. While the best wine often comes from the harshest and most unpromising soil, and the greatest individuation often appears in the toughest and least tolerant organizations, nevertheless I feel it is worthwhile to try improving organizational life and to assist its development toward greater consciousness. Ultimately, as I imagine things, this assists in the evolution of human consciousness generally.

### REFERENCES

Dogen, and Kosho Uchiyama. 1983. *Refining Your Life*. New York: Weatherhill.
Eliade, M. 1959. *Cosmos and History: The Myth of the Eternal Return*. New York: Harper Torchbooks.
Ellenberger, H. 1970. *The Discovery of the Unconscious*. New York: Basic Books.
Jung, C. G. 1936. Wotan. In *CW* 10: 179–93. New York: Pantheon Books.
———. 1948. The Spirit Mercurius. In *CW* 13: 193–250. Princeton: Princeton University Press, 1967.
———. 1961. *Memories, Dreams, Reflections*. New York: Random House.
———. 1966. *Two Essays in Analytical Psychology*, 2nd ed. New York: Pantheon Books.
———. 1970. *Mysterium Coniunctionis. CW*, vol. 14. Princeton: Princeton University Press.
Neumann, E. 1955. *The Great Mother*. Princeton: Princeton University Press.
Robinson, J., ed. 1977. The Apocalypse of Peter. In *The Nag Hammadi Library*. New York: Harper & Row, pp. 339–45.
Stein, M. 1983. *In MidLife*. Dallas: Spring Publications.

. . . . . . . . . . .

# PART 2

# Practicing
# Wholeness
# Clinically

## *six*

. . . . . . . . . . . . . . . . . . . . . . . . .

# Nature and the Analytic
# Practice of Wholeness

A wit once proclaimed that the art of the physician is to entertain the patient while nature heals. This may be as true for psychotherapeutic analysis as it is for medicine. "The best the analyst can do is not to disturb the natural evolution of this [healing] process," Jung wrote in a letter in 1960. "The process consists in becoming whole or integrated, and that is never produced by words or interpretations but wholly by the nature of Psyche itself" (1975, p. 583).

Today most experienced analysts of all theoretical persuasions would agree that they are not healers of psyche but are at best only allies of the healing processes within it. All but the most inflated clinicians recognize their limitations of skill and technique in the therapeutic process. What actually heals in psychotherapy remains a mystery. Perhaps it is a certain kind of love.

What some commentators (like Ellenberger, for instance) have seen as a holdover of German Nature Romanticism in Jung's works actually turns out to be a realistic assessment of what happens in analysis. Jung's reliance on nature to supply the healing forces is not some sort of woolly mysticism but a physician's recognition that human art and science have limitations. Analysts are not omnipotent, and they certainly need the cooperation of nature if healing is to occur.

Yet the practiced skill and masterful technique of the trained analyst are also important in analysis, and in some cases they are even crucial. Otherwise the training of analysts would be unnecessary and training institutes a lavish waste of time. While there may exist natural therapists and healing personalities, good training is still essential since the most difficult analytic cases require a great deal of expertise and skill. But this has been true since time immemorial. Shamanic healers too were and are highly trained technicians, albeit of traditional and not modern scientific methods.

In order for nature to do its healing, it is often the case that the pathways by which it can do this work are blocked and need to be opened and cleared of obstacles. In some cases, new bridges need to be built up into solid, workable psychic structures. Often a new psychic infrastructure must be constructed in order for nature to have a chance to work its healing effects. Faulty and malignant conscious attitudes and developments, acquired usually through traumatic and hurtful experiences in early life, prevent nature's healing processes from having much effect.

Actually many things can get in the way of the psyche's natural healing processes. To quote Jung from a very late work, entitled "Symbols and the Interpretation of Dreams":

> [T]hrough dreams, intuitions, impulses, and other spontaneous happenings, instinctive forces influence the activity of consciousness. Whether that influence is for better or worse depends on the actual contents of the unconscious. If it contains too many things that normally ought to be conscious, then its function becomes twisted and prejudiced; motives appear that are not based on true instincts, but owe their activity to the fact that they have been consigned to the unconscious by repression or neglect. They overlay, as it were, the normal unconscious psyche and distort its natural symbol-producing function.
>
> (1976, par. 512)

This overlay of repressed psychic material is maintained and held in place by all of the psychic splits, vertical and horizontal, that are revealed through the careful scrutiny of analysis. In large measure, the work of analysis has to do with bringing together the psychic pieces (so-called opposites) that have been split and pushed apart, so that the normal psychic equilibriating force can take over and offer its creative and healing potential. This knitting together of bits of consciousness is the work of integration in a Jungian analysis.

## The Nature of the Psyche

Jung's vision of the psyche and his approach to the theory and practice of analysis unfolded over a period of some sixty years. Beginning with psychiatric studies in 1900 and continuing through his close collaboration with Freud between 1907 and 1913, Jung went on to extend the scope of what he believed to be the true range of the unconscious from a one- (or two-) drive theory to a theory that encompasses a wide array of instinctual and archetypal centers. He also reconceptualized the relations between conscious and unconscious in a more dynamic and less mechanical way than had Freud. His early argument with Freud about the nature of libido (Is it purely sexual or a more general type of psychic energy?) turned into a thoroughgoing revision of the psychoanalytic theory that he had received from Vienna (see chapter 4, above).

The nature of the human psyche embraces, in Jung's view, instinctual-somatic elements (i.e., impulses) at the one end of a spectrum and spiritual-archetypal elements (i.e., images and ideas) at the other. At both extremes, the psyche fades through a psychoid barrier into nonpsychic areas: into physical matter at the somatic end and into pure spirit at the archetypal end (Jung *1954*, para. 420). The psyche itself is defined by the range of the will: Whatever the will can effect or influence in principle belongs to the psychic realm, and whatever it cannot reach even in principle (e.g., autonomic system functions) lies outside of the psyche. The psyche is bounded by body and instincts on the one side and by spirit and archetypes on the other: "[T]he will cannot transgress the bounds of the psychic sphere: it cannot coerce the instinct, nor has it power over the spirit, in so far as we understand by this something more than the intellect. Spirit and instinct are by nature autonomous and both limit in equal measure the applied field of the will" (1954, par. 379).

The view that Jung was a mystic has been a willful political distortion, but it does contain the truth that he did take spirit into account in his theory of the psyche. In analytic therapy, it is seen as important to release spiritual elements into consciousness as it is somatic instinctual impulses. But contrary to the erroneous opinion that Jung denied or downplayed the biological and instinctual side of psychic life, he actually gives it equal weight to the spiritual and archetypal. Jung's is not a purely spiritual psychology, though it takes spiritual matters more seriously perhaps than other modern depth psychologies.

For Jung the unconscious contains much more than the sexual drive (the famous *Lustprincip* of Freud) and its associated materials and more even than the total mass of repressed psychic contents of all kinds. The unconscious contains thoughts and images, impulses and desires that have not yet seen the light of day in an individual's life, as well as those that have been experienced and were rejected for one reason or another. While Jung did not deny the importance of sexuality in psychic life, he found that other somatic instinctual factors also play significantly upon the psyche, not to mention the panoply of contents and factors that have more a spiritual or purely psychological identity than a biologically based one.

Jung theorized that there are a number of instinct groups, in fact five of them. In a key but much neglected essay entitled "Psychological Factors Determining Human Behavior," which was written in 1936 for presentation at the Harvard Tercentenary Conference of Arts and Sciences when he received an honorary doctorate, Jung postulated the five "instinctive factors" of hunger, sexuality, activity, reflection, and creativity. These deep human impulses, which lie beyond the levels of acculturation and cannot be controlled by the will, belong to human biological nature itself. They influence human behavior and supply energy and motive force ("libido") to the psyche. They are themselves in turn shaped by several other physical, psychological and cultural factors that Jung calls "modalities." These include the physical factors of gender, age, and hereditary disposition, and the more psychological ones of typology, spiritual vs. physical orientation to the world, and the degree to which a person behaves consciously or unconsciously. Culture and history play a role in forming these latter three modalities and thereby influencing the ways in which the instinct groups may be deployed in an individual's life. For Jung, history and culture play a large role in shaping and forming the canalization of both instinctual and archetypal factors in the psyche.

Jung's Harvard paper underscores his appreciation for the multitude of ways in which the individual psyche is embedded in and influenced by the surrounding social world. The individual is subject to social forces from both internal and external sources. As history and culture shape family life and attitudes, so families shape individuals and, due to the process of introjection, the ego becomes subject to culture from within the psychic matrix itself. Social disruption, war, and economic hardship are factors that contribute to the construction of an inner world that the individual carries throughout life.

Jung's theory is nonsolipsistic in another sense as well. Through the psychological functions, such as sensation, thinking and feeling, the ego is able to make adjustments to the environment and to fashion a conscious response that is not determined by the instincts or complexes. While Jung's vision is profoundly appreciative of the importance of the psyche in making judgments and formulating responses and ideas about the world, it does not paint the human being as locked into a dark box from which only projections can emanate and grope at a totally unknown and unknowable "outer world." For Jung the human being is highly adaptive and takes cues both from intrapsychic factors such as instinctually based impulses and archetypally derived ideational processes and from the surrounding environment.

It is surely significant too that Jung does not list aggression (Freud's second drive, *thanatos*) or the wish for power (Adler's core drive) as basic human instincts. In this respect, his conception of the human condition differs from Freud's more pessimistic view, not to mention Melanie Klein's further extensions of *thanatos* theory into earliest childhood and infancy, as for instance in her theory of envy. He also sets himself apart from Adler, for whom the power drive was the key force in human life and who saw the human experience of inferiority and powerlessness as central.

This is not to say that Jung's conception of the human condition is one-sidedly and naively optimistic or depicts a psyche that is free of internal conflict or power needs. Jung recognizes in many places that the instincts often compete with one another (e.g., "the system of instincts is not truly harmonious in composition and is exposed to numerous internal collisions"—1954, par. 378) and that constellations of polarities and internal conflict within the psyche are inevitable. He also is cognizant of the power issue and its importance, especially for introverts. In fact, the existence of inner conflict is bedrock in Jungian doctrine. Conflict, inner and outer, is a normal part of human life and even provides the necessary condition for ego growth and development. Politics is inevitable and universal because of the insecurity of the ego, but it is not instinctual. Insofar as the ego needs greater security or recognition or even conflict for growth and development, it may search out opportunities to engage in politics, but for Jung this is not the enactment of an instinctual impulse. Politics is driven more by the ego's need for power and grandiosity than it is by instinct.

If Jung does not root aggression and the power need in instinct, he does nevertheless have a strong conception of evil. The shadow, for Jung a technical psychological term that refers to repressed traits like (typically) envy, greed, and aggression, belongs to the human personality at all levels, personal and impersonal, individual and collective. But the shadow is not invariably defined by "sex and aggression," the Freudian id. It is Mercurial and depends upon the particular aspects of personality that an individual and/or a culture choose to denigrate and attempt to eliminate. The shadow is that which does not belong in polite company, is shaming and embarrassing, and is rejected by the individual and by society as unacceptable and even intolerable. It is made up of the traits, feelings, and harbored fantasies that analysands confess to their analysts with great shame and reluctance. The shadow is complementary to the persona (another technical term, which refers to a person's official psychosocial identity): as the one side shows the face we want to be seen, the other conceals the face we do not wish to show. Both exist inevitably and form two sides of a psychic coin. But the shadow is not drive-based and is not associated or shaped by a specific instinct.

There is in Jung's theory, then, no specific drive towards destruction or aggression for its own sake, and the shadow does not inevitably tend in that direction. Destructiveness and aggressivity are universal among humans, or so it seems, but they are the by-products of other factors: ego frustration, traumatic childhood, the need to create, the urge to mate, etc. There is no inherent human need to destroy. Jung rejected this central Freudian notion (the Thanatos drive) because it did not make sense from a biological or psychological standpoint, even though the idea seems to have originated in connection with his early student, Sabina Spielrein, who wrote of it in her doctoral dissertation (supervised by Jung) and passed it on to Freud (see Kerr). In *Symbole und Wandlungen* Jung considers the idea but later deletes it from subsequent versions of this work.

Belonging to the same deep level of the psyche as the instinctive factors are the archetypes. If instincts are the drives, archetypes are the shapers of the drives. Together they make up the famous Jungian collective unconscious. In an essay entitled "On the Nature of the Psyche," which is perhaps his greatest single theoretical paper, Jung speculates about the relation between instincts and archetypes. He concludes that they are best conceived as lying along a spectrum, like the color spectrum, with the instincts at the infrared end and the archetypes at the ultraviolet end (1954, par. 414). But archetypes and instincts are also intimately related to one another, the first shaping and giving form to the second. By themselves the instincts would be without form and void, like the Biblical *te'hom* (Genesis 1:1); the spirit (archetype) broods above this amorphous chaos and gives it shape. The archetypes structure the deep unconscious, where matter and spirit come together and meet as instinctual urge and archetypal image. In fact one never encounters in the psyche an instinct without an archetypally formed structure.

Jung would sometimes hold that the archetype is the image of the instinct. So intimately are they related that he often refers to archetypes and archetypal patterns without explicit or even implicit reference to instinct, simply assuming the link between instinct and archetype that drives the "pattern of behavior" that is the archetype (cf. 1954, par. 352). Without such a source of somatic energy, archetypal images would be lifeless and without embodiment, pure mental spectra that float around in the psyche without emotional connection or impact. Taken this way, archetypes become mental abstractions and schemas for thinking rather than the numinous powers that Jung has in mind whenever he uses the term.

Without an image, on the other hand, an instinct would lack direction, it would be diffuse, it would not know how to find a suitable object. While instincts give energy and drive to archetypal images, archetypes generate the images that allow instincts to become related to fitting objects, which is what they inherently seek.

In Jungian theory, this linkage between instinct and archetype is the presupposition for all satisfactory object relations, beginning with the infant-breast unit (nurturance), extending through the formation of a sexual love bond with a mate (sexuality), and including the discovery and recognition of a vocation (activity, creativity) and of the persons and tools necessary for deriving meaning from experience (reflection). For Jungians these key experiences of a "fit" in life are archetypal, meaning that there is a good match between internal and external worlds (between need and fulfillment) and between nature and culture (between self and other, individual and society). There is also the factor of innateness: these fits are not learned, they are discovered.

Jung would not reject the point of the object relations theorists who wish to insist that humans are innately and inherently object-oriented and related from the beginning of life, but he would add that the psychic ground for this relatedness lies in the still more fundamental link between instinct and archetype. When this linkage is disrupted or broken, object relations are inevitably disturbed, perhaps even from the period of intrauterine life but certainly from the moment of birth onward. Without the guidance of the archetypal image, the psychic energy pouring in from the somatic base is disorganized and unfocused.

Neither instincts nor archetypes are contained within the psyche itself, according to Jung's theory, and therefore they cannot be experienced directly. The instinct groups are rooted in the somatic base, and the archetypes are formative factors that exist in a spiritual realm beyond the range of the human psyche (1954, par. 420). From both extremes of the spectrum, the psyche receives signals: from the instinct groups these come as feelings of desire and as impulses, and from the archetypes they appear in consciousness as images, fantasies, ideas, visions, and intuitions. By the time they enter the psyche and even more so reach ego consciousness, both types of signal have been "psychized" and each related to the other type.

The empirical consciousness of individuals tends to slide back and forth between the somatic and archetypal poles of the spectrum, now experiencing desires, impulses and the libidinal fires of passion more strongly, now images, ideas, and intuitions more intensely. Emotion can equally attach itself to either end of this polarity, and either one can at times overwhelm or swallow the other. But in the healthy psyche, which is the balanced psyche for Jung, instinct and archetype are held in tension. In the psyche they are coordinated and work together, the one providing impulse and drive and the other contributing direction and meaning. Precisely how this coordination comes into being and operates or fails to operate successfully were topics pursued by Jung late in life, particularly in his last great opus *Mysterium Coniunctionis*. The great "union of opposites" that the psyche is asked to host is that between matter and spirit. The human condition as we experience it at this point in evolutionary history is fundamentally shaped by this tension of opposites between the soma-based instincts on the one hand and the spirit-based archetypes on the other. The meeting place (or the battleground) where they converge is the psyche. As Jung saw it, the meaning of human existence in the temporal universe lies in this precise function of the psyche: to unite spirit and matter within the space-time continuum of an individual human life.

When these two poles of the psyche, the material body and the transcendent spirit, are adequately coordinated, it makes for healthful psychic compensation from the unconscious. Jung's view of compensation is vastly different from Adler's. The term "compensation" for Jung does not refer to the outcome of a sense of inferiority or the attempt to overcome the feeling of smallness by imagining the opposite: It is not a "protest." Rather, compensation is conceptualized by Jung as a psychic mechanism that aims at directing a balanced dynamic movement toward individuation and wholeness. Ego consciousness needs this compensation from the unconscious because on its own and without benefit of such a relationship with "nature" it becomes rigid, sterile, and one-sided. "True instincts" or "nature" can adjust, balance, and heal the conscious personality if the way is clear for compensation to have its proper effect.

## Complexes, Pathology, and Analysis

Early in his psychiatric career, Jung noticed the wonders of dissociation in his psychotic and neurotic patients. Repression is but one of several means by which consciousness is prevented from integrating parts of the psyche and extracting meaning and benefit from experience. It became clear to him that the main hindrance to the successful functioning of nature's psychological ecosystem lies in the personal complexes. These are psychic bodies that are developed throughout a person's life history, most importantly in childhood. They are instigated by interpersonal traumata like emotional abandonment, sexual abuse, and lack of adequate mirroring, and then they grow by gathering associations of a similar nature around themselves and by binding them to the core of the complex with emotion. The complexes are highly charged with affect, behave autonomously (i.e., are not under the ego's control), and possess a kind of consciousness of their own. They are highly reactive to external stimuli, and when stimulated they cause both physiological and psychological distress and confusion. They are our emotional "buttons"; when pushed they can drive us to the brink (or over it) of irrationality. In analysis they are interpreted reductionistically. That is, the emotional reactions generated by complexes are placed in the context of their point of origination, usually in childhood.

As important as their interference with the ego's so-called reality testing may be, however, a perhaps even more severe problem comes about as the result of their eventual buildup into a sort of psychic barrier, often impenetrable, between the ego and the deeper, instinctive/archetypal levels of the psyche. It is this barrier layer of complexes that can severely block the healing compensations of the natural psyche from reaching ego consciousness.

The complexes also create fracture points in the structure of the developing ego. They allow for ego fragmentation and dissociation along certain predictable line of cleavage. When strongly stimulated, they splinter the psyche and cause splits within consciousness (vertical split) and between conscious and unconscious (horizontal split). When this happens, a person experiences a state of dissociation, high affectivity, and physiological stress. Consciousness is disturbed and the integration of experience is blocked. Memory, too, is disrupted, and distortions of every variety intrude in the ego's construction of reality.

These points of vulnerability in the psyche call for ego defenses, which are meant to distance the subject from suffering and pain. Unfortunately, they at the same time distance the person from valuable psychic experience and from parts of the Self that are called into play at the moment of complex stimulus. They interfere with useful instinctual responses to stressful and even dangerous situations, and they cut down on the ego's capacity to take advantage of opportunities in the environment with adaptative responses. They make us into the sick animals we are when caught in neurotic patterns of thinking and responding. The resultant defenses against psychic pain prevent integration and foster the chronicity of psychic patterns and partialness. The Self is not unified but rather becomes compartmentalized and dissociative.

As much as the fragmentariness of a poorly formed and vulnerable ego interferes with healthy functioning and utilization of healing compensation from the deep unconscious, the existence of a thick, unbreachable layer of complexes between ego consciousness and the deeper layers of the unconscious, along with the defenses employed by the ego to keep psychic pain at bay, creates a psyche that cannot utilize the healing powers of the unconscious when they happen to break through in dreams, impulses, or fantasies. In analytic practice it is not uncommon to find a person who reports a numinous archetypal dream that should have the effect of moving the subject toward greater wholeness and meaning. But the analyst sees that the dream that should have a profound healing influence upon consciousness has no discernible effect at all, and not even the added weight of the analyst's most empathic and inspired interpretation will move consciousness very far in the direction of health. The dream and the interpretation simply carry too little force within this psychic matrix to make much difference.

The normal and optimal function of the unconscious is to compensate the ego and to orient it thereby in the direction of psychic equilibrium and balance, but this is thwarted by faulty ego development and the formation of complexes. This is what needs to be rectified by analytic treatment. At the heart of treatment lies the analysis (analysis = dismemberment) of the complexes and the synthesis of an ego attitude that can support what Jung called the transcendent function, the bridge between ego consciousness and the deeper layers of the unconscious.

## Ego and Self in Analysis

The ego is the primary object of all practical therapeutic and analytic endeavors. It is to the ego that we psychotherapists must answer, for it is the ego that defines a person's consciousness and is the felt center of a life. It would be foolish to attempt the healing of the psyche without healing the ego: Should the procedure succeed, the patient would not know the difference!

And yet we also know that the ego is merely a partial aspect of the whole psyche. The whole, of which the ego is a part, consists of the Self in its totality of polarities, the most essential of which is the spectrum that stretches between the instinctual-somatic and the archetypal-spiritual extremes. This mind-body totality is what Jung conceived of as the Self. The Self is the God principle, as it were, and the ego is the human reality principle.

The ego is defined as a complex that constitutes a focal center for consciousness. Like all other complexes, the ego has an archetypal core, and in the case of the ego this archetypal core is very special. It is the Self. This sets the ego apart from the other complexes. The ego's consciousness is privileged within the psychic universe because of its unique link to the Self.

Being a complex, however, means that the ego is also deeply constituted by trauma. In fact, Jung theorizes that the ego comes into being through "collisions" that inevitably take place between an individual and the world. He was familiar with Rank's notion of the importance of the birth trauma for ego development, and, while he did not give this early experience quite the weight that Rank did, he would concede that traumata suffered at birth have a fundamental constituting force in ego formation. The ego is born in and through pain, and at its heart lies anxiety. The "reality principle" by which the ego is supposed to operate (according to Freud) in fact amounts to little more than an anxiety principle, but this is (for Jung too) key to the ego and its functioning.

Like all complexes the ego is made up of a variety of associated contents clustered around a bipolar core, and as such it is subject to fragmentation and to splitting processes that can easily break it apart into states of dissociation. In a sense, modern depth psychology begins with the study of ego dissociation. Mesmer and his followers employed "artificial somnambulism," or hypnosis (Braid's term), to create special altered states of consciousness and to induce intense rapport between "magnetizer" and subject (cf. Ellenberger, p. 112ff). What these early practitioners of depth therapy had stumbled upon was the phenomenon of ego dissociation through hypnosis. Hypnotism became what Ellenberger has termed a "royal road to the unknown mind" (p. 112) because it opened a way through the normally defended rational ego into uncharted territory. From Mesmer the trail leads to Janet, who explored the phenomena of dissociation in great detail at the Salpetriere and is often credited as the founder of modern dynamic psychiatry (Ellenberger, p. 331). Jung, like Freud, studied Janet's methods and employed both some of his techniques and some of his theories in his early work.

The existence of variety in ego states fascinated Jung from an early age. His doctoral dissertation was the study of a medium (in fact his cousin, Helene Preiswerk) who had an amazing ability to acquire personalities during seances that had vivid historical features about which she consciously knew very little. Such states of possession by foreign psychic bodies (complexes and archetypal images), Jung found in his later investigations with psychotic patients at the Burgholzli, can be transitory or relatively long-lasting. One goal of therapeutic analysis is to become aware of these various states and part personalities and to knit them together into a relatively cohesive whole, so that an umbrella of consciousness and personal identity can surround the parts and hold them together. This is different from merging them into a hybrid. Jungians speak of containing the opposites within consciousness, of maintaining the tensions inherent in the interplay and dynamics between the various pieces of the psyche, and of not allowing them to fall back into dissociation.

As the virtual center of consciousness, the ego is responsible for playing the role of container of these polarities and splinters of consciousness, as well as having the adaptational function of responding to changing environments. The archetypal core of the ego complex comes into being even before the physical birth of the infant. This virtual center of incipient consciousness is in place and functioning already in utero, as the fetus orients itself to its environment and begins to sense the world. The Self, which is the central organizing archetype of the psyche as a whole, contributes to the ego this same quality of centrality as the organism emerges into the world and gains more consciousness.

The deep connection to the Self at the ego's core makes the ego a paradoxical psychic figure. On the one hand, it is the seat of conscious anxiety and pain, originating and awakening through trauma. On the other hand, it is divine and godlike because of its identity as the Self. The ego is at once the incarnation of the Self in the time-space continuum and the fragile register of existential anxiety.

Clustered around this central bipolar core at the heart of the ego are associations that make up a person's remembered history and personal identity. Mother, father and all the other significant figures of personal history are woven into the fabric of consciousness and ego identity. These can be supportive and life enhancing associations, or they can be debilitating and toxic ones. Analysis attempts to separate the ego from the pathological associations wrapped into the structure of the ego complex and to recover and support the beneficent ones.

Being a complex, however, the ego is of only relative size and importance in the psychic universe. It is not its center and not even its major body. As the center of consciousness, though, it easily succumbs to the illusion that it is the center of the whole psychic universe and therefore in control of the other lesser parts. This state of inflation, which is based on too close an identification between the ego and the archetypal Self, can lead to psychic symptoms, to dangerous overestimation of mastery and control, and to illusions of grandiosity vis-a-vis the world at large. While such archetypal inflation is normal in childhood, it is obviously dangerous in adolescence and adulthood. The ego learns through hard experience that it is not the master of the psychic household and that it is subject to fluctuations in the psychic economy. It may seek someone to blame for this at first, a scapegoat, but eventually it can come to accept psychic reality. This displacement of the ego from illusions of centrality is sought as an outcome of analysis.

The ego that has not disentangled itself sufficiently from the Self can behave like the executive of an organization who fails to realize that the organization as a whole needs the cooperation of even the humblest workers in order to function well. This ego takes too much credit for the success of the organization and usually tries to avoid blame if the organization fails. The workers, on the other hand, also need the executive; if sane executive decisions and judgments are made, all may survive and prosper. This perception of interrelatedness among the parts of the intrapsychic world is where the ego needs to arrive in its awareness in order for sanity and optimal functioning to become possible. It is a position of considerable humility.

If, because of its deep internal association with the Self, the ego has a tendency to assume centrality in the psychic world and to fall into grandiose illusions of specialness and importance in the world at large, it can also suffer the opposite problem if the connection between ego and Self is too tenuous and distant. Then the ego feels abandoned and unmoored in a frightening world of impersonal forces. It feels inadequate and suffers from low self-confidence and self-doubt.

The proper balance in this relation between ego and Self is discussed in Jungian literature under the heading of the ego-Self axis. If the ego-Self axis is sufficiently and properly developed, a person has the feeling of possessing a solid core of inner strength, identity and value and has access to resources for self-esteem and confidence, but the ego is not puffed up and unrealistically inflated.

By hearing the soul's cry for help and taking a stand on the side of the native drive for wholeness, the therapist can aid and abet the deeper unconscious processes that are striving for health. What Jung refers to as "soul" (the anima and animus in his writings) is a level of psyche that forms a link between ego consciousness and the instinctual-archetypal, natural psyche, which ultimately is also the link between the ego and the Self. The anima/animus structure is a "function" (see chapter 12, below) that corresponds to what Jung calls the transcendent function, and its purpose is to provide a channel of communication between the ego and the deepest levels of the collective unconscious. It is also roughly equivalent to the ego-Self axis if one imagines this axis as a function. To advance this cause of establishing a vital contact with the soul, any technique that does the job is good technique. In analytic practice, the usual Jungian move in trying to facilitate this recovery of the soul connection is to work intensively on dreams and to engage in active imagination.

## Dream Analysis and Active Imagination

Dreams and fantasies are subverters of hardened and entrenched psychic structure. Many dreams bypass the blockages created by the complexes and lead directly to the layer of soul that is the connecting link to the depths of the instinctual/archetypal psyche. It is not surprising that some analysands will resist bringing dreams into analysis or giving them much credence when they do. This is a resistance to the decentering process that threatens an inflated and defensive ego.

The Jungian approach to analysis is oriented largely by working with dreams and inner images and taking cues from them as to what kinds of intervention would be useful on the analyst's part. Dream analysis was and remains a cornerstone of classical and also of much neoclassical or post–Jungian analysis.

Dreams require interpretation, however, and a method for rendering their often puzzling themes and images useful in analysis. Jung's method of dream interpretation is basically twofold: reductive and synthetic. If the clinical picture and the dream themes point for the need to interpret dreams reductively, i.e., in terms of the past and especially of childhood and pathological developmental issues, then the analyst takes this approach. Reductive analysis is caustic and burns away ego inflation and the distortions due to complexes. On the other hand, when the clinical picture and the dreams point toward the need for a prospective, synthetic approach, the analyst will interpret in terms of future possibilities, untapped potentialities, and larger symbolic meanings. This is usually recommended for cases of depression and chronic low self-esteem. Striking the balance between these two approaches, which are typically both used at one point or another in most lengthy analyses, is a clinical art. Timing and appropriateness depend greatly upon the analyst's trained intuition and the accuracy of empathic knowledge of the analysand's inner states.

In a departure from Freud's method of interpretation, Jung did not place much value upon free association as a means for discovering the meaning of dreams. Free association, he felt, does not break free of the controlling complexes and the dominant ego attitude. It goes in a circle of the already more or less well known. For Jung, the dream is not meaningful until it is brought to the point of telling the dreamer something new. If you can easily think a particular thought, he felt, there is no need to dream it. So the interpretive strategy is to stay with the dream images as presented until they begin to reveal ideas, insights, patterns, or feeling states that are not already familiar to the ego. At that point, the ego can begin to benefit from the compensatory function of dreaming and can open a pathway to the deeper healing influences of the natural psyche, the instinctual and archetypal layers. The dream then begins to function as a pathway to the soul of the analysand.

A second method, besides dream interpretation, for reaching past the personal complexes and ego defenses into the deeper layers of the psyche is active imagination. In active imagination, the analysand (in private, not in the analytic session) opens a dialogue with figures of the unconscious as they have appeared either in earlier dreams or as they appear in the active imagination itself. These imaginal figures do not represent the personal complexes—e.g., mother and father—but rather figures of the archetypal, collective unconscious. Active imagination figures function much like icons on a computer screen, opening the way to programs locked deeply away in the hidden layers of the unconscious. By stimulating these iconic images, the ego is exposed to a stream of messages and information from sources of energy and insight in the unconscious that lie beyond the individual's neurotic patterns, acquired complexes, and conventional ego attitudes.

Active imagination was classically a technique invoked in analysis to help resolve intransigent transferences. It does this by replacing an outer icon (i.e., the analyst) with an inner one. As an analytic technique, active imagination may be used throughout treatment or become more emphasized toward the end of analysis as a way of preparing for termination.

## Conclusion

Practice follows vision and theory in Jung's psychology, but practice also feeds theory and keeps it growing and evolving. The Jungian vision is a continuously expanding one. What Jung himself lays down as a powerful and compelling view of the wondrous complexity and nuanced subtlety of the human psyche is based on a polarity of body and spirit. The full human being is a union of animal and spiritual nature and energy. Jung's theory of the psyche, therefore, spans the heights and depths of human experience and accounts for the similarities and differences that can be found among human beings throughout recorded history. The rich territory where instincts and archetypes meet, the psyche, is a vast and nearly inexhaustible wonderland of figures and potency.

Jung's is also a theory that allows for human evolution and emergence. Neither the individual nor the human race is a static, "given" entity but rather an evolving process. The final goal of this evolution is unknown and can only be surmised on the basis of what is known about the basic structures of the psyche as we come to understand them. What Jung concluded is that there is in the individual an implacable drive toward wholeness.

Pathology is caused by a departure from this basic groundplan. In its milder forms it amounts to simple one-sidedness that needs correction. In its more difficult and complex forms, it presents obstacles to living a full existence that need serious, sustained analytic treatment. Even in such cases, however, the deepest assistance comes from nature itself, for healing has its source within nature and not directly in the healing ministrations of therapists, as important and catalytic of healing as these may be.

For Jung the fundamental human struggle is to become oneself as fully and completely as possible. What this means is living the basic plan of the psyche, which is written into the fabric of nature itself. This is not without many inherent conflicts that produce necessary suffering (as opposed to neurotic suffering) and severe limitation. The narrative that unfolds from this struggle with limitations is the story of individuation, a story of accepting limitation on the one hand and of realizing potentials that lie hidden in the depths of the unconscious on the other. The latter await the quickening summons of auspiciously timed constellating life events, of which therapy may be one.

### REFERENCES

Dieckmann, H. 1991. *Methods in Analytical Psychology.* Wilmette, IL.: Chiron Publications.

Ellenberger, H. 1970. *The Discovery of the Unconscious.* New York: Basic Books.

Fordham, M. 1957. *New Developments in Analytical Psychology.* London: Routledge.

Frey-Rohn, L. 1974. *From Freud to Jung.* New York: Putnam.

Galimberti, U. 1989. Analytical Psychology in an Age of Technology. In *Zeitschrift fuer Analytische Psychologie und ihre Grenzgebiete* 20:87–120 (Author's translation).

Hoganson, G. 1994. *Jung's Struggle with Freud.* Wilmette, IL.: Chiron Publications.

Jung, C. G. 1916. The Transcendent Function. In *Collected Works*, vol. 8, pp. 67–90. Princeton: Princeton University Press.

———. 1931. Problems of Modern Psychotherapy. In *Collected Works*, vol. 16. Princeton: Princeton University Press, 1966.

———. 1936. Psychological Factors Determining Human Behavior. In *Collected Works*, vol. 8, pp. 114–25. Princeton: Princeton University Press, 1969.

———. 1954. On the Nature of the Psyche. In *Collected Works*, vol. 8, pp. 159–234. Princeton: Princeton University Press, 1969.

———. 1966. *Two Essays on Analytical Psychology. Collected Works*, vol. 7. Princeton: Princeton University Press.

———. 1970. *Mysterium Coniunctionis. Collected Works*, vol. 14. Princeton: Princeton University Press.

———. 1975. *Letters*, Vol. 2. Princeton: Princeton University Press.

———. 1976. *The Symbolic Life.* Volume 18 of *The Collected Works.* Princeton: Princeton University Press.

———. 1995. *Jung on Evil* (ed. by Murray Stein). London and Boston: Routledge.

Kerr, J. 1993. *A Most Dangerous Method.* New York: Knopf.

Samuels, A. 1985. *Jung and the Post-Jungians.* London and Boston: Routledge.

———. 1993. *The Political Psyche.* London and Boston: Routledge.

Schwartz-Salant, N. 1989. *The Borderline Personality.* Wilmette, IL.: Chiron Publications.

Stein, M. 1992a. Power, Shamanism, and Maieutics in the Countertransference. In *Transference/Countertransference* (eds. N. Schwartz-Salant and M. Stein), pp. 67–88. Wilmette, IL.: Chiron Publications.

———. 1992b. The Role of Anima/Animus Structures and Archetypes in the Psychology of Narcissism and Some Borderline States. In *Gender and Soul in Psychotherapy* (eds. N. Schwartz-Salant and M. Stein), pp. 233–50. Wilmette, IL.: Chiron Publications.

Van Eenwyk, J. 1991. The Analysis of Defenses. In *Journal of Analytical Psychology* 36:2, pp. 141–63.

# seven

· · · · · · · · · · · · · · · · · · · · · · · · · · ·

# *Amor Fati:* Analysis and the Search for Personal Destiny

Is it possible to come to love one's own history and to develop a sense of personal destiny as a result of analysis? This question takes us a step further into the discussion of meaning as it crops up in and around the therapeutic process. To a considerable degree, a person's sense of wholeness depends upon realizing meaning in life. And this in turn depends upon recognizing and sensing archetypal factors at work in one's own personal history. To love one's fate (*amor fati*) is to have felt and embraced the whole complexity of one's life, one's wholeness.

In one of his greatest essays, "On the Psychology of the Transference," Jung showed how the constellation of the *coniunctio* archetype in analysis gives rise to a sense that the analytic encounter has meaning for the whole of one's life history. There is a feeling of momentousness when this happens. Both partners in this relationship are deeply affected and both are changed and transformed. Both are touched by agape love and infused by the energy of the love union. The healing that comes about through this experience is due to a profound conjunction of personal and archetypal factors, which fuse and create the experience of meaning and destiny. Jung speaks here of the activation of kinship libido.

While many other analyst authors have followed Jung's lead in locating archetypal factors in transference and countertransference processes in analysis, none has to my knowledge noted that archetypes also play an essential role in the creation of historical narrative in analysis. This aspect of analytic work, which goes under the heading of reconstruction, offers opportunities to recognize archetypal images and indeed to feel cosmic meaning at work in one's personal life history. It will be my contention in this chapter that remembering and reconstructing the past, as this takes place within the context of analysis, can be as important for transformation as the transference/countertransference process, because reconstruction also rests upon and is informed by archetypal processes and factors. Archetypes can be experienced in memory and in the construction of a personal narrative.

A preliminary point needs to be made and underscored. Narrative creation and historical reconstruction as this is done within the context of an analytic transference are special and perhaps unique, because the transference/countertransference relationship makes the past deeply accessible and helps to constellate the archetypal factors latent and available within the psyche. Without these elements we would have a different genre and a different experience, one that may be with or without archetypal dimensions. Reconstruction in analysis is quite different from taking a history or anamnesis at the outset of analysis or engaging in a simple recollection of the past. It occurs piecemeal over the long course of analysis and is put together bit by bit from emerging memories and interpretations. A new sense of personal history is constellated in the course of analysis. This constellation depends importantly upon the energy of the transference/countertransference process. At the beginning of analysis, the full scope of the final picture is largely unknown by both analyst and analysand. An early anamnesis often leaves out the most essential parts of the story, the repressed and denied pieces, which will enter into consciousness and become prominent as the analysis proceeds.

Furthermore, an essential role in the experience of analytic reconstruction is played by the witness, the analyst. The narrative that is constructed in analysis is told to a singular audience, the analyst. The analyst's role in creating the setting and the atmosphere in which the story emerges is crucial. Moreover, by assisting in the tasks of reconstructing and understanding this history and of bringing the most deeply hidden and personal elements of the psyche into consciousness, the analyst is a key catalyst in the narrative-creating process. Reconstruction of personal history in analysis emerges within the context of the interactive field between analyst and analysand.

Analysis is in a sense continuous history making, which calls for the active participation of both analyst and analysand. In the Jungian literature, however, there has been little rigorous discussion of the technique and place of reconstruction in analysis. Jung himself rarely uses the term (para. 595 in Volume 4 of *The Collected Works* is the only instance noted in the *General Index*). Occasionally Jung speaks of "recollection" in a vague and nontechnical way. And later Jungian authors have not focused much on reconstruction in analysis either. Such standard texts as Edward Whitmont's *The Symbolic Quest*, June Singer's *Boundaries of the Soul*, Hans Dieckmann's *Methods in Analytical Psychology*, and my own (edited) *Jungian Analysis* skirt this subject. Instead, the center of Jungian discussions of analytic practice has been occupied by consideration of various methods of interpreting dreams and other contents of the unconscious and of the transference/countertransference process. Educational tools in therapy, such as amplification from myth and religion, and the various means available for evoking symbolic material—active imagination, sandplay, dance/movement, bodywork, painting—have found a place in the standard texts. Reconstruction, however, has been a stepchild and largely ignored. Only the British authors of the developmentalist orientation, particularly Michael Fordham and Kenneth Lambert, have given it more than passing attention.

This general neglect originated in Jung's divergence from Freudian technique and in his own differing theoretical interests. One of Jung's criticisms of Freud's early psychoanalysis was that it ran the risk—and often succumbed to it—of paying too much attention to patients' stories about childhood. In Jung's Fordham University lectures of 1913, for example, he criticized psychoanalysts for sometimes following their patients endlessly into the maze of their dubious meanderings and ruminations about childhood, thus getting lost in the neurosis themselves. By focusing so much on childhood and on the reconstruction of repressed traumatic scenes from that period, Jung felt, psychoanalysis was in danger of coming to resemble the neurotic diseases it was intended to cure. At that time, Jung regarded the most important cause of neurosis to be a person's unwillingness to face up to the emotional demands of the present. Analysis, therefore, should keep a careful eye on what the patient is avoiding in the present and should interpret the patient's flights into childhood memory or into incestuous transference fantasies as regressions and evasions from the life tasks at hand. Unless the patient manages to surmount this obstacle, Jung argued, neurosis will maintain its grip (1913, pars. 291–313). With this attitude it was unlikely that Jung would give himself with great enthusiasm to the work of reconstruction in analysis. Memories of the distant past were seen as a clever trap laid by the neurotic mind to divert attention from the real problems at hand. To become caught up in endless remembrances of things past, not to mention the intensely intriguing possibility of "screen memories," would play into the crafty patient's already too-well-developed tendency to evade the responsibilities of the present. Analysis would become mere woolgathering.

A second early trend in Jung's thinking that led him to look away from the role and value of reconstruction in analysis was his fascination with myth and symbol. In *Psychology of the Unconscious*, written in 1911–12 as he was distancing himself from Freud, this strong interest in myth and symbol is fully apparent. This tendency has been further emphasized by many of Jung's followers. When archetypal themes are elaborated in the clinical literature of analytical psychology, one often hears little about a patient's personal history. We come into the territory of impersonal, or transpersonal, or archetypal psychology, where personal matters become obscured not to say insignificant. The distinction between "personal" and "archetypal" has been used by some authors to create a breach between a person's history and the objective psyche, by dividing them into two separated realms of mental life. On the clinical level, then, the personal aspects of history tend to be separated from larger, even cosmic, meanings, and the result is an impression of ungroundedness.

This polarization between personal and archetypal levels of psychic experience has been created by careless usage and thinking, but it has also been used for defensive purposes. To claim archetypicality avoids the hazard of claiming personal responsibility. Jung himself does not actually polarize these dimensions either clinically or theoretically, nor do most practicing Jungian analysts, but the theory of analytical psychology can provide a handy means by which this kind of defensive thinking can be fostered. As I will show later, Jung himself actually used a method of reconstruction in his clinical practice, and he certainly assumed it in his general discussions of the therapeutic process.

What is meant, then, by the term "reconstruction"? In the broadest and simplest sense, it refers to the activity in analysis of telling and hearing the life story of the analysand. In a more precise sense, it means piecing together the inner history, the emotional life story, of the analysand, often with particular emphasis on childhood and on repressed or lost memories, by using the means of dream interpretation, interpretation of the transference/countertransference dynamics, emerging memory images, and general theoretical understandings of development and psychodynamics. What Jungians perhaps add to this generic understanding of reconstruction in analysis is the archetypal dimension, the dimension of meaning. What is the meaning of the story? Why and to what end has this individual's life played itself out in a particular fashion?

When a person enters analysis and begins to reveal what has led to this step of consulting an analyst, to speak personally about the sufferings and problems that present themselves at this precise moment in life, it is not long before the historical antecedents come to the fore. Certain events from the past have converged to create a troublesome situation; images of earlier times and places come to mind; even dreams and experiences from childhood and adolescence may be related in an initial session. The stories of relationships, of work, and of many significant life events are told. As time goes on and session

follows session, the analyst perceives an increasingly sharp picture of
the analysand's psychological patterns and of how they have grown
and developed in the past, as well as of how they operate in the present.
The analyst's interpretations often then take on a historical cast: this
dream image or that transference reaction is linked to an earlier scene
or relationship. In this fashion the present comes to be seen as a con-
tinuation, even sometimes an unconscious repetition, of the past.
When these kinds of continuity and repetition have been established
such that even the subtlest feelings and emotional reactions and images, as they are experienced in the present, can be related to older,
established themes, the work of reconstruction has been undertaken
and to some extent completed. Lambert quotes Novey as saying that
reconstruction is "an attempt . . . to see the patient and have him see
himself in some continuing context in which his present modes of
experiencing and dealing with himself and others are a logical out-
growth" (Lambert 1981, p. 115).

But tying the present to the past in this way may be too reductive.
Should the psyche be so tightly bound to history? What about the
psyche's creativity and the emergence of new potentials? Binding the
psyche to history and to the patterns of thought and feeling that come
about in the course of development places it in Procrustes' bed. Reconstruction may hamper the freedom of the psyche to soar, to create, to
resurrect and begin again. History chains the soul to a corpse. In fact,
history must be defeated and transcended if one's full freedom and
potential for spiritual awareness are to be realized. The psyche is discontinuous, illogical, and free, as much as it is continuous, logical,
and bound to the past. Attempts to create tight linkages between the
operations of the autonomous psyche and its surroundings—interpersonal, cultural, or historical—must acknowledge also the prospective
or future-oriented drive of the psyche. Otherwise they fall into the pit
of reductionism.

What I would like to show in this chapter is a way to combine a
historical approach in analysis with an archetypal, prospective approach. My argument is that when the activity of reconstruction in
analysis reaches an archetypal level it takes up the question of meaning and purpose. Personal history and narrative then become infil-
trated with archetypal elements and take on the nature of personal
destiny. The Jungian contribution to reconstruction and narrative
creation lies precisely in this sense of the deeper background processes
active both in analytical reconstruction itself and in the lineaments
of personal fate and destiny as they appear in the story that is gathered
and told in analysis.

In speaking about archetypal dimensions of reconstruction, 1 will be speaking then of several different things: of the archetypal basis of processing data historically, of archetypal features of the act of remembering, of archetypal elements within the remembered events of one's personal history, and of archetypal elements in countertransference feeling and imagery that can be used for reconstruction. All of these dimensions have a place in reconstruction and narrative building.

## On the Archetypal Basis of Thinking Historically

One basis for claiming archetypicality for any human activity is its ubiquity. Historical thinking is ancient and universal. Every known human group has a story of its origins and history, a narrative, be it historical in the modern sense or mythic and traditional. Generally the origin of a group's history is situated *in illo tempore* (Eliade), in a mythical creation event, a cultural big bang from which history unfolds. In the Biblical tradition, for instance, prehistory is occupied by God and His brooding over the waters of chaos; He creates the heavens and the earth and its creatures, the humans, the garden, and history begins from there. Rome's history begins with its founding by the orphans, Romulus and Remus. American history begins with a story of revolution against the parent country. After such more or less mythic beginnings, the story of the nation or tribe goes on and the various significant human and divine figures are recalled by the historian in detail as they appear on the stage of history and influence the historical process. Historians remember the story.

"History" derives from the Greek adjective *histor*, meaning "knowing, hence erudite, itself an agent . . . from *eidenai* . . . to know" (Partridge 1966, p. 289). At the root is *weld-*, "connoting vision, which subserves knowledge; cf. Gr *eidos*, form . . . akin to Skt *vedas-*, knowledge" (ibid.). The knowing, erudite ones, the original historians, were poets and storytellers who could remember history back to the very walls of Troy or to the days of the patriarchs, all the way back to the mythic source of history itself, and could then come forward into the present. This was not scientific history in the modern sense, but it was equally based on the human urge to know by having a history. The "idea of history" (an archetype) was at work in an archaic way in the minds of these early historians.

After the storytellers came the historians proper—Biblical, Greek, Indian, etc. Every human group, including our nation, our ethnic tribe, as well as our individual families, has a history. It is a sad and broken group indeed that has lost its story. The same is true of individuals.

There is other evidence as well for the archetypicality of thinking historically. It is a fact that a historical record of sorts is kept by the unconscious quite independently of conscious intent. One of the original insights of psychoanalysis was that the mind does not simply erase the past. One may forget or even repress a memory trace, but events are not permanently lost. They are stored in the unconscious. The memory bank is only partially conscious; much of it is unconscious. The unconscious keeps an historical record, and thus it can also anticipate events because it houses a time-keeping device. This timekeeper in the unconscious has a sense of historical pattern and duration and thus imparts to the individual an intuitive sense of how long things should take. Many people report, for instance, that they can easily awaken without an alarm clock if they tell themselves before falling asleep when they need to get up.

Jung gives an example of this internal timekeeper in reference to a case that he alludes to in "The Psychology of the Transference." He says that when the transference is initiated, "a queer unconscious time-reckoning, lasting for months or even longer" begins (1946, par. 376). The example he cites is from the dreams of a sixty-year-old woman patient who was having dreams of a baby, "a child hero or divine child" (par. 378). In the dreams, this child was six months old. Upon investigation, it turned out that six months earlier the analysand had had a birth dream. Nine months before that she had painted a picture of "a naked female figure from whose genital region [a serpent] rears up towards the heart, where it burst into a five-pointed, gorgeously flashing golden star" (par. 380). Jung comments: "The serpent represents the hissing ascent of Kundalini, and in the corresponding yoga this marks the first moment in a process which ends with deification in the divine Self, the syzygy of Shiva and Shakti. It is obviously the moment of symbolical conception." (par. 380). This whole sequence of conception, birth, and growth had occurred spontaneously in the unconscious and had unfolded in a time frame that matched that of actual historical time, had it been a physical process. The unconscious was keeping time.

A similar example of unconscious time reckoning occurred in the case of a sixteen year-old daughter of one of my analysands. She had had a secret abortion in early summer, which she confessed to her parents in August. In September she returned to school and was doing quite well until late October, when she developed a peculiar and undiagnosable illness. She consistently ran a temperature of 100 + F, which did not respond to medical treatment. As a result she could not go to school. The parents took her to the best diagnosticians in the city, and none could find evidence of disease. Everything was tried, to no avail, and she was forced to stay at home, mostly in bed. The theory was that the fever was caused by a pelvic infection and that it was located in the reproductive organs, but no evidence could be found. She stayed in bed from October onward. In mid-February a new doctor decided it was time for exploratory surgery. This was done, and the girl responded poorly, having to be hospitalized for two full days rather than only overnight. She came home, took a week to recover, but then developed a case of common flu. This disappeared in a week, and with it all signs of illness. There was no more fever, and she returned to school. The doctors had found no evidence of disease in the exploratory surgery. The peculiar fact was that the operation and hospitalization coincidentally took place exactly nine months after conception, just when she would have been going into the hospital to give birth. It was as though the unconscious had kept time, knew it was now time to release her from her pelvic distress, and recognized the surgery as equivalent to birth.

Anecdotes such as these do not prove the existence of a time-keeping function in the unconscious, but they do strongly suggest this to be the case. It is this psychic factor, 1 would guess, that underlies the pervasive human tendency to think historically in a conscious way.

It is important to make this point about the archetypal basis of reconstruction, because it can appear that it is merely the times, and the peculiar modern bent toward historicism, that has captured the minds of therapists as well as of educated persons generally. Historical thinking in the academy has certainly flowered in the last several centuries. The nineteenth century saw a great burgeoning of it, and our own century has continued the tradition. This tendency toward historicism in the intellectual community has produced great stress and conflict because of the ways in which secular historians have rendered sacred history. Their accounts have, generally speaking, left out the dimension of purpose and meaning. The basic conflict has been joined between the mythic, religious thinkers on one side and the scientific, empirical thinkers on the other. For the former, history is grounded in and profoundly shaped by divine interventions; for the latter, such mythic elements need to be ferreted out of the historical record. Meaning has no place in the record. The debate has not been so much about whether or not history is important or should be pursued as an intellectual discipline, but about what can be counted as a part of the record. Do dreams and revelations count? What is one to do with historical accounts of divine intervention? The secular historian has been stuck and has not known what to do with this problem, except to ignore it in favor of the "facts."

The same argument can be transposed to the psychological and clinical level. Almost everyone would agree that history and development are molar ideas in psychology and in the practice of psychotherapy, but not all would agree on what counts as valid historical data. Should important dreams be included in the developmental story? Should synchronistic events be given an important place? Or should one count only the unfolding of a genetically based developmental sequence and the influences of the environment? The conflict between views of history and views of what makes up the fabric of history should be as intense in psychological circles as it has been in philosophical and theological ones. If creative acts of God (synchronistic events) are excluded from the historical process, the record will bear no evidence of transcendence or meaning, and the soul will inevitably be reduced to a shimmering epiphenomenon of genes and environment.

At one level, Jung broadened the scope of history in its application to clinical practice. Included in the analysand's history are not only genetic factors of inheritance, childhood events and the immediate family's influence, but also the much larger matrix of culture, of generational patterns, and of archaic history as this is embedded in the collective unconscious. Jung's interpretation of history and his account of psychological development includes the psychological dynamics of identification, introjection, participation mystique, and complex formation, all of which together move toward the inclusion of large amounts of collective material in the developmental process. But he also deepened the notion of history by including the archetypal dynamics of constellation, synchronicity, and spontaneous influences from beyond the horizon of external causal factors. If anything, Jung is a more rigorous and consistent historian than most other clinical theorists, because he recognizes that the individual's life is deeply formed by these many factors, all of which play a part in development and, more importantly, lean toward a destined goal.

This understanding of history should give the Jungian analyst a particularly keen appreciation for the importance of reconstruction in clinical work. Reconstruction is a key part of becoming conscious and of discovering meaning in one's own personal existence. Reconstruction is healing because it restores consciousness to an archetypal base and connects it to its deeper wholeness in the psyche. Its healing power derives not only from the benefit of regaining a sense of one's own history and thereby solidifying an identity, but even more from the healing effect of remembering one's wholeness.

## On Jung's Use of Reconstruction in Clinical Practice

One reason many readers come away from Jung's *Collected Works* with the impression that he did little reconstruction in analysis and that he preferred to amplify archetypal aspects of his patients' dreams and unconscious contents is that he spends so few pages actually detailing his analytic cases. I am convinced that if he had written up his cases, the surprise would be the importance of personal history in them. One reason I am confident of this is that in the several cases he does describe, the personal historical details that are uncovered are always critical for understanding the case and its outcome. I will cite three such instances.

The earliest of these cases (1961, pp. 115–17; 1935, pars. 107–8) comes from the time of Jung's residency at the Burgholzli. Jung recounts that a woman was admitted to the hospital and diagnosed as schizophrenic. He disagreed with the diagnosis and thought it was a major depression, a much less serious psychiatric illness. By using the word-association test and analyzing her dreams, he discovered her story: She had unconsciously killed her child by giving it contaminated water to drink. The reconstruction of this piece of repressed personal history led to a full recovery, according to Jung, and constituted the whole of her treatment.

The second case is of a young Jewish woman with an anxiety neurosis (1939, pars. 635–36). Jung recounts that she had been in analysis before, and the analyst had fallen in love with her. The treatment had failed to relieve her symptoms or to cure her mental anguish. Jung says that he dreamed of her the night before he met her and realized in the dream that she had a debilitating father complex. When he interviewed her, however, he could find little evidence of this problem, so he dug deeper into her history and found that she was the granddaughter of a Hasidic rabbi. This bit of personal history proved to be the key to a cure. Jung told her, "Look here . . . you have been untrue to your God. Your grandfather led the right life, but you are worse than a heretic; you have forsaken the mystery of your race. You belong to holy people." Upon hearing this she was able to accept her Jewishness and her religious identity, and within one week the anxiety neurosis was cured (par. 636). In this instance, the reconstruction of family history led not only to a stronger sense of personal identity but also to realizing the symbolic, religious tendency and need of the psyche. The retrieval of an important piece of personal history and the reconnection to the archetypal psyche happened in one and the same realization. Again, reconstruction represented the key to therapeutic healing.

A third case reported by Jung is more extensive. He refers to it several times in the *Collected Works* (1942, par. 189; 1950, pars. 656ff.; 1937, pars. 546–63; 1935, pars. 334–37), as well as in the Kundalini Seminar (Autumn 1932, pp. 91ff.). This is the case of a young woman who spent her childhood in Java. She was twenty-five years old when Jung began to see her. Jung was her third analyst, the former two treatments having ended in impasse and failure. In the course of treatment, Jung reports, he was at first put off by her vulgar persona and then extremely puzzled by the physical symptoms she developed as they worked together. He was ultimately able to amplify these physical maladies by using the Kundalini yoga symbolic chakra system, which he had discovered independently while she was in treatment. His extensive knowledge of the historical details of this patient's life and his evaluation of their central importance in her psychology (see especially 1937, pars. 546–63) make it evident that he did a great deal of reconstruction of her early years, particularly of her childhood in Java and the relationship she had with a Javanese ayah, a nanny or native nurse. Jung was able to understand her bizarre dream images and physical symptoms and to explain their meaning to her, because he could relate her Javanese childhood to the symbol system of tantric yoga. Treatment broke off, he says, when she reached the *manipura* center and experienced a bird descending and piercing through the fontanelle to the diaphragm. At this point she realized she wanted to have a child, literally, and gave up psychological treatment without explanation. A year later she returned to Jung and explained why she had abruptly terminated; he, in turn, was able to amplify her motives by using tantric philosophy.

> This little bit of Tantric philosophy helped that patient to make a normal human life for herself, as a wife and mother, and to get out of the local demonology she had sucked in with her ayah's milk, and to do so without losing touch with the inner, psychic figures which had been called awake by the long forgotten influences of her childhood. What she experienced as a child, and what later estranged her from European consciousness and entangled her in a neurosis, was, with the help of analysis, transformed not into nebulous fantasies but into a lasting spiritual possession in no way incompatible with an ordinary human existence, a husband, children, and housewifely duties.
>
> (Jung 1937, par. 563)

This paragraph, as clearly as any single passage in Jung's written works, illustrates the intimate blending of personal and archetypal factors in his method of reconstruction. The personal elements and the archetypal ones are seen as making up a whole, and they are held closely together in the fabric of a person's history.

Others cases of Jung's could be cited to make the same point. In practice, the line of demarcation between personal and archetypal aspects in the personality is much less straight than it sometimes is made to seem in theory. And historical reconstruction is deeply woven into the process of analysis, alongside the other aspects of treatment. More than that, the product of reconstruction—the narrative—often occupies the center of clinical treatment, forming a kind of center pole that supports the whole analytic edifice.

It is sometimes supposed that the strength of Jungian analysts lies in our ability to see things archetypally. Give us a grain of sand and we will find a world in it. Indeed, one of the current understandings of what the term "archetypal" means is that it has to do with a way of seeing: "archetypal" is an attribute of the eye of the beholder (Samuels 1985), or a term used to indicate the great importance of something (Hillman 1983). Jungians are supposed to have archetypally oriented eyes. The problem with this usage of the term archetypal is that it sacrifices the connection to the underlying reality of archetypes, like paper money that is no longer related to real property. Consequently the term can become inflated, devalued, and meaningless. The more usual Jungian usage is that "archetypal" means that a psychic fact— an image, a dream, an idea, a perception, or a pattern of behavior— reflects an archetype, which is a structure that is rooted in a reality beyond the psyche. Such patterns can be regarded as generally human and innate, and the trained clinical eye can see these elemental forms in the welter of facts presented by a patient.

The surface through which one peers in analysis is the analysand's life story. The clinician with an eye trained to perceive archetypal factors at work in the analysand's history may reverse the background/ foreground fields, perhaps thus missing some detail but looking more deeply into the underlying patterns that have organized the details in a person's life. In the background one can see evidence of archetypal dynamic/developmental themes, individuation phases and their typical movements through time: the constellation of the *puer aeternus*, of the hero, of the romance with the father, or the *coniunctio*, or the death and rebirth motif. One can also find the typical archetypal figures in personal history: mother, father, child, hero, witch, trickster, clown, anima/animus, the old ones. Gazing into psychic background has the sense of studying life's fate.

The activity of reconstructing history and building narrative in analysis can be carried out on a completely personal basis: this mother, this father, this set of siblings, this school, etc. The result will be a complete set of facts, a story, but it will not include the fatedness of this life to be this way and not that. It is recollection, but it has less therapeutic value than it will have if it includes the spiritual purpose of this life, its meaning. It will also miss its deepest suffering, such as was experienced by a fifty-year-old woman who, racked with sobs and outrage, whispered through her hot tears: "When I was seven years old and my mother gave me that doll with my sister's dress on it, I knew I would never have children and she would. This is my fate." The therapist feels inclined to look away from such finality, but a chord of truth is struck. The sensitive therapist shudders at the thought of such limitation. Who has dictated this course? And are we not in the business of helping people to change, to grow, to become what they are not and want to be? If we look for archetypal patterns, however, we come upon limits, sometimes cruel destinies, also sometimes inexplicable charm and good luck. It does not always seem fair. "The doctor knows that always, wherever he turns, man is dogged by his fate," writes Jung in his seventies (1946, par. 463).

I once worked in analysis with a young man whose presenting problem was intense jealousy. He thought that his beautiful girlfriend was always looking at other young men in their high school class and that she secretly hoped he would get lost. Despite much reassurance from her, his gloomy thoughts persisted. We began by looking at his dreams and putting together his history and trying to understand his suspicions, which he often confessed were bizarre and out of his rational control. After a few months we had assembled the main features of his life story. He was the only child of a couple in which the mother felt far superior to the father, who was a common worker. The mother doted on her son, and he grew up feeling special. At an early age, however, he had been sent to the country to live with grandparents because his mother had to return to work and did not have time to care for a small child. So until he was old enough to enter primary school, he lived several hours away and saw his parents on weekends when they came to visit him. This absence increased the intensity of the bond, but also created feelings of abandonment and lack of self-worth.

As he grew up, he became much more closely identified with his mother than his father. She was musical, poetic, artistic, as he was, while his father was seen by them both as gross and uneducated. His father favored rough sports like football and wished the son were more athletic. By the time I saw him, he had decided to become a high school teacher. He enjoyed writing and painting, and his particular pleasure was sculpture. At one point he had written a poem in which he expressed his feelings of inferiority by depicting himself as a hunchback who lived underground. He was despised by passersby, and occasionally they would spit on him. He felt that his body was "too thick" and often wished that he were more slender and small in build. He felt particularly oversized in his chest, his upper torso, and his hips. He felt womanish and unmasculine, rejected by "real men" like his father.

One night as he was sitting at the desk in his room and dwelling on his jealous thoughts, he looked at his leg and noticed it had turned blue from the foot to an area above the ankle. Greatly upset, he got up and went over to his bed. As he sat there he saw footprints moving across the carpet and thought they might be his father's. Then the vision passed and his foot returned to normal. This highly disturbing experience brought him into therapy with me. He had no other such experiences after that, and a physical examination had revealed nothing of concern.

Some months after therapy began, he took a brief holiday by himself. His girlfriend had gone on a school trip to another city. While camping out, he dreamed that she was having an affair with a young man in the city she was visiting. This dream, which was a highly disturbing nightmare, occurred during a thunderstorm, and he awoke in a panic.

After all of these details had been set out, it occurred to me one day in a session that there were a number of elements in his story that reminded me of the Greek god Hephaestus. He had been cast out of heaven shortly after birth and was crippled. He hobbled, alone of all the gods imperfect. He was also an artistic craftsman and a sculptor. Scoffed at by the other gods for his physical awkwardness and betrayed by his beautiful wife Aphrodite, who went to bed with his half-brother Ares, he suffered from jealousy and low self-esteem. I mentioned this association to my young analysand and told him I did not know much about Hephaestus, which was true at the time, but since he was interested in myth perhaps he could look it up and get some more information on his own. In the next session he told me that he had indeed looked up everything he could on Hephaestus, and that he was strangely moved by this figure. In fact, he had been so taken by the stories about this god that he had shared some of them with his girlfriend over the weekend. When he came to the story of Hephaestus discovering Aphrodite in bed with Ares, he began to weep. Surprisingly, his girlfriend also began to cry, and she confessed that she had indeed had a sexual affair with a classmate during her school holidays. As it turned out, the timing of it coincided precisely with his dream during the thunderstorm in the mountains. This confession had actually relieved him a great deal, because he now knew he was not just crazy. His girlfriend was unreliable sexually, and it was better to know this than to keep wondering about it.

It would be preposterous to claim that this amplification of certain facts in his life history and experience with the Hephaestus myth cured him completely of his jealousy. The roots of his jealousy were fed by deep and persistent forces in his psyche. His self-esteem was certainly improved by this association, however, and the wider context of meaning supplied by the myth helped him place his life experience into the context of an archetypal pattern. The sense of a deeper pattern and meaning for the crippled craftsman that he was provided a redeeming frame of reference. It also gave us a direction to work toward in therapy. There is a good deal of strength and potential for life in the Hephaestian character, but this sense of archetypal pattern also brings awareness of limitations: Hephaestus will never be Hermes, or Zeus, or Apollo. He will always have to struggle with lameness, with fears of rejection, with vulnerability to threats of abandonment. Reflecting later on this case, it occurred to me that this pattern is fairly typical of young men who are intensely introverted and also artistic and creative. Their salvation lies in staying true to their introversion, to their creative vocation, and to their capacity for eventually filling themselves out as adult males, as Hephaestus does after his failure with Aphrodite.

The discovery of a mythic pattern in this case was important as an orientation device. It also reassured us that beneath all the facts of this particular history an archetype was operative. This meant we could have faith in history's unfolding.

### Amor Fati

The key clinical move in Jungian reconstruction is to where and how concrete personal and historical data of an individual's life are joined to archetypal images and themes, either through an archetypal "intervention" in history (synchronicity) or through the effective union of personal and archetypal data and figures such that personal history takes on the feeling of religious meaning and destiny. This is a type of reconstruction that attempts to hold the personal and the archetypal dimensions of history together in a single vision. It is a *mysterium coniunctionis* at the level of history.

Jung quotes the Rosarium:

> Whiten the lato and rend the books lest your hearts be rent asunder.
> For this is the synthesis of the wise and third part of the whole opus.
> Join therefore, as is said in the Turba, the dry to the moist, the black

earth with its water, and cook till it whitens. In this manner you will have the essence of water and earth, having whitened the earth with water: but that whiteness is called air.

(1946, par. 484)

This summarizes, symbolically, the operation I am speaking of in this chapter, where the personal aspects of one's history (the "lato," a black substance) are given the fullness of analytic attention (the "water," which is the divine gift of illumination) until that history rises from the concrete to the symbolic (the "whiteness," the "air") and personal history and archetypal images and meanings become united. This is the stage of the opus referred to by Jung as "Purification," and is accompanied by the lines: "Here falls the heavenly dew to lave / The soiled black body in the grave." (1946, p. 273)

Religious thinkers have developed the idea of a "sacred history," a *Heilsgeschichte* ("salvation-history"), to speak about the inner story of how a people was chosen by God, formed into a holy nation, and given a vocation and a meaning on the stage of world history. This is the inner history of religious communities (Niebuhr 1960), the story of how God has guided, intervened, tended, driven, criticized, and blessed them. It is quite different from the outer history as written by noninvolved, dispassionate, objective academic historians. An inner history is the story of meaning, in which time and eternity, consciousness and unconsciousness, specific historical and archetypal forces together perform their roles and produce a particular configuration in time. To be totally inside such a history is to be quite unconscious and ignorant of other historical trends, of objective history. To be totally outside any such history, however, is to be unconscious and ignorant of transcendent factors at play within the historical process. Traditional persons live wholly inside such a sacred history; modern persons live wholly outside; postmodern persons, such as Jung was, dwell both inside and outside, carrying the tension of these opposing perspectives in a single paradoxical vision.

In analysis these three stages may also be traversed, at least to some extent. The psychological beginner is wholly enclosed in conscious subjectivity, and the objectivity of the unconscious and its influence are completely unknown. Analysis brings about some measure of awareness of this "other" within, an objective psychic reality made up of complexes and archetypes, which dwells alongside conscious subjectivity and impinges on it in innumerable ways. Analysis seeks to achieve some detachment from one's own biases and perspectives and limited history. This is generally what it means to be analyzed. But can analysis also take the third step? This would occur when in the course of reconstructing history and constructing a personal narrative in which the personal and impersonal past, subjective and objective elements, would fuse in such a way that both remained within consciousness. Archetypal elements would not be used to obliterate personal ones or get placed in the service of the ego defenses, nor would the personal elements obscure and hide the archetypal ones. Both would appear and be held in consciousness simultaneously. In this instance, the symbolic becomes personal, and the personal is symbolic.

Jung's woman patient with the Javanese childhood illustrates the synchronistic confluence between an archetypal process and a personal history, and this is uncovered and understood and accepted in the reconstructive work of analysis. The final psychic product of the stage of reconstruction I am describing here is *amor fati:* not only knowledge of one's history, but a full embrace and love of it, as that which has been archetypally meant to be.

### REFERENCES

Dieckmann, H. 1979. *Methods in Analytical Psychology.* Wilmette, IL.: Chiron Publications.

Eliade, M. 1959. *Cosmos and History: The Myth of the Eternal Return.* New York and Evanston: Harper & Row.

Fordham, M. 1978. *Jungian Psychotherapy.* Chichester, New York; Brisbane, Toronto: John Wiley & Sons.

Franz, M.-L. von. 1972. *Creation Myths.* Dallas: Spring Publications.

Harvey, Van A. 1966. *The Historian and the Believer.* New York: Macmillan.

Hillman, J. 1983. *Archetypal Psychology: A Brief Account.* Dallas: Spring Publications.

Jung, C. G. 1913. The Theory of Psychoanalysis. In *Collected Works,* 4:83–226. Princeton: Princeton University Press, 1961.

———. 1916a. *Psychology of the Unconscious.* Supplementary Volume B of *Collected Works.* Princeton: Princeton University Press, 1991.

———. 1932. Psychological Commentary on Kundalini Yoga. Unpublished seminar notes.

———. 1935. The Tavistock Lectures. In *Collected Works,* 18:267–90. Princeton: Princeton University Press, 1976.

———. 1937. The Realities of Practical Psychotherapy. In *Collected Works,* 16:327–38. New York: Pantheon, second edition, 1966.

———. 1939. The Symbolic Life. In *Collected Works,* 18:267–90. Princeton: Princeton University Press, 1976.

———. 1940. The Psychology of the Child Archetype. In *Collected Works,* 9/1:151–81. Princeton: Princeton University Press, second edition, 1969.

———. 1942a. On the Psychology of the Unconscious. In *Collected Works,* 7:3–119. New York: Random House, second edition, 1966.

———. 1946. On the Psychology of the Transference. In *Collected Works,* 16:163–324. New York: Pantheon Books, second edition, 1966.

———. 1950. Concerning Mandala Symbolism. In *Collected Works,* 9/1:355–84. Princeton: Princeton University Press, second edition, 1968.

————. 1952b. Answer to Job. In *Collected Works*, 11:355–472. Princeton: Princeton University Press, second edition,1969.

————. 1954. On the Nature of the Psyche. In *Collected Works*, 8:159–234. Princeton: Princeton University Press, second edition, 1969.

————. 1961. *Memories, Dreams, Reflections.* New York: Random House.

————. 1966. The Practice of Psychotherapy. In *Collected Works*, vol. 16. Princeton: Princeton University Press, 1966.

Lambert, K. 1981. *Analysis, Repair and Individuation.* London, New York, Toronto, Sydney, San Francisco: Academic Press.

Niebuhr, H. R. 1960. *The Meaning of Revelation.* New York: Macmillan.

Partridge, E. 1966. *Origins.* New York: Macmillan.

Samuels, A. 1985. *Jung and the Post-Jungians.* London, Boston, Melbourne and Henley: Routledge & Kegan Paul.

Schwartz-Salant, N. 1986. On the Subtle-Body Concept in Clinical Practice. In *The Body in Analysis*, N. Schwartz-Salant and M. Stein, eds., pp. 19–58. Wilmette, IL.: Chiron Publications.

Schwartz-Salant, N., and M. Stein (eds.), 1984. *Transference and Countertransference Processes in Analysis.* Wilmette, IL.: Chiron Publications.

Singer, J. 1972. *Boundaries of the Soul.* Garden City: Doubleday.

Stein, M. 1980. Hephaistos: A Pattern of Introversion. In *Facing the Gods*, J. Hillman, ed. Dallas: Spring Publications.

————. 1985. *Jung's Treatment of Christianity: The Psychotherapy of a Religious Tradition.* Wilmette, IL.: Chiron Publications.

————. (ed.). 1995. *Jungian Analysis*, second edition. LaSalle and London: Open Court.

Whitmont, E. 1969. *The Symbolic Quest.* New York: G. P. Putnam.

## *eight*

. . . . . . . . . . . . . . . . . . . . . . . . . . . .

# Dreams in the Creation
# of Personal Narrative

There is a history in all men's lives,
Figuring the nature of the times deceased.
Shakespeare, *Henry IV* Pt. II

W hen Jung was breaking with Freud, he announced in his Fordham University lectures that in his opinion the cause of neurosis lay in the present and not in the past. It was useless for the
analyst to follow a neurotic into endless ruminations about past
slights, injuries, and possible traumas, he argued. What the neurotic
needed to do was, in so many words, to pull up his socks and face the
challenge of present life, to quit shirking (1955, pars. 373–381).

Anyone who has tried following the neurotic patient into the
twisted trails of past miseries can sympathize with Jung's Jovian impa-
tience. His view around 1913 had an unusually strong Adlerian tone
to it and may also have resulted from the internal dynamics of the
psychoanalytic group at that time. It is a remarkable ahistorical and
pragmatic position for Jung to have taken precisely at a time when he
was beginning to investigate the greater depths of the unconscious
psyche. Yet it was also the case that in investigating the deeper meanings of Miss Frank Miller's fantasies in *Psychology of the Unconscious*
he gave little attention to her personal history; indeed, he knew almost
nothing about it. His focus was on mythic parallels and themes in the
fantasy material, a focus that he was to repeat again in the 1930s when
he commented on a lengthy dream series using alchemical imagery
and ideas (Jung 1944, pars. 44–331). Again, in that later work, he neglected personal history and associations in favor of a symbolic/arche-
typal interpretation.

It must be pointed out that both of these texts were meant to represent scientific investigations of the unconscious psyche, not to serve
as models for therapeutic analysis. When it came to analytic treatment

of individuals, Jung was not quite so unambiguously nonhistorical (see chapter 6, above). And, from a theoretical point of view, he could not be. Analysis deals with complexes, and what are complexes but personal history recorded in the unconscious? The theory of complexes insists on the practical necessity for historical reconstruction in analysis.

According to Jung's formulations both early and late, complexes are basic building blocks of the personal psyche and make up the contents of the personal unconscious. These are the emotional factors that disturb waking life with their autonomous vagaries and populate our dreams with their images. The dream is the theater in which the complexes, dressed up in a multitude of guises from everyday life, express themselves. According to the subjective approach of dream interpretation, dream figures are to be read as recurrent complexes. It is impossible, therefore, for a Jungian analysis, based as it is on Jungian theory and emphasizing the importance of dreams, to avoid the issue of personal history. Dream figures bring history trailing after them.

If one is a consistent Jungian analyst, then, the rule should be that historical reconstruction would play a central role in analysis precisely because dream interpretation is so central a feature of it. Why is this not always, or perhaps even typically, the case?

As Jung separated from Freud, he developed what he came to call the symbolic and teleological view of the psyche. This view holds that expressions of the unconscious should be interpreted symbolically and teleologically, not reductively and historically. A historical view, or a developmental approach, came to be regarded as overly reductive, while the symbolical view was associated with *telos*, a goal. Instead of reflecting the past, dreams were seen to anticipate the future. From this arose the notion, for example, that the first important dream in analysis is an "initial dream" that forecasts important developments and issues that are likely to arise in the course of the analysis ahead. This does not necessarily mean, of course, that a future as presaged by the unconscious is discontinuous with the past. It may be held, indeed, that the unconscious is able to lay out the future because it contains the complexes as formed in the past and because, furthermore, there is a strong tendency for complexes to repeat the past in the present and future. The repetition compulsion, seen through Jungian eyes, is simply the complexes discharging themselves over and over again upon the passive ego from out of their own inner necessity to repeat. So, on the assumption that dreams are based on complexes and on their internal relations with one another, and that psychological patterns of repetition are formed by complexes, which behave mostly autonomously and require a discharge of energy time and time

again, one could argue that dreams do indeed have a prospective, forward looking agenda: namely, to repeat the past. The task of analysis
would be to strengthen a tendency in the psyche to produce an *opus
contra naturam*, which would free the individual from these historical
patterns and help to dissolve the complexes through interpretation
and working through the emotional issues housed in the complexes.

Yet, because dreams have been seen as symbolic in another sense,
this analytic task of psychological deconstruction has often assumed
a secondary position. In Jung's later theorizing, the complex was seen
to have an archetypal core. And archetypes are ahistorical, at least to
some degree; that is, they are not produced by personal experience but
are rather inborn potentials for experiencing. Thus the mother complex is a mixture of one's personal experiences with one's own mother,
plus the innate potential for receiving and relating to a mother. When
one comes to interpret the mother complex, both of these elements
are taken into account. On the one hand there is mom, on the other
there is the Great Mother. When the accent falls on the Great Mother,
the interpreter tends to look away from personal history to a collective
history of the race or, even further, to the idea of Mothering Itself.
This leads to the meaning of Mothering, to the inner Mother as She
impinges on the psyche here and now. This naturally draws attention
away from historical concerns, from interpreting the individual
mother-child relationship and its ramifications in the particular case
at hand. In this way, dream interpretation runs exactly counter to
historical reconstruction and to working out personal issues with
childhood and/or projection of childhood into present situations such
as in transference.

The dichotomy between symbolic/archetypal interpretations of
dreams and historical/personal interpretations has lead the field of
analytical psychology into one of its central dilemmas (cf. Dieckmann
1986). Questions such as: Should one take a symbolic view of case
material, or should one be "clinical," i.e., reductive and historical?
Should one treat dreams as oracles and auguries of meaning or as
statements of the psyche that require analysis back into a personal
context of history and relationships? Is the psyche fundamentally
mythic and mythproducing, weaving a personal myth out of a warp
and woof of archetypal elements with the intention of giving the individual life its meaning, or is the psyche fundamentally repetitious and
pattern-restating and therefore in need of assistance when it gets stuck
in its old ways? From this difference flows the archetypal school on
one side and the developmentalist school on the other (see Samuels),
the former treating the psyche as fundamentally unconnected to history and history itself as fundamentally of the imagination; the other

considering imagination and emotional life as deeply controlled by history and its impasses. The classical Jungian school tries to straddle this fence by taking a both/and position: the dream is both a statement of historically created complexes and a symbolic statement of the psyche's drive for wholeness. The dream compensates one-sided ego consciousness and thereby pushes for wholeness.

In the classic approach to analysis, the doctrine has been to practice reductive, historical analysis of complexes first (the "Freudian" phase) and the symbolic, synthetic method second (the Jungian phase); or (and this is an important conditional clause) as indicated by dreams themselves. The notion here is that dreams themselves indicate when they are to be taken historically and when teleologically and symbolically.

It is fair to say, I think, that an analyst trained in the developmentalist school will take dreams historically and reductively first and foremost; one trained in archetypalist ways will never take the dream historically but always in its own terms of image and internal structure; one trained classically will look to the dream itself to indicate how to take it, whether personalistically, historically, reductively, or symbolically and teleologically. This means, concretely, that these three analyses will be significantly different. The first will have great historical coherence, the second none, the third some but unsystematically (see Samuels 1985, for a full treatment of these three schools).

In this chapter I will be assuming a modified classical position, in that I will be taking cues about when and how to pursue the search for wholeness from dreams themselves. My hope is that the therapeutic value of this approach will become clear.

## Dreams of History

Some dreams simply cry out for historical reflection and demand it. In this group are recurrent dreams that bring up the past by reliving it. This dream classically replays a traumatic event, such as a battle scene, which recurs repeatedly in almost identical form and insists on the dreamer's once again going through the moment of terror. But there are other dreams, much less physically threatening and less dramatic, that fall into this same genre.

A number of men I have worked with in analysis have reported recurrent dreams of this sort that center on high school sports teams and events. In these dreams of football, basketball, or baseball, there is a particular setting, an important game, often a particular old coach, and a critical moment: "I am driving for the goal line and drop the ball"; "I tell the coach to put me in, but he won't"; "I am suiting up and can't find my shoes," etc.

Collecting the associations and the history represented in this recurring dream, one comes to the feeling that an essential psychic fact of this personality is being presented. This fact cannot be exposed and investigated without the historical setting, without the detail and exact associations. In one case, this psychic fact was expressed by the figure of the coach and by his conflicted relationship with the dreamer. The recurrent dream revolved on the centrality of this figure. Reflecting on this coach, who appeared in many dreams throughout this young man's analysis, we would eventually conclude that the central psychic fact depicted in these dreams again and again was a failed male initiation ritual and its aftermath. Left in the wake of this arrested psychological development were distrust of male authority, tendencies toward a *puer aeternus* character structure, compulsive sexuality, and a search for adequate mentoring that invariably concluded in disappointment. While our analysis of this psychic fact was going on, the dreams began to change. The coach came down from his throne of power and authority and eventually appeared as a pathetic, down and out character in need of help and sympathy. Behind this coach, or rather buried in this image, was a father figure and a father problem that antedated the coach. This young man also reported many dreams of his father, more or less parallel in theme with the coach dreams but often less dramatic and less frozen in content. The father appeared to be a more realistic figure, the coach more set in a specific time period and therefore also more symbolic.

If we say, now, that the coach, or rather this particular coach, was an important dream symbol for this young man, we are using the term in a different way from the sense of "symbolic" as understood when it is contrasted with "historical." The coach clearly symbolizes an essential psychic fact in this man's personality, in that he represents a central complex in dream after dream. This image from dreams could be used with effectiveness, in analyzing other relationships, including (to some extent) the transference. Had it not been for these recurrent dreams of the coach, it would never have occurred to this analysand to use his memories of the coach in such a central and psychologically illuminating fashion. The dreams presented the coach as a symbol, and as a symbol this figure had general applicability for interpreting other similar structures of relationship and life experience.

The complex represented by the coach figure also has an archetypal core, in which resides the Father. This complex was arranged in such a way that it impinged upon the ego as the Father archetype would: a male authority blocking or facilitating the way to work and libido commitments in the world. The dream figure here was symbolic in that it pointed beyond itself to greater psychic meanings, and yet it was also purely historical: this man had actually been the dreamer's coach some twenty years earlier.

The realization that a recurrent dream of this kind, containing a clearly marked and recalled historical figure or event, also carries symbolic significance is achieved when one gets a sense of its greater psychological meaning. It is more than a simple repetition of a memory or an attempt to work through an emotional trauma from the past. Perhaps a symbol could be defined as an event plus its meaning. If we say for example, that a dream is a symbol, this means that we have captured this combination of the dream as an historical event and its meaning. Once rendered symbolic, the meaning of the event can also be transferred to other contexts.

A general hypothesis for dream analysis can be suggested: when a person or figure or motif from an individual's history recurs to a noticeable extent in a long dream series, it contains symbolic import. Symbolic import means that the extent and range of possible meaningful reference to which this image can be applied is greatly increased.

In a long dream series, too, where one can witness a gradual change in the structures and figures of the dreams' dramas, one can also often glimpse how the psyche deals with history. The dreams rework a bit of history until it both becomes symbolic and transforms its shape. In this respect, we can affirm that psychological growth can be charted in dream sequences. The transformation of personal history into symbol makes it possible for past events that have inhibited or blocked psychological functioning, split the psyche, or limited the self in externalizing its functions in space and time to be gradually overcome.

A second kind of dream that calls insistently for historical reflection and reconstruction is one that hints symbolically at a historical event. This was Freud's insight and his use of the term symbolical. Here a historical event is hidden by an image, barely alluded to, yet dreamed in a way that associations can lead to it quite directly and easily. Typically these hidden events are of a shaming, embarrassing, and painful nature, such as incest experiences that have been covered up and to some extent repressed.

A young woman came to see me because she felt overwhelmed by powerful dreams that she could not understand. The dreams were charged with emotion, they would often awaken her, and they were often innocuous in content. In our second or third session, she reported dreaming of her childhood home. She is exploring the back yard and comes upon a tree she has not seen before, a young tree about to bear fruit for the first time. Her associations to the dream took us quickly and forcefully back into her early adolescence, when her family had moved into this house and her father had purchased the land next door for a garden. It was a garden rich with orchards and berry bushes. She had spent many hours roaming through it and playing there with girlfriends. At the place of the unknown tree in the dream, she recalled, she had had an early sexual encounter: another girl had shown her her pubescent breasts, and they had touched one another. This association led quickly to others, and particularly to painful memories of discovering that her divorced and lonely father would spy on her as she undressed in her room and would sometimes come into her room at night and sit on her bed. Suddenly her whole terrified adolescence sprang back into memory. From the innocence of a young fruit tree in the garden we came suddenly upon the serpent, upon an original sin, upon the fall from grace of her father in her eyes, and upon years and years of holding in a terrible secret. In this instance, an ingenuous dream, an Eden image, yields up a secret of personal shame, not on the mythic symbolic level but on the concretely historical level.

One interesting feature of this case is that it conforms to Jung's early formulation of the etiology of neurosis (Jung 1955, pars. 203–522). There was a task in the present that this young woman was avoiding: she was stuck in writing her dissertation. Libido would not flow to it. Furthermore, there was also a problem in her relationship with her husband: libido did not want to flow there either. The damming up of libido and the ensuing regression produced symptoms: overcharged dreams, nightmares, and anxiety. Following the above-mentioned dream back into her personal history, the path led to incest scenes with her father, and after these were uncovered and the traumas and feelings were brought into consciousness, libido was released for a new progression of libido. In fact, after some discussion of these memories that came flooding back, she was able to take up her dissertation and finish it. She also tackled her relationship with her husband. What started out seeming like a dream symbol in this case, namely the garden, the tree, the fruit, turned into history and lost its symbolic meaning. This deconstruction of symbolic into historical meanings follows the old-fashioned notion of psychoanalysis as undoing repressions and working through incest issues. This dream presented a dream symbol in the Freudian sense of disguise rather than in the sense of event plus meaning.

And yet there was one detail in the dream, which did not seem particularly significant at the time because of all the material that flowed from the associations, that did have symbolic import as well. It was the new fruit of the tree. Unlike any of the trees in the actual orchard back home, this was a pear tree; the fruit was an incipient pear. Historically this referred to the period of adolescence when she became initiated into female sexuality, but it had a teleological reference as well. From a clinical viewpoint one could readily assess that she needed to further her feminine identity and maturity as a woman. As for the interpretive work, the deconstructive move in taking apart the symbol-as-disguise serves the prospective function of the dream, which is to advance the cause of personal psychological development.

## History as Metaphor

When Freud abandoned the seduction theory and replaced it with the notion that childhood incest fantasies disguise themselves as historical memory, he was pointing to one of the ways in which the mind uses history metaphorically. Jung certainly supported this view of the psyche as creator of metaphor to express its essence and meanings. History can be used to this purpose.

In a metaphor, two things are compared in such a way that one can stand for the other and illuminate its significance. But it also may come to replace it. If I say, "My love is a red, red rose," this may engender some confusion about the object of my love. You could ask, "Does this mean that you love a red rose?" I would protest that I was speaking poetically. But when we speak or think in metaphors we are not far from a potential muddle. Straightening out this muddle and making the meaning come clear is one function of interpretation. A good interpretation will render the meaning of the metaphorical expression in a language that is considerate of poetic values; it will carefully suggest the meaning of the metaphor.

In a sense, every dream is a metaphor and needs to be so interpreted. Freud and Jung agreed on this. A dream interpretation says in prose what the dream says in poetry. Reading or hearing dreams, I often ask myself, "If I were to state this dream story as a thought, what would the thought be?" The mind dreaming is the mind thinking in images. (Equally, one could say that the mind thinking is the mind dreaming in thoughts.) This does not answer the question of where these thoughts come from or what they mean, but it does take us toward a theory of dream interpretation. To understand dream language requires us to translate it into the thoughts that it represents metaphorically. A dream can move us emotionally without this, of course, but it cannot be understood cognitively unless we make this translation.

There is a large group of dreams that begin something like this: "I was back home." The dream report opens with a statement of place, and that place is from the long ago: the childhood home, the school, the grandparents' place, the summer home, but in any case a place of origin where much important, formative experience took place. Then, after this typical opening, we are introduced to a cast of characters, often mixing the old and the new: some from the old home town, some from more recent days, some from the present. The dream then proceeds to develop into a drama that often has little or nothing to do with the past even though it is set there. While it has more to do with present matters, these are surprisingly stated in historical terms and images. It is as though one were to read about a current political campaign in terms of the Civil War or the Revolutionary period, of formative times.

A man in his late fifties was studying for a new profession, psychotherapy. He was in the midst of a practicum with a number of low-fee patients when he dreamed of being back in the town where he had been born and spent the first fifty years of his life. (This was the usual setting of nearly all of his dreams.) In this dream, he was playing the role of doorkeeper in a saloon. A sting operation was being conducted to capture drug dealers and users, and his job was to escort the potential customers to the back of the place, where they would be busted. Finally the operation was completed, and he was free to leave, which he did with trepidation, fearing an attack from the drug people. In associating to the dream, he identified this location as the snake pit of his hometown. Other associations led to his practicum, where he was dealing with a number of substance abusers. One of these had canceled a session on the day of the dream, and he feared the patient was regressing to his old habit. Others of his patients were sociopathic court cases.

It is a cardinal tenet of analytical psychology that the unconscious assimilates experience by comparing it to the past. New experience is integrated by chewing it up with old teeth in an old mouth and digesting it in an old stomach with old gases and juices. As far as the psyche is concerned, new wine is always put into old casks. If this operation does not work, there is a breakdown and subsequent reorganization. This is the basis of transference: the patient assimilates the analyst, this new figure of importance, libidinal attachment, and authority, to former authority figures (usually parental, they being the earliest), along lines that were laid down long ago along an archetypal roadbed of truly ancient vintage. In a dream like the one quoted above, we see this process at work. The practicum was a new, and in many ways threatening, experience for the dreamer. He was not a novice to the world of work and to membership in the service industry, but this activity and role were new for him. He was an old dog learning a new trick, and in this dream we see his unconscious groping to grasp this new role on the basis of former life experience. The dream thought is something like this: "In your new job you are one part of a larger effort to change some antisocial behavior and to try to clean things up. This is a somewhat dangerous job, and you could be easily misunderstood and attacked by the people you are trying to help change. The kind of people you are dealing with are a lot like those characters who hung around on that corner back home where drugs were bought and sold. You are dealing with the shadowy side of life. Be careful and stay alert."

In this dream, the historical setting makes the statement that the present moment is something like it was back then. This assimilation of the present to past models is part of the adjustment and adaptation to a new situation that is challenging and somewhat frightening.

I am reminded of an observation that Miss Marples, the foxy old detective in some of Agatha Christie's novels, makes about how she is able to sleuth so well. She says that back in her small English village there were just enough characters to learn all she needed to know about human nature. What she does when she goes into a new situation is to get a sense of what the people are like by comparing them to the characters in the village. Her observation was that if you thoroughly know the people in one small village, you can understand any human situation.

What Miss Marples did was assimilate the new to the old through comparing them. This is the use of history as metaphor: for a moment the past stands in for the present so that one can understand the present more clearly.

"My love is a red, red rose" only works if one has earlier come to know roses and to love them; otherwise the metaphor is meaningless and could confuse the reader into thinking the poet is a gardener. Sometimes the would-be interpreter of a dream that contains a strong historical reference acts like such a reader. If the historical reference is taken literally, as making a concrete reference to a past event or person, when this historical reference is actually meant to be taken metaphorically, the muddle becomes complete.

In the example given above, it would have been foolish to pursue the notion that the dreamer was in the process of uncovering some shadow activity that had actually happened back in his old hometown. Not that this tack would be "wrong" necessarily; one could indeed look, perhaps even with some profit, at shadow issues from those past years. Similarly, one could also take the line, "My love is a red, red rose," and speculate that the poet's selection of precisely this metaphor had to do with a strong preference for red roses. Or was his mother's name Rose? But this would be missing the point of this poem, which is not really about roses but about his beloved. Similarly, in the instance of the dream, it would be missing the point to go woolgathering on that street from the old hometown.

The historical element in dreams where history is metaphor points to old and long-standing patterns of structure, identification, habit. The dream is saying: this is an old pattern that is now being applied to a new situation; this is a pattern that was laid down in that place because of the circumstances, identifications, persons involved there and your relationship to them. The unconscious is trying to assimilate the present by devouring it in the stomach of the past.

These dreams raise a further question, particularly if they are habitual and recurrent. Is this a good thing? Is assimilation of the present by the past the way of individuation, or is it a sign of defense? We come here upon the uses of memory. Memory can be a means of cognition, but it can also be an instrument of defense.

## *History as Oppression*

"We are our complexes; they are our memory," writes Elie Humbert in an article in which he discusses how analysis attempts to dissolve the repetition compulsion through regression. His notion is that in order for change to take place, the complexes must be dissolved and reformed through a therapeutic regression. This forms new structures. The implication is that memory alters as well. This brings us to the question: Do dreams indicate a process at work in the psyche that can alter the structure of complexes and change memory as well?

It is too facile an equation to say, simply, that our complexes are our memory. Memory is more than complexes. And yet there is certainly an important connection. Memory, in the sense depth psychologists understand it, goes beyond the conscious memory bank, short or long term. It extends to body memories and unconscious memories as well. The evidence that memory exceeds consciousness and its powers of recall is extensive and compelling. We dream of persons and places we would never retrieve through conscious effort. Too, after a long and arduous process of association and interpretation, we often realize that dreams contain memory images: then we are surprised that this is the case. In recent years, body therapy has demonstrated that the very body tissues, when pressed and massaged in certain ways, can be made to give up the dead in the form of memory images of early childhood. Hypnosis has long been used to demonstrate the existence of memory far beyond the range of conscious recall, and it has even entered areas that may pertain to previous lives. Here we verge on the edge of a memory bank that extends through the ages. The collective unconscious is thought to contain memory traces of an ancestral origin.

As far as the contents of memory are concerned, therefore, we can say, with a fair degree of confidence, that they exceed consciousness and conscious control. We cannot control or retrieve what we remember at all levels. Freud's theory of repression deals with the human need to forget, while it simultaneously testifies that we do not forget the very things we want to: the memory of traumata and fantasies lives on. This is also true of Jung's theory of complexes. Complexes are made up of largely unconscious memories clustered around an archetypal core, and complexes are autonomous and free from ego control. Thus memory is controlled by the psyche, not by the ego.

When we consider how memory is structured we come upon a further set of considerations. Elie Humbert claims that memory is structured by complexes. This is to say that memory is structured largely by emotional dynamics, such as the operation of defenses. Moreover, the nature of complexes is to repeat their patterns, unchanged, until an intervention from outside alters them. The tendency of complexes to rigidify, to resist change, and to repeat was an early observation. Jung's differentiation between neurosis and schizophrenia rested on the relative malleability of complexes in the former and their utter imperviousness to change in the latter (1960, par. 141). In neurosis, the complexes will yield somewhat to treatment and to conscious intervention; in schizophrenia they are intractable. This is another way of saying, perhaps, that for normal neurotics memory can be changed and restructured somewhat; for the more seriously ill, it cannot. A sense of personal history, then, is structured by emotion (i.e., the complexes), at least to some degree, and the harder that emotion is frozen the less likely it is that memory will change.

As one observes dreams, it becomes evident that they both reconstitute memory and attempt to restructure and to change it. If memory changes in its contents, its repetitions, its structuring, then personal identity also changes, patterns of behavior and reaction and perception change, and personality undergoes a transformation. The change of memory, in content and structure, is an essential component of therapeutic transformation. More precisely, the change in affective charge, or valence, around certain areas of an individual's sense of personal history—mother, father, childhood, identity, etc.—is the critical factor in psychological transformation. An autobiography written after analysis is typically quite different from one written beforehand, both because of the additional detail and because of the rearrangement of the valued contents.

Dreams can be seen working on the emotional valences of past figures, presenting "positive figures" from the past in a negative light
and "negative figures" with more positive cast and feature. Within
dream dynamics there is an attempt to change the complexes, which
are the emotional basis of memory and its structuring.

One class of dreams that shows this effort is the toilet dream. This
dream has a more or less standard structure and two or three predictable outcomes. The dreamer typically realizes, suddenly, a need to go
to the toilet, usually to defecate. Either this occurs successfully, or it
runs into one of several problems. There are other people in the bathroom, and this interrupts the act; the toilets are stopped up and the
place is a mess, and again this leads to difficulties in obeying nature's
commands; the toilet is full and will not hold more content. In my
experience, the people who have this dream recurrently are somewhat
compulsive, rather unhappily entrenched in their habits and styles of
living, and find themselves in a crisis that demands change. Their
being stuck in the midst of a transformation process manifests itself
in this dream: the toilet is stopped up, and the dreamer cannot get rid
of a used-up past.

This dream indicates a need and a problem: the need is to get rid of
some worthless material, the problem is doing it. An impasse results.

This dreamer is typically a person with high control needs, along
with a strong fear of letting go of a secure position that in the past
was of value but now no longer serves the needs of individuation. As
a thought, the dream images would say: In the past this identity was
of great value, but you have gotten what you can out of it. Now you
must let it go. But you are not letting it go; something in your character (the plumbing) has created a blockage.

Both the requirement for change and the resistance to it belong to
this same personality, of course, but they arise from different areas.
The requirement derives from the Self's need for something new, for
new sources of nourishment. The resistance comes from the ego's
defenses against the anxiety created by change. The complexes (i.e.,
emotionally structured memories) make up the material in the
blockage, and they insist on repeating the past for emotional security.
They constrict the personality and thereby create the blockage in the
toilet. The complexes themselves are imaged as shit by the dream.

The message is unmistakable: it is time to remove this bit of outworn history and memory from the psychic body. What was once
perhaps a nourishing repast is now chewed up, worked over by the
digestive system, useless, and if retained will poison the whole body.
The used-up past needs to be eliminated. Toilet dreams can, of course,
also give clues about transference issues that revolve around holding

back and controlling emotion. Beneath this trait lie the intractable complexes and their repetitions. In a sense, memory will not let go. Our history will not be denied, and it insists on repeating itself. The complexes form a character structure. The separation anxiety constellated in losing a grip on personal history is enormous, and this anxiety provides the glue between ego consciousness and its outworn past.

This may take the form of persona anxiety—"What will people say, or think, if I make such a change and release the past in this way?" Or the issue may revolve on security and display the notion of clinging to history for comfort and identity. This anxiety may also be an expression of a collective, clan, or family problem, reflecting the fact that many others, too, cannot make the necessary change and all are blocked, the whole interpersonal system may be stagnant and poisoned. The issue for analysis in all of these instances is separation anxiety, which presents itself with excruciating impact during periods of deep inner change. The analyst who is similarly blocked may contribute to the problem rather than help to relieve it.

At the conclusion of his paper "The Spirit Mercurius" (1948, pars. 299–303), Jung discusses two kinds of knowledge, following St. Augustine: *cognitio vespertina* ("evening knowledge") and *cognitio matutina* ("morning knowledge"). The first is the kind of knowledge that becomes ego syntonic and eventually grows old and stale, losing its savor and value; the second remains eternally fresh. When insight and experience that were once inspired and fresh becomes integrated into ego consciousness as personal history and identity, the need arises to renew oneself in a wellspring of fresh vision and awareness. The sense of a personal history runs this course. At first it is a feast and supplies the basic material for a personal identity. Personal history and identity rest, however, upon a set of complexes, which make up the emotional glue of memory and of its structuring. This emotional glue becomes hardened by anxiety, and history thus becomes fixated. It turns into a burden. The tyranny of a too fixed sense of personal history blocks life and new direction. So the husk of history must be shed, the complexes dissolved. The archetypal core of the personality, however, remains eternally fresh, filled with nourishment and value. The ego can renew itself in this level, in the Self. This "regression," according to Humbert, is the secret of therapeutic healing. We can add that it is also the key to all psychological renewal. From the Self flows the *cognitio matutina*, a fountain of youth that also has the detergent power to flush the toilet clean.

## The Child, Childhood, and Nostalgia

If one follows the lead of dreams and associations in analysis, one comes rapidly and inevitably upon images and memories of childhood.

When these begin to crowd into consciousness, it is the dawning of *cognitio matutina*. Dreams of childhood, of being a child again, of returning to important places of childhood, of caring for small children and infants, are indicators that analysis is reaching the soul. This reentry into childhood is essential for the healing process that we anticipate and count on in analysis.

The constellation of this inner child is essential for healing the fundamental split in the modern adult psyche. This is the split between consciousness and the unconscious, between reality and imagination. The healthy child within is our capacity to dwell in a world of whole symbols, where the divisions between these elements are not yet existent. Whether this world is called "transitional space" (Winnicott 1971) "liminality" (Turner 1967), the operation of the transcendent function (Jung 1916), the "imaginal" (Hillman 1983), or the "secured symbolizing field" (Goodheart 1980), it is a kind of consciousness in which the literal and the imaginal are combined and allowed to mingle in such a way that the dichotomy between them, created by later ego developments, is suspended. This healing of the rift between inner and outer, real and imaginal, ego and unconscious is the function of the symbol and the constellation of this healing symbol is the generally accepted ultimate goal of Jungian treatment. Jung spoke of the transcendent function as the means by which the opposites are reconciled and attitudes changed, and this function at work is represented by the child at play.

The return of childhood images in dreams in the course of analysis therefore indicates operation of the healing function. Dreams that speak of loss of the child, damage to the child, threats to the child, neglect of the child, etc., indicate potential hazards facing the working of this healing function. One recalls that Jung himself returned to childhood and to childhood games in his search for healing during midlife, and it was through these activities that imagination was released and the transcendent function discovered and allowed to release symbols of reconciliation (Jung 1961, p. 174).

At the heart of every analysand's history lies childhood. Dreams of childhood imply a particular story of childhood, a history, and remembering childhood has the psychological value of helping to constellate the transcendent function.

A woman in her mid-forties suffering from the turmoil created by a conflict between physical and emotional desire on the one hand and spiritual aspiration and commitment on the other, dreamed that she was playing a game with her younger brother, as they had often done in childhood. Suddenly she was no longer playing with him but with a favorite doll. This dream released a flood of memories from childhood, both of her brother and their relationship and of this favorite doll that she had kept with her into teenage years. The dream also occurred at a point in her life when rational problem-solving methods for tackling her conflict had become useless, and she was simply ruminating over the same old ground. She was caught in her complexes. The dream suggested the activation of the transcendent function, first of all by drawing her back to scenes of childhood and, even more importantly, by providing her with recall of a transitional object. This magical object has the power to transform the ego's time- and space-bounded reality into transitional space, where play allows new combinations of old elements to form. From this dream she proceeded to try sandplay. In the sand tray she created a scene of conflict and resolution. This activity, in turn, coincided with a general lightening of the rending effects of the conflict, with a return of her sense of humor, and with the disappearance of some rather severe and embarrassing physical symptoms.

When a dream brings back childhood, the feeling tones evoked by it can smack strongly of nostalgia. One may awaken from such a dream with a sense of nostalgia so compelling that hours or even days may pass before mood and emotional tone return to normal. Typically these are dream reminiscences of times and places that emotionally contained and nurtured the dreamer in a particularly effective way. With such a dream, one is drawn into a set of feelings and images that smell of attachment and intimate familiarity and induce longing and sometimes short separation depressions. Separation from the mother is recapitulated, and there is a reminder that one cannot go back home again. A longing for paradise suffuses nostalgia, and the dreams tease us, seemingly, with a glimpse of what we once had and forever lost.

This type of dream represents a brief symbolic return to the mother. The significance of this return is not fully noted by pointing out that one cannot actually do that, that it is a romantic delusion and needs to be shunned. These dreams are not so much symptomatic of an unwillingness to accept present reality as they are an effort to return to a source of life and nourishment to gather energy for a new beginning. They speak of renewal. For nostalgia is both a sentimental attachment to the past and a hope for another chance at a future.

The Child and childhood itself are evocative of nostalgia. One can recall them as times of comfort, safety, and creativity, as existing beyond serious conflict and the experience of loss and limitation. But as Jung points out, the child archetype fundamentally signifies futurity (1951, par. 278). The child faces into the future, not back to the past and, paradoxically, the return of the child in analysis is a means of approaching the future via the past.

The reason this is possible and actually happens is that as the past recedes and becomes the distant past it becomes assimilated to the archetypes (see chapter 6, above). Thus, my own personal childhood becomes Childhood itself; the home of my childhood becomes the Garden of Eden or that mythic and much sought after place called Home; my personal parents become Mother and Father. As memories recede, they sink further into the unconscious and come into contact with the archetypal substratum. Eventually they become assimilated to it. Another way to conceptualize this phenomenon is to see the archetype, which lies at the core of the complex, gradually absorbing the personal associations into itself; enriched by these, this memory trace more and more reveals itself as archetypal image in dreams and recollected associations. The emotional aura around memory changes with age. This is how personal history becomes personal myth.

Often this phenomenon is interpreted as defensive. In order to convert a painful and troubled childhood into something acceptable, or at least neutral, the ego defenses take off the edges, distort the memories through association with archetypal structures, and leave the individual with a defensively reconstructed memory of childhood. Traumas are repressed, injuries suffered at the hands of borderline or narcissistic parents are disguised, and a kind of sentimental haze conceals the realities of childhood in order to hide its gloomy and fearful truth. As these defenses are dismantled, the person who entered analysis with a glowing account of parents and childhood leaves with a Graham Wilson vision of torture chambers and monsters. The ego has been strengthened to a point where it can now accept this harsh reality.

The advantage of following dreams rather than memories or free associations into childhood is that they do not lie. The ego and its defenses may well give a distorted account, in the form of a pasted together set of idealized or horrific memories, but the unconscious does not much cooperate in this. Dreams of childhood are both warm and exceedingly unpleasant. Witches, fires, floods, dismembered dolls frightening animals such as vicious dogs and clawing cats, disemboweled and otherwise sick farmyard animals, scenes of violence and destruction are as common as teddy bears and Gardens of Eden. The painful dynamics of childhood do become manifest in dreams: separation and loss, oedipal rivalries, double binds that injure and maim. Dreams do not hide any of these in the course of a complete dream series in analysis.

But there is also a child at play, which feels like the soul's essence. This is the object of nostalgia; to return to this child is its goal. In order to preserve this sense of childhood, all the defenses of the Self are mobilized. These are Self defenses (Fordham 1985, pp. 152–60) rather than ego defenses, which merely guard against ego pain. Only when conditions of safety are in place can these defenses be dismantled and this child be allowed to come out of the closet or basement.

This child of play is a fusion of archetype and personal memory, mediating imagination and historical existence in a particular zone of time and space. And gathered around this child are the places and persons who are also symbols: Mother, Father, Home, Animals.

A woman in her late thirties who had been in analysis for about twelve months and had recently become bedridden with an anomalous illness, dreamed that she was in church. As she walked to the door, a gigantic butterfly flew past her and out into the fresh air. She steps out herself and is suddenly in a winter landscape. The place is Russia, and she is standing on a road that runs through a forest for hundreds of miles. As she looks down the road she sees a horse-drawn sleigh approaching and is surprised to see her mother and father coming her way. Associations to this dream only recalled that her father was a second-generation Russian American, that she had always been fascinated with stories told by her grandfather about Russia, and that she had read and reread the great Russian novels. But why the giant butterfly, why this landscape, why her own parents and not her grandparents or great-grandparents?

Quite evidently this is a symbolic, archetypal dream as indicated by the soul figure in the butterfly, the gesture of passing through a doorway, the land of ancestors. At the time of the dream, she was feverish and worried about the seriousness of her illness. A question of survival even occurred, although she was not hypochondriacal. Her parents called from time to time throughout the illness to encourage her. She has lived out a sort of counterdependent defensive relationship with them, in which they gladly colluded.

While this dream is clearly a return of sorts to childhood and to feelings of vulnerability, in short an image of regression during illness, it goes beyond that to represent transitional and archetypal space: the church as sacred temenos and place of souls; the butterfly as departing soul, flying off into another world; her own entry into that other world, the world of the ancestors; the experience of nostalgic reunion with parental imagoes. One could almost think this was anticipatory of death: the soul leaves the body and enters another world, where those who have loved one most deeply come to greet and lead one on into the other life. In this return to childhood, there is a penetration beyond it into Childhood, the childhood of her own genetic line and race, the point of origin, the source of life. In this respect, the dream implies birth, the renewal of life through a return to the point of origin, and entry into the realm of *cognitio matutina*.

The timing of the illness and of this dream was meaningful as well. They occurred precisely during the period when a child would have been born to her had she not aborted it. The decision to have an abortion had been a sound one, practically speaking, but her psyche and her body had not given up the agenda of pregnancy and birth and followed through, after a manner. The dream, with its escaping butterfly and return to the world of the ancestors, charted the course of this unborn soul. It also brought the dreamer, the lost child's mother, to the place of her ancestral origins and roots. The implication of a return to "deep childhood," to the point of ancestry even beyond one's own personal beginning, is futurity. Because the archetypes are engaged at this level, the psyche's progressive movement toward wholeness can be touched.

### REFERENCES

Dieckmann, H. 1986. Opening Address. In *Symbolic and Clinical Approaches in Theory and Practice*. Zurich: Daimon Verlag.

Fordham, M. 1985. *Explorations into the Self*. London: Academic Press.

Goodheart, W. 1980. Theory of the Analytic Interaction. *The San Francisco Jung Institute Library Journal* 1:2–39.

Hillman, J. 1983. *Archetypal Psychology: A Brief Account*. Dallas: Spring Publications.

Humbert, E. 1988. The Wellsprings of Memory. *Journal of Analytical Psychology* 33:3–20.

Jung, C. G. 1907. *The Psychology of Dementia Praecox*. In *Collected Works* 3:1–151. Princeton: Princeton University Press, 1960.

———. 1913. The Theory of Psychoanalysis. In *Collected Works* 4:83–226. Princeton: Princeton University Press, 1961.

———. 1916. The Transcendent Function. In *Collected Works* 8:67–91. Princeton: Princeton University Press, 1969.

———. 1944. *Psychology and Alchemy*. In *Collected Works*, vol. 12. Princeton: Princeton University Press, 1968.

———. 1948. The Spirit Mercurius. In *Collected Works*, vol. 13. Princeton: Princeton University Press, 1967.

———. 1951b. The Psychology of the Child Archetype. In *Collected Works* 9/1:151–181. Princeton: Princeton University Press, 1969.

———. 1952a. *Symbols of Transformation*. In *Collected Works*, vol. 5. Princeton: Princeton University Press, 1956.

Samuels, A. 1985. *Jung and Post-Jungians*. London: Routledge and Kegan Paul.

Stein, M. 1985. *Jung's Treatment of Christianity*. Wilmette, IL.: Chiron Publications.

———. 1987. Looking Backward: Archetypes in Reconstruction. In *Archetypal Processes in Psychotherapy*, N. Schwartz-Salant and M. Stein, eds. Wilmette, IL.: Chiron Publications, pp. 51–74.

Turner, Victor. 1967. *The Forest of Symbols*. Ithaca: Cornell University Press.

Winnicott, D. W. 1971. *Playing and Reality*. New York: Basic Books.

*nine*

. . . . . . . . . . . . . . . . . . . . . . . . . .

# The Analyst's Part: Three
# Types of Countertransference

In 1982, Harriet Machtiger issued a provocative challenge for greater disclosure of countertransference reactions on the part of analysts. It has been known for a long time that analysts can get in the way of their patients' development and search for wholeness, but this is not easy to admit and may not be welcome news to some inflated analysts. In fact, Machtiger pointed to the "almost phobic response" of analysts to questions about "the revelation of what transpires in the counter-transference or in the analysis itself" (p. 93).

In the past several years, there have been a number of courageous works that have taken up this challenge and a good deal of headway has been made, much of which has been admirably summarized by Sedgwick in his book, *The Wounded Healer*. The reason such a stunning lacuna existed in the literature of analytical psychology, I believe, is that countertransference has been and to some extent still remains lodged in the shadow of analytic practice. If we are to come close to understanding what happens in analysis, more confessional work on the part of analysts, like that of Sedgwick, must be produced.

Our field does seem to have reached the point of agreeing that countertransference is inevitable in analysis and can be extremely useful for therapy if correctly understood and handled. Machtiger even asserts that "it is the analyst's reaction in the countertransference that is the essential therapeutic factor in analysis" (1982, p. 90), making the point that the reaction of the analyst can become a model for the patient's own integrity and wholeness. Machtiger insists that countertransference must be interpreted in analysis:

> One of Jung's basic premises was that the patient's illness needs to be met by the analyst's health. This interaction requires the confrontation and conscious interpretation of the conscious and uncon-

scious countertransference/transference position of both analyst and patient, and the subsequent integration of the contents.

(p. 100)

By interpreting countertransference forthrightly and courageously, therefore, the analyst is demonstrating basic health as well as modeling a way to work on transference. In this way, what had perhaps appeared as the very block to a patient's psychological movement becomes the means for facilitating that movement.

As a discipline, however, analytical psychology is still at the beginning of its thinking about countertransference. Once this is more advanced it should make things less awkward for analysts who find they need to work at this level with their patients. What is needed is better orientation in emotional waters that are often confusing and frightening. The great sea of unconsciousness in which this factor of analytic work washes about still needs much further exploration. We also need to describe more fully and accurately the stupefying variety of images, feelings, psychological dynamics, and structures involved in countertransference attitudes and reactions. We need both theory and experiential accounts to help sort out the confused tangles that often infest the analytic relationship.

A few important basic discriminations about countertransference have been made in the analytic literature. There is the easy almost conversational distinction between positive and negative countertransference, which mirrors the notion of positive and negative transference. This seems to say, basically, that an analyst likes the analysand or does not. As a point of reference this is not altogether useless or beside the point, but it leaves a lot to be desired in the way of detail. A more interesting and analytically useful distinction has been made between countertransference that originates autonomously in the analyst's psyche (Fordham's [1978] "illusory," Dieckmann's [1976] "projective," Racker's [1968] "neurotic" countertransference) and countertransference that originates in response to the analysand's psyche (Fordham's "syntonic," Dieckmann's "objective," Racker's "concordant" countertransference). This distinction often breaks down, however, because, as many analysts have pointed out, the two subjects involved in this relationship cannot be separated so neatly. It is impossible to tell with complete assurance who owns which psychic contents in the transference/countertransference process. Nor is it possible to be sure who is being reactive to whom, or to what. Is the analyst reacting to the analysand's unconscious, or activating it? Plaut has put forward the suggestion of mutual transferences in analysis rather than speaking of transference on the patient's side and *counter-*

transference on the analyst's part. Jung pointed out long since that in the complex process of analysis the analyst and analysand "find themselves in a relationship founded on mutual unconsciousness" (1946, par. 367), and both contribute unconscious impetus to it. Countertransferences are often both illusory and syntonic at one and the same time. And yet these discriminations need to be made if we are ever to raise consciousness about the contents and dynamics of countertransference.

## Methodology

An added complication to the project of investigating countertransference is methodological. The method commonly used by analysts, a combination of introspection and self-analysis, is not able to discriminate very well "who owns which" bits of psychic material in analytic processes. So even if analysts valiantly attempt consciously to examine their countertransference by use of this method, the goal is not within reach because the method is inadequate. By themselves, analysts are unlikely to get to the truth. All of the analyst's secret thoughts and fantasies can be exposed to light and still not reveal the actual countertransference, precisely because it is unconscious. So self-analysis and confession are not enough. A method up to the task of analyzing countertransference would have to have the power to search out the analyst's unconscious as well as conscious attitudes and reactions.

Such a method might look to several sources for information. Analysands are highly sensitive (consciously or unconsciously) to countertransference, and they reveal it to their analysts either in fantasies and dreams or through associations and indirect communications. Their testimony could be a primary source of data. Second, analysts' unconscious reactions to analysands, as indicated in dreams and spontaneous fantasies and in associations to analysands' material as well as derivatives in the form of interpretations, could be collected and examined. Analysts' interventions in the actual setting of therapy should be carefully observed most of all, since they are the strongest and most immediate indicators of countertransference. If analysts gathered and analyzed these materials, we would come much closer to an accurate appraisal of countertransference than we have.

## Three Types of Countertransference

Allusions to the three types of countertransference I am going to discuss here are scattered about in the Jungian literature, as my references indicate. So while this delineation is not completely new, I believe considerable detail and coherence can be added to the portraits. What I am offering here are three containers into which empirical material can be entered. These containers can offer images and models that will help others sort through their countertransference attitudes and reactions and perhaps find some clarification, or they may find a challenge to elaborate quite other containers. At any rate, I am hoping this will be a beginning for the kind of work I have described.

The names of the three types of countertransference I will describe—the power-oriented, the shamanic, and the maieutic—suggest their core values and dynamics as well as the kind of dyadic relationships they help to create. Each one produces its own characteristic images and anxieties and shows a distinctive, archetypally based patterning. Each can be employed defensively by the analyst to discharge tensions and pressures that build up during analysis; each can also provide an (often partly unconscious) orientation for what he or she is doing; and each can release a satisfying stream of inner meaning and fulfillment when its positive requirements are met. They can all heal and facilitate the search for wholeness, but each can also create distortions and do harm. This is to say that none is all good, none all bad. Each needs to be analyzed when it appears to be getting in the way of therapy.

By no means do these three types cover the whole gamut of countertransference reactions. Countertransferences based on maternal—nurturant patterns (cf. Machtiger) and eros-sexual (cf. Schwartz-Salant) patterns are more widely recognized and commonly discussed in the literature. The hope in naming these other three and reflecting on them is that this will help analysts to identify countertransference reactions and attitudes that are not fundamentally maternal or sexual, and will also encourage the description and discussion of still other types.

THE POWER TYPE

In the course of analysis, the analyst will frequently feel strong or subtle pressure to take command of the situation and to wield power over the analysand. Power, by which I mean the need or desire to have control, is never absent from human relationships, and the therapeutic relationship between analyst and analysand is no exception. Evidence of this type of countertransference reaction are many: giving the analysand unsolicited advice about how to improve a mental attitude; recommending auxiliary types of therapy, medication, or hospitalization; insisting on rigid compliance regarding time and place of treatment; making aggressive interpretations that establish dominance; trivializing other people's therapeutic effects on the analysand; terminating unilaterally. Every analyst knows the impulse to get and maintain control over analysands and over the analytic process, and most feel somewhat guilty about asserting power, at least blatantly, within the analytic context. Analysts are supposed to be without desire (Bion teaches to be without memory or desire).

Analysands are not immune from the wish for power either. It is not unknown that analysands sometimes actually take control and assume the power position. When they succeed, the analyst's countertransference position may in turn rest on the relinquishment of power and the acceptance of helplessness. If this complete sacrifice of the wish to have power over the analysand and the analytic process sounds like an approximation to the ideal of the ascetic analyst, it may in fact be rooted in a counterwish to be controlled and led in a masochistic style or in fear of the analysand.

This is to say that the power problem is not solved by giving control to the analysand. Analysands will gradually become upset about their compulsive attacks on the analyst and about their need to keep control of the analytic process, and become anxious about their success in doing this, but the behavior will not stop until the need to control is interpreted and metabolized. It cannot be analyzed, however, from the masochistic position: from there the analyst has no analytic power.

It is relatively useless to berate oneself or others for becoming involved in this type of transference/countertransference process, either on the one side of the power play or the other. More difficult, but analytically more helpful, is understanding why it happened and perceiving the dynamics that sustain it. How can the analyst interpret this type of countertransference effectively?

Guggenbühl-Craig (1971), a leading Jungian expositor of the power theme, holds that when the quest for power becomes paramount in the helping situation, an archetypal image has become split into two parts. One can roughly designate these parts as the lesser and the greater: the ill patient versus the healthy doctor; the poor client versus the established, dominant social worker; the sinful penitent versus the holy confessor; the ignorant student versus the learned teacher, and so forth. (Or, vice versa: the healthy patient vs. the ill doctor, etc.) In analysis this may be played out in many ways when an archetypal pattern gets split and the analysand accepts and carries one side of it, and the analyst the other. This takes place through mutual, usually unconscious, collaboration in which projection and projective identification are the key dynamics.

The psychological effect of this splitting of an archetypal pattern is emotional distance: analyst and analysand become very different, and their relationship is colored by this feeling of otherness. The analyst or the analysand (whoever is in the power position) seems transcendent from the process, affecting it from far away.

The analyst wants to know when and why this (or any other) kind of countertransference/transference process gets set up in analysis. It may be due to the analyst's original countertransference attitude, which is established and in place before a particular analysand ever walks into the office. This is simply a professional attitude, perhaps one of power and command. The analysand either accepts it and adapts, or rejects it and leaves. More often, though, the power dynamic becomes established as analysis proceeds, as the personal emotional complexes of each partner become engaged with those of the other. Here the power pattern derives from the psychodynamics that operate between two specific individuals, while other areas of each person's life may remain relatively free of this pattern.

Certain personalities tend to bring out the sadist (or the masochist) in the analyst: They are unconsciously looking for someone to take charge of their lives and to assert power over them, to tell them what to do, to give them tough advice, to punish them for their inadequacy; or, conversely, they are unconsciously driven to overcome and to dominate others. Analysts can be co-opted by these unconscious pushes and pulls to perform the relevant partnership role, identifying with one side of the split in the archetypal pattern and projecting the other. The ensuing relationship enacts a psychodynamic that is internal to each partner but externalized and now shared between them. The cooperation, or collusion, of each partner is what needs to be analyzed and worked through. The analyst may need to confess to the analysand that such fantasies and tendencies seem to have entered the field between them. "I suddenly feel a need to control you. I want to prevent you from hurting yourself. I wonder if this means anything to you? Can you relate to this kind of a situation? Am I becoming your overprotective, controlling parent?"

When the power dynamic takes over in analysis, it is not usually very effective simply to say that an archetype has become split. The specific details of the transference/countertransference process that led to this point need to become conscious. What unconscious elements of both analysand and analyst played a part in this splitting? What belongs to whom? Both sides of the interaction need to be openly analyzed and worked through in the course of therapy. Usually the analyst will need to take the initiative in bringing the dynamic or the fantasy to consciousness.

In the dreams of female analysands who assume the masochistic position and offer a sadistic projection to the male analyst, for example, a sexual theme is often associated with this pattern. In the resulting transference/countertransference field an erotic relationship is played out in subtle relational dynamics through the drama of domination and submission. Masochistic submission gains the bondage of love. Meanwhile the analyst finds himself unaccountably stimulated as he feels impelled to take the upper position, to control, perhaps at times to point out the analysand's shortcomings or to make harsh or even sarcastic interpretations. His countertransference reaction is partly syntonic and can therefore shed insight into the analysand's intrapsychic processes: In the countertransference he can feel the sadistic rage of the animus and directly experience the analysand's rejecting and punitive (usually early and parental) inner figures. This information can yield rich genetic and dynamic interpretations, as it can also provide the material for empathic interpretations: "You must have felt very tightly monitored and controlled by your parents, even humiliated."

When the power theme becomes a strong countertransference reaction and truly engages the emotions of the analyst, it has an illusory side as well. When the analyst feels stuck and angry, unworthy of his fee, disinclined to go on with the analysand unless she begins snapping out of it and getting better, he is generally in the grips of this countertransference reaction and under threat of being overcome by his own internal self-attacks. The analyst is struggling to get control over his own chaotic unconscious, generally over a willful and unruly anima or mother factor that creates moods of inadequacy and self-denigration with respect to infantile components in the ego (shadow elements). He projects this infantile (shadow) image onto the female analysand and attacks her, or tries to shape her up, in the same way his internal mother or anima-sister attacks him and tries to make him grow up. The analysand is inflicted with the analyst's self-punishment and attempts at self-mastery.

While this countertransference reaction may be seen as deriving from a response to a specific analysand's unconscious, it is also derivative from the analyst's own unresolved ego and anima problems. Pulling out of the analytic process at this point would be the analyst's ultimate power play.

In analyzing the transference/countertransference process, both sides of the relationship need to be interpreted, the one in light of the other. This can perhaps be best done with a fantasy image. An image that suggests the nature of the current relational field can offer a rich item for reflection and interpretation. In the complexity of this process, there are no purely individual or intrapsychic factors having no connecting synapses to the partner's personality. Power happens in a field with at least two parties involved. If the transference is analyzed without reference to the analyst's complex participation in it, analysands are likely to get the message that all the sickness is theirs. This will feed the masochistic position rather than offer any manner of insight into how that position triggers a sadistic attack or how as a strategy for achieving love it ends up in a loss of power. Without this insight, the pattern cannot be transformed because the underlying unconscious assumptions and splits are not brought to light in a therapeutically effective way. By analyzing the countertransference/ transference process as a complex whole, on the other hand, the analysand can discover how this pattern operates and how it generates the interpersonal and intrapsychic stalemate that follows.

I once had a case in which the image that symbolized the interactive field was the chess match. We sat on opposite sides of the board and struggled to see who could outplay whom. The analysand was also a therapist, so competiveness was not surprising, but more deeply this dynamic had origins in his father complex. He had to overcome his father to prove that he was worthy of his mother's high estimation of him. For my part, I was caught in the chess match as well, struggling with a parallel issue in my history. This image, which came from a dream, offered a precise way of talking about our difficulties and understanding them. There was also a prospective meaning to this, since this therapist was training to become an analyst and was finding his strength in tests with me.

Whether one is analyzing the syntonic or the illusory aspects of a power countertransference, the job is not an easy one. But the two types present different problems. In the first, the countertransference is used to interpret the inner states of the analysand, and here it seems relatively easy to link countertransference to transference dynamics. In the case of an illusory countertransference, however, the analyst is called on to analyze projections upon the analysand, which have in turn produced complex discharge and emotional reactions in the analysand. The first type of analysis provides the analysand with insight into his or her intrapsychic, genetic, and interpersonal patterns; the second relieves the analysand of the burden of carrying the analyst's projections.

Countertransference is never completely illusory, however, so the interpretation of it can always also be linked to transference. In the constellation of analyst-on-top power countertransferences, the analysand is in some sense unconsciously asking to be on the bottom and to be cured passively. So a countertransference/transference interpretation can be used to point to these features of the transference and to link them to the rage beneath the masochistic position, which the analysand feels about having to meet the world on its terms and having to engage life actively.

While it is important to recognize that power assertions—whether in the form of brow beating, advice giving, technique teaching, or pill pushing—never cured anyone of a deep psychological problem and have often done a lot of harm, it is equally essential to realize that sometimes the analyst's conscious assertion of power is exactly the correct and helpful thing to do. Power assertions for the sake of containing and for keeping an analysand to task are gestures of care and therapeutic concern. Generally an assertion of power is not well aimed when it comes from a chronic countertransference attitude or from a shadow response. It may work out quite well, however, when it is compensatory to an analyst's earlier too passive approach that has gotten stuck. Here the impulse to take control and to get things moving can provide the force needed to interpret the earlier transference/countertransference process and to move beyond it.

A personal observation is that the power countertransference appears as a shadow aspect of analysts who claim consciously to operate out of an "Eros model." In principle, of course, this makes sense, since power and love often form a pair of complementary opposites. Carotenuto writes masterfully about this pair of opposites in his book *The Difficult Art.* Perhaps not for him but certainly for me it is still always a cause for wonder to see how glaring an unconscious power countertransference attitude can be without the eros analyst having the slightest inkling of it. Since this is genuinely of the shadow, these analysts are not able to discover it through conscious introspection or self-scrutiny, and the reactions of analysands only leave them puzzled. They are always surprised and nonplused, and become exceedingly defensive when analysands or supervisors attempt to point it out to them.

One such analyst had a dream in which she was driving a powerful car and terrifying everyone in the vicinity by shooting a pistol out the window. She was not shooting directly at the people, however, but at an object off in another direction. Nevertheless the people were terrified, and the driver could not understand why they should be afraid of her; after all, she was not shooting at them, she was firing in another direction! If the analyst could have interpreted this dream, or could have accepted a supervisor's interpetation of it, she would have realized what was going wrong with so many of her patients: they were reacting to her unconscious power discharges, which were terrifying them, while her conscious intentions were not at all harmful or malicious. In fact, she was consciously committed to the idea of healing through love and intimate relationship.

THE SHAMANIC TYPE

In his written discussions of transference and countertransference Jung does not include much consideration of the power dynamic, although he does occasionally tilt his hat to Adler. But as much as he tends to gloss over the issue of power dynamics in the analytic setting, he is equally inclined to emphasize a shamanic model of healing in the countertransference (see, for instance, Jung 1921, par. 486; 1931, par. 163; McGuire and Hull 1977, p. 345). His numerous scattered remarks about transference/countertransference dynamics in analysis are cast largely in this mold: Analysts become infected by their analysands' illnesses and then effect a cure by healing themselves and administering the medicine they manufacture in themselves to the analysand via "influence." In analysis this shamanic healing process is, of course, carried out on a psychic rather than physical plane. As Jung depicts it, this is a very complex and subtle interaction, involving the whole personality of both partners in a kind of alchemical combination of psychic elements (see 1946).

If power dynamics create distance between analyst and analysand and a sharpened sense of their differences in value, the shamanic process yields the opposite result. Difference is smudged and distance collapsed in favor of psychological identification. Analyst and analysand experience each other as sames not as opposites. As this process of psychological identification takes hold, the empathy flowing between the partners tends to intensify; what happens in the one also occurs in the other; they resonate psychologically to one another. And this is when the analyst becomes infected. Psychic ailments like depression, anxiety, schizoid withdrawal, invasions of unconscious figures and impulses are experienced, often simultaneously, by the analyst as well as by the analysand because the two psychic systems run on parallel lines, the analyst's psyche bending to the features of the analysand's inner landscape. Through this kind of mirroring, the analyst's psyche absorbs and comes to reflect the analysand's illness.

This type of countertransference, it might be imagined, occurs only with analysts who have excessively permeable ego boundaries and a sort of elastic sense of personal identity. But many analysts relax their ego defenses in therapy and open themselves to the other person's psyche, and psychotherapeutic training generally fosters their doing this to some extent. So this type of interactional process is not as rare as might be thought, particularly since these identifications often take place at a level that is deeply unconscious for both analyst and analysand, bypassing ego defenses altogether.

As a shamanic healer, however, the analyst not only becomes infected by the analysand's illness but also finds a way to cure it. As the illness is taken in and suffered, the analyst begins searching for a cure: analyzing the inner psychological constellation created by this illness; scrutinizing dreams, associations, and other unconscious material relevant to the suffering; looking for symbols that emerge from the unconscious and represent the healing factor at work; active imagination. The unconscious responds to the healer's suffering, and the analyst applies the curative symbols to the wound, thereby healing the illness. Out of a personal need for healing, then, the analyst has been forced to develop further by dealing with the effects created by the analysand's illness.

I once worked with a young man who was given to serious depressive episodes. After a point he trusted me enough to allow me to share in his moods. In session he would visibly sink into his pit of despair and his body would show the pain of his emotions in vivid gestures and grimaces. As I went into these spaces with him I too began to feel the hopelessness, the sheer blankness, the physical pain of depression. These were incredibly painful sessions for me, and at times I wondered if I would survive. Would my usual spirit of optimism and enthusiasm about the future entirely crumble? I had to let it go in order to know internally what he was feeling. Together we journeyed to the place of his suicidal fantasies, and together we felt the relief of easing our wasted spirits into the welcome embrace of death. From these sessions he unaccountably got better. His functioning and mood in life generally improved a great deal, to the point where he could find a new challenging job and get married. His healing came about not by interpretation so much as by the realization that I had survived these intense states of despair with him. In some mysterious way our joint survival innoculated him against the worst ravages of depression. They also helped to prepare me for times of despair later in life.

The therapeutic task is to pass the psychic medicine over to the analysand. Like catching the original infection, administering the medicine occurs by way of the countertransference/transference process. The analyst, Jung says, "influences" the analysand (1931, par. 169). Influence in this case implies not only the effects that can be achieved simply by giving good advice or recommending some healing rituals or even making acutely empathic interpretations, but it also embraces the notion that the unconscious is deeply involved in this interactional nexus. Analyst and analysand are bonded as much unconsciously as they are connected consciously, and it is through this channel, too, via the unconscious, that the *medicina* passes to the analysand. This is the meaning of the hackneyed observation that the whole being of the analyst is sometimes involved in the countertransference/transference process. The influence of the analyst's healing substance is carried to the analysand through many subtle capillaries that run between the two partners in this complex relationship.

In modern analytic terms, this shamanic cycle can be understood as a mixture of mutual identification, projective identification, and introjection between analyst and analysand. Analyst and analysand enter into a state of identification; they project psychic contents into one another, and each identifies with these; each is introjected at some point by the other. (All of these dynamics were covered by Jung in the concept of *participation mystique*. Through *participation mystique*, which is largely unconscious, the analyst and analysand affect and are affected by each other.) The healing influence of the analyst's personality, which is constellated in response to the internalized illness of analysand, creates a curative effect within the analysand, because the analyst's self-healing process triggers a parallel healing process in the analysand's psyche. The analysand's own inner healing forces become activated by, or around, the healing analyst-imago.

This type of countertransference/transference process seems ideal in many ways for achieving the goal of psychological healing that many analysts seek. But shamanic wizardry in analysis is seductive and has its pitfalls. It can misfire and end in *folie à deux* and analytic stalemate, particularly when the dynamic sources of mutual identification remain hidden and unconscious. There is a strong temptation simply to fall into the flow of this process and to let it go on unanalyzed in the hope that it will create a magical cure. The shamanic process is not necessarily an ideal one, and analysts should be able to recognize it when it occurs, understand what it means and how it works, and foresee some of its dangers. For it creates many blind spots and can easily become anchored in the analyst's shadow, which in turn creates fierce resistance to analyzing this type of countertransference. Sometimes medication is needed, and the shamanic analyst refuses to consider this option because of an inflated attitude about the healing capacity of the analytic process.

I pointed out earlier that when power is the issue, opposites are split and a sense of sharp difference and opposition between analyst and analysand is constellated. The shamanic mode, on the other hand, is based on a constellation of identity between analyst and analysand. Here each psyche becomes oriented by an impulse to be as similar as possible to the other, with the result that each also becomes unconscious at the same points. Each shares, or tries to, the same psychological typology, the same level of maturity, the same masculine/feminine, ego/shadow constellations; even various inner objects—such as mother and father imagoes and complexes—become so thoroughly confused that the personal history of one can hardly be told from the other. Mutual idealization and denigration may occur, each person representing the other's alter ego or psychological twin. The analyst's assumption that identity prevails in so many conscious and unconscious areas of course obscures analytic vision and enfeebles the analytic grip. Analysis becomes a sort of self-analysis, with the same penchant for blindness to the shadow, and the real sickness and pathology are excluded from consciousness by mutual consent.

Shamanic countertransference, too, can easily veer toward becoming Fordham's (1978) "illusory" type. What the analyst is seeking to treat and to heal—a "bad mother" imago, for example—is actually being projected onto the analysand, who may comply by identifying with it and presenting it back to the analyst for treatment. The illusion is that the analysand is the source of the illness from which the analyst is suffering. Actually, the analyst's attempts at self-healing are not shamanic in this instance but simply efforts at self-healing, in which analysands act as receivers of projected unconscious material and as catalysts for self-therapy.

An ongoing shamanic countertransference/transference process can never be purely illusory, however, because the analysand must have an internal capacity to accept the analyst's projection and to identify with it, which implies similar inner structures. But in the countertransference itself, as this transpires during therapeutic sessions, the analyst is striving for self-healing through working on what is identified as originally being the analysand's illness. (The analyst may feel better after these sessions, while the analysand feels worse.) Thus a reversal can occur by which the analysand becomes the shamanic healer, suffering in order to cure the analyst's illness. The transference need to cure the analyst has been recognized (see Searles 1979), but the countertransference side of this, wherein the analyst unconsciously offers his illness to the analysand for shamanic treatment, has not been recognized. This reversal of the therapeutic direction is the great unanalyzed shadow of the shamanic type of countertransference.

THE MAIEUTIC TYPE

In his 1912 paper, "Neue Bahnen der Psychologie" ("New Paths in Psychology"), Jung first used the term maieutics to characterize psychoanalysis:

> It is a catharsis of a special kind, something like the maieutics of Socrates, the "art of the midwife." It is only to be expected that for many people who have adopted a certain pose towards themselves,

in which they violently believe, psychoanalysis is a veritable torture. For, in accordance with the old mystical saying, "Give up what thou hast, then shalt thou receive!" they are called upon to abandon all their cherished illusions in order that something deeper, fairer, and more embracing may arise within them. Only through the mystery of self-sacrifice can a man find himself anew. It is a genuine old wisdom that comes to light again in psychoanalytical treatment, and it is especially curious that this kind of psychic education should prove necessary in the heyday of our culture. In more than one respect it may be compared with the Socratic method, though it must be said that psychoanalysis penetrates to far greater depths.

(par. 437)

Imaged in this statement is a type of countertransference: The analyst sits as midwife to a psychological birthing process, in which "something deeper, fairer and more embracing" than the former (persona-dominated) conscious attitude arises within the analysand. In this type of countertransference/transference relationship, analysts experience themselves as assistants to a creative process that is taking place within their analysands.

In this maieutic process, the central exchanges within the analytic relationship are seen as revolving around creativity and the revelation of the Self. Not mastery (power) or healing (shamanism) but birthing is the root metaphor for what is taking place. The analyst's task is to assist what is within the analysand's unconscious to reveal itself; then, receiving and accepting this Self into the world, the analyst facilitates its incorporation into the patterns of daily life.

In this countertransference, the analyst typically sinks into a state of deep receptivity to the analysand's unconscious; background becomes foreground and the unconscious becomes palpable. The analysand is meant to follow suit and also to become receptive to the unconscious, becoming self-maieutic to the unfolding drama of creativity and the Self's revelation. During times of struggle in this birth giving, the analyst may want to attend to ego anxieties, but the basic commitment remains to a creative process that is appearing out of the invisible recesses of the unconscious. Often the analyst is captivated by a vision of the analysand's wholeness and futurity (the "child"), of a still largely unconscious Selfhood that must be brought to light and integrated. The analyst sees beyond the surface to the hidden core of a symptom's meaning. A divinity is perceived, a call heard for its recognition.

Jung's comparison of psychoanalysis to maieutics draws on the clinical experience of the differing images between what an analysand may hold consciously as a sense of Self at the beginning of analysis and the portrait of the Self that gradually emerges through a conscious exploration of the unconscious. The first is a persona-based false self, which has been constructed by a long process of identification and introjection; the second is the innate, autochthonous Self, which emerges in analysis as the unconscious is consulted and allowed to reveal its contents. Wholeness comes gradually into view. As Jung points out in the passage quoted, a person's separation from a persona-based self and the recognition of another quite different image of the Self can be an extremely painful process. But it is one that can be ameliorated by the careful empathic holding of the maieutic analyst.

Analytic work is different of course from midwifery in many respects. One of them is that after midwives help to bring children into the world, their job is done, whereas analysis (like education) goes on and on. Unlike childbirth, the emergence of the Self is not a one-time event, numinous as a glimpse of it in a dream or in the animated field in analysis may be. On the other hand, every analytic hour can be partly a maieutic event, in which an aspect of the unconscious Self is brought more into the light. Over a long period of time, many such mini-birthings add up to consciousness of the Self's vast complexity and richness. This conscious sense of wholeness is the baby whom the analyst hopes the analysand will carry away and take home at the end of analysis.

I once had the experience of observing such a happening early in an analysis. The middle-aged woman analysand brought in an initial dream in which a large animal came up out of the ocean, transformed into a wise old woman on shore, and took a long walk with her. During this walk they discussed the woman's life to date. As this woman and I considered the meaning of this dream for her we entered a field of consciousness that can best be described as mutual reverie. The dream almost became recreated and relived between us. If I squinted my eyes just a little I could see the image of the dream and could feel the powerful presence of this wise old woman. I said, You have had a great difficulty accepting your womanhood, living your feminine reality fully and freely. It was as though I were speaking for the old woman myself. These words came to me intuitively, and as I said them the analysand's eyes welled with tears and she nodded agreement. We sat for much of the session in the presence of this archetypal figure, and I could feel its reality taking hold palpably in her psyche. The Self visited us that day, and we received it in the space between us. It was a birthing. As this woman left my office she said "Wow! Thank you." And I replied, "Thank you." I felt that I had been privileged to witness a mystery.

"Psychoanalysis, considered as a therapeutic technique" Jung writes, "consists in the main of numerous dream-analyses" (1912, par. 437). In the maieutic process, these have several key functions: to reveal where the "baby" is, at what stage of readiness for birth, how close to emerging into ego consciousness, and also where the ego's defenses lie and where the tight spots of the passage to consciousness will be. Dreams function as X rays, and the job of the maieut is to read them for information concerning the development of the process underway. Each dream interpretation is also, though, one of the many mini-births necessary to bring the Self up into the full light of day.

In the maieutic countertransference position, the analyst listens primarily for messages from the unconscious as they are spoken through dreams and through the noise of the ego's communications, often ignoring or discounting the ego's manifest meanings. The analysand, who too becomes involved in this maieutic process, may experience a gradual opening of the ego to the unconscious. Optimally he or she will develop feelings of profound trust in the capabilities of the analyst, who is fixed on penetrating beneath the surface to the unconscious core of meaning within the presented associations, images, words, and symptoms. The analyst is primarily focused on gathering together aspects of the unconscious Self—the complexes and archetypal images—and on glimpsing their internal unity and structure. This requires hearing and seeing through the play of words on the surface of conscious communication and taking sonarlike soundings of the depths beneath. Eventually a bit of truth about the analysand's unconscious Self comes clear and can be raised into consciousness.

While this countertransference position is based on a medical model of sorts—attending to the biological process of birthing—it is quite different from what we usually think of as such. The medical model normally implies clinical distance on the analyst's part, the image of a surgeon coolly detaching pathological tissue and afterwards leaving the patient to recover more or less on independently. In the surgical model the analyst hunts down pathology, attacks it, and tries to remove it from the analysand's personality. The maieutic attitude is very different: The analyst assumes a basically healthy process and is present to assist normal functioning. The sort of analysis that results from the maieutic stance may include some reductive analysis (which Jung called "caustics"—1917, p. 394) of ego defenses, even though an eye is kept all the while on the emerging Self as it is growing and moving toward consciousness. The attitude of the analyst in the maieutic position is not purely passive and receptive, since there is an active role to be played in forcefully engaging defenses and resistances and sometimes in pushing through, or removing, them if they interfere with the birth.

The major pitfall in this countertransference attitude is that it may be illusory. The analyst may be gripped by a vision of the unconscious Self that is more his or her own than the analysand's. Birthing efforts are therefore unconsciously governed by the analyst's personal need to be creative and to give birth to a still unconscious Self. In this event, the analyst is projecting a creative process into the analysand, expecting to find a baby where there may even be no pregnancy, or, if so, only a false one.

In a sense, it is always partly the case that analysis is maieutic for the analyst too. Through its action, and especially through the analysis of the countertransference, the analyst becomes more conscious of the Self that is forever somewhat unconscious. The analyst is also always still in the process of piecing together a greater awareness of the Self.

But it can happen that a chronic maieutic type of countertransference attitude occludes the analyst's vision. It may be intolerable for someone who operates habitually out of this attitude to realize that the unconscious of an analysand is not always pregnant and abundantly creative, and that some analysands are so riddled with ego deficits and encased in pathological defenses that pregnancy and birth giving are out of the question until these issues are resolved. It may well be that the analysand's ego is the infant that needs careful attention and holding rather than a still-to-be-born Self. The analysand for whom this is the case may attempt to comply with the analyst's expectations by producing something that looks like psychic pregnancy and new birth, but which is really playacting and adaptation to the analyst's expectation and never addresses the real person. A *puer aeternus* can produce one false rebirth after another, none of which moves the psyche ahead. In a maieutic countertransference, the analyst can unconsciously collude with this resistance to analysis.

The analysis of this countertransference/transference process is no less tedious and repellent for the analyst than that of the others I have discussed. Examining one's own illusory and projective involvement in it is not an enviable task. It is particularly difficult when the countertransference lies primarily in the shadow of the analyst's conscious therapeutic stance. Consciously an analyst may support that he or she is working from a neutral objective attitude, for example, while unconsciously operating from a maieutic countertransference. This unconscious attitude will exert pressure on the analysand to conform to type: If the analyst is going to be maieutic, the analysand must be, or rapidly become, pregnant. This unconscious message is communicated in many ways, among them through the interpretation of dreams, associations, and images. When the analyst is intent on birthing, the analysand had better come up with a fetus.

Analyzing this countertransference/transference process is no less important than analyzing the other types. Indeed this phase of analysis may be the only means by which a therapeutic process that has gotten stuck in this impasse can be freed for a more honest and exact analysis. Once the pressure to be pregnant and creative has been removed, the analysand can afford to be conflicted and sterile, if that is indeed the true psychological picture. The analyst is then able to see, accept, and work with a real person. When the maieutic countertransference is analyzed and put aside, the analysand is free to be whatever he or she is, and if pregnancy is in the cards, a true birth can take place in its own time.

I have worked with a male analysand who seemed to be filled with a pregnant future. Oddly he kept refusing to recognize this. His resistence proved to be salutary and caused me to take back my projection into his future. He needed to be freed from my need to give birth to a transformation. Once I performed this caustic reduction of the countertransference, he was freed to explore his own directions. The new freedom in the space between us was fresh and lively. He could become himself.

Unless the analyst is utterly delusional, however, the maieutic countertransference is never altogether illusory. The analyst is at least partly responding to something in the analysand of which the analysand may not yet be aware. The constellation of the maieutic countertransference, therefore, may be an early sign of psychic pregnancy, a bit of clinical evidence that the Self is approaching. When it is syntonic, this countertransference response informs the analyst that the infantile aspects and future potential of the analysand's psyche are approaching and will soon reveal themselves. These will require empathic holding and containment, another maieutic function. So the stimulation of this countertransference as a reaction can be a harbinger of things that are still hidden in the womb of time and gestating silently in the unconscious.

## A Postscript

The unclarity of the discussion of countertransference—whether this term indicates all of the analyst's reactions to an analysand or only the more unconscious, complex-determined ones—could be resolved in part, it seems to me, by distinguishing between countertransference *attitudes, phases,* and *reactions.* By a countertransference attitude I would understand an enduring, persistent set of conscious and unconscious images, values, and thought patterns, a psychological structure that continues through long periods of time and is present before, during, and after a particular analysis. Countertransference reactions, on the other hand, are temporary and fleeting, chiefly rooted in unconscious complexes and not under ego control, disruptive of the countertransference attitude. Countertransference phases are longer lasting than reactions, but they are contained within the overall structure of the countertransference attitude, often lasting throughout a phase of the analysis.

Each of these is made up of elements that derive from an analyst's psychological history. The countertransference attitude has roots in childhood, because an analyst will instinctively care for others as he or she was cared for originally. The analyst's psychological typology as well is a piece of this attitude. The countertransference attitude is also rooted in an archetypal core, whose specific nature (mother, father, hero, etc.) depends on the personal complexes in which the attitude is set. In addition to parental and archetypal figures, introjects of personal analysts and control analysts hold key positions in the makeup of the countertransference attitude: One treats others analytically as one was treated oneself. (Where parental and later analytic inner figures clash, a fundamental rift exists in the countertransference attitude, which creates an axis of vacillation that often disturbs the analyst and will frequently be observed and challenged by analysands who are particularly sensitive due to nuances of relationship.) The same can be said about the elements making up countertransference phases and reactions: They too are rooted in the analyst's history, only they do not constitute the usual state of (professional) consciousness.

The specific elements that go into making up the countertransference attitude form the special features of an individual analyst's style of working and relating to analysands. Through training and experience, this attitude is adjusted, sharpened, made more conscious, but probably not changed fundamentally. The countertransference attitude is a more or less constant presence throughout analysis, a relatively stable factor among all the analyses an individual analyst conducts. This is the analyst's face, so to speak.

A countertransference reaction, on the other hand, is more limited, extending through a few minutes of a session or through a few sessions, or limited to the analysis of particular kinds of persons. A reaction is distinct from the countertransference attitude, which it disrupts. It is a grimace on the analytic face. Whether syntonic or illusory, it may be reactive to the transference, and it is usually derived from a fairly limited area of the analyst's unconscious. It can generally be dissolved by analysis.

A countertransference phase, in contrast to a reaction, stays within the structures of the more pervasive and enduring countertransference attitude and does not disrupt it. In a particular analysis, there are often periods when the analyst's attitude shifts subtly and, without being broken or disrupted, is augmented by a new attitude. A phase may perseverate for some sessions or even months, but one would not be inclined to say that the analyst had changed the basic countertransference attitude, only that some elements within it had been augmented, rearranged, or displaced. Like the more fleeting reaction, the phase is a reactive product within the analyst to the analysand's transference.

Each of the three types of countertransference discussed in this chapter could, in a particular instance, be an attitude, a reaction, or a phase. Each type can constitute the relatively stable substructure on which the entire analytic practice rests; each can appear as a temporary countertransference reaction that disrupts the analyst's usual attitude; or each can form a phase within the context of another type of countertransference attitude. If we follow Jung's (1961, p. 133) insight on countertransference reactions, they are often products of unconscious compensation, which occur chiefly to modify an analyst's one-sided or distorted attitude toward a particular analysand.

The psychological dynamics operating within the analyst in transference/countertransference processes are different for countertransference attitudes, reactions, and phases. For useful analysis, the analyst should know what his or her countertransference attitude is, and what is a reactive, possibly a compensatory, departure from it. The main objective of control supervision, it seems to me, is to analyze the features of the countertransference attitude and to become familiar with the most frequently constellated types of countertransference reaction and phase. These insights will be of great value for the analysis of countertransference/transference processes in the course of the analyst's subsequent therapeutic work.

### REFERENCES

Dieckmann, H. 1976. Transference and Countertransference: Results of a Berlin Research Group. *Journal of Analytical Psychology* 21/1 :25–36.
Fordham, M. 1978. *Jungian Psychotherapy.* New York: John Wiley & Sons.
Goodheart, W. 1980. Theory of the Analytic Interaction. *The San Francisco Jung Institute Library Journal* 1/4 :2–39.
Guggenbühl-Craig, A. 1971. *Power in the Helping Professions.* New York: Spring Publications.

Jung, C. G. 1912b. New Paths in Psychology. In *Collected Works*, vol. 7. Princeton: Princeton University Press, 1966.

———. 1917. *Collected Papers on Analytical Psychology*. New York: Moffat, Yard.

———. 1921. *Psychological Types*. In *Collected Works*, vol. 6. Princeton: Princeton University Press,1971.

———. 1931. Problems of Modern Psychotherapy. In *Collected Works*, vol. 16. Princeton: Princeton University Press, 1966.

———. 1946. On the Psychology of the Transference. In *Collected Works*, vol. 16. Princeton: Princeton University Press, 1966.

———. 1961a. *Memories, Dreams, Reflections*. New York: Random House.

Machtiger, H. 1982. Countertransference/Transference. In *Jungian Analysis*, M. Stein, ed. LaSalle and London: Open Court.

McGuire, W., and Hull, R. F. C., eds. 1977. *C. G. Jung Speaking*. Princeton: Princeton University Press.

Plaut, A. 1994. *Analysis Analyzed*. New York and London: Routledge.

Racker, H. 1968. *Transference and Countertransference*. New York: International Universities Press.

Searles, H. 1979. The Patient as Therapist to his Analyst. In *Countertransference and Related Subjects*. New York: International Universities Press.

Sedgwick, D. 1995. *The Wounded Healer*. New York and London: Routledge.

## *ten*

. . . . . . . . . . . . . . . . . . . . . . . . . . .

# The Muddle in Analysis

> When I was working on my book about the libido and
> approaching the end of the chapter "The Sacrifice," I
> knew in advance that its publication would cost me my
> friendship with Freud. For I planned to set down in it my
> own conception of incest, the decisive transformation of
> the concept of libido, and various other ideas in which
> I differed from Freud. . . . But Freud clung to the literal
> interpretation of it and could not grasp the spiritual sig-
> nificance of incest as a symbol.
>
> C. G. Jung, *Memories, Dreams, Reflections,* p. 167

A woman enters analysis and declares at the outset that she's a feeling intuitive type, but she behaves, as it turns out, like a sensation/thinking type. This is compensatory to her natural functioning. It is an obsessive/compulsive defense, which both affords her protection in the real world and conceals her true inner being even from herself. In addition to this, in the early phase of analysis she shows evidence of developing a split transference, such that women (the "feminine") are taken to be the caretakers of feelings and relationships while men (the "masculine") take care of the outer world. The male analyst is expected to respond (a) to her true self-functioning and (b) as a man with concrete, outer-world concerns and interests on her behalf.

Instead, the analyst responds with puzzlement and frustration. So many mixed messages pour out of this woman, beginning with her twisted typology. Frequently he feels maneuvered first into taking an obsessive amount of interest in her real-world concerns, then pushed toward giving up his analytic attitude and neutrality, then tugged toward counseling and instructing and advice giving, all the while continuing to be expected to recognize her true, feminine core. Resisting these pressures the analyst sometimes makes negative interpretations:

she is resisting analysis by these diversions, he thinks, and sometimes he says so.

The analysand, who at first feels uneasy at being in analysis at all, eventually comes to feel betrayed and complains that she is not being helped. At times she even feels she's being abused by interpretations that feel demeaning and demonstrate to her a lack of understanding of her real needs for help. She dreams that men are betraying her, even that her own husband is going behind her back and consorting with the enemy.

Communications in analysis become fraught with misunderstanding; an undertone of suspicion and accusation gathers force. Meanwhile, the analysand has found a woman analyst with whom she wants to consult on her feminine parts, in addition to continuing (but less frequently) with the male analyst, to "balance out my growth process." The analyst feels abandoned and debased. He wanted to be a full-service analyst, not an adjunct.

This muddle derives from the transference, by which he is assigned the role of the father/masculine who takes care of outer-world concerns, so that the analysand can relax the compulsiveness of her sensation/thinking functioning in order to experience and eventually to become her true Self. He is supposed to replace her obsessive/compulsive defenses. When he does not play the role of her extraverted sensation/thinking adaptation, he falls into her negative father complex and looks to her like her inadequate father: crippled, unable to assert himself in and through the world, ineffective in making a place for her in it. She's been trying to repeat her childhood, to make it right this time. Instead she's ended up simply repeating it and feeling no better off after the analysis than before.

Straightening out this muddle would involve both of them understanding this transference dynamic and relating to one another symbolically rather than concretely and protectively. If she could treat the analyst as though he were her defective father, then she could mourn him as well as her failed childhood and use the analyst as a symbolic carrier of her father problem. The ramifications of this problem in her life generally would be grasped and perhaps worked through to a resolution involving a change of transference expectations from men and from life generally. For his part, the analyst could, in the symbolic "as if" mode, express his countertransference reactions, and these could be used to unpack further her totally compacted inner life. "I'm feeling like you're asking the impossible of me" in the countertransference would become "You put myself into impossible situations and feel frustrated and helpless," or "When you get put into impossible situations, you feel helpless, abandoned, betrayed, and angry at yourself." "I feel like you want me to break the rules for you" would become "You feel like you want to break the rules and destroy everything so you can have it your own way, but without guilt." These kinds of interventions, made in the symbolic as-if space of the analytic vessel, would be extremely useful in both elucidating and transforming this analysand's inner life. The meaning of the negative father complex would ultimately unfold into the image of the wounded Father, the suffering and helpless God.

## The Muddle as Betwixt and Between

This movement into psychic space—where the transference projections and the countertransference reactions can be taken up in the as-if attitude and made conscious, and where archetypal images can take form and their meaning be recovered—is the nub of the problem. This transition is exceedingly difficult with analysands whose transference interferes in the way described above. They want to keep everything concrete. The muddle, occurring in the space between the literal/contractual side of analysis and the psychic/symbolic as-if side, creates a hazard for the entire analytic enterprise. To get from concrete, literal communications and their univocal meaning to a symbolic as-if field of communicating with its multivocal meanings, one must often pass through the valley of the muddle, a state of confusion between these other two types of communication. Typically it is the transference that accounts for the hangup in muddle-land.

Naively, one would expect the transition from literal communication to the symbolic field of communication to be easy because this is what analysis is explicitly about, after all. Who would think otherwise? Who could possibly come to a Jungian analyst, of all types of therapist, for help in dealing with situational problems on the concrete level? Jungian analysts are as far from vocational counselors, behavior modifiers, activistic social workers, evangelical preachers, drug-pushing physicians, or professional mentors in the world of work and taxes as one would expect to find in the spectrum of mental health professionals. Surely anyone who consciously chooses a Jungian analyst would know, implicitly, that what we concern ourselves with is the inner world: images not people, memories not events, conflicts not family squabbles, fantasies not careers. And yet transference is able to interfere with this conscious knowledge and to create the muddle. Jungian analysts are not immune from the muddle just because they explicitly state their way to be symbolic.

The muddle lies in the realm of "betwixt and between" (Turner 1969): between concrete communication ("waiting room behavior," as a therapist friend once aptly termed it) on the one side, and symbolic communication on the other. The analyst naturally also knows that concrete communication is necessary but is for the "world out there" and for certain concrete aspects of analysis (time, place, fee, ethical matters), while the analytic area is filled mostly with symbolic communication. This difference is parallel to the distinction Jung made between signs and symbols: signs are univocal, referring to one thing clearly and explicitly; symbols are polysemous, cannot be defined exactly or interpreted completely, and create a bridge between consciousness and the unconscious. When we listen concretely, it is with only one ear, and what we hear are clear tones and signals; when we listen symbolically, it is in stereo and we hear resonances, reverberations, depths, dimensions, and we sense a mysterious core of meaning that remains elusive and unspeakable. Listening to the muddle, however, requires yet a third ear, which can hear a latent signal dimly beneath the misleading and deceptive surface of static and disinformation. The muddle is neither concrete nor symbolic communication, but both. It pretends to be concrete but is actually symbolic in disguise, and it therefore creates misunderstanding, puzzlement, and confusion.

In the muddle, we ask questions like, "What's going on here?" "I don't understand this; are we out of control?" Or one might defend against it: "This is nonsense; let it go." Yet, however we confront it, it opens into an abyss of liminality and generates an urgent demand for understanding the dynamics at work. It throws us into a desperate need to sort things out and to get to the bottom. This experience of liminality is quite different from the kind one finds in the "secured symbolic field" (Goodheart). There one experiences a kind of liminality that belongs to transitional space (Winnicott 1971), and the distinction between literal fact and symbolic meaning is not relevant; it is suspended. Illusion and reality are simply accepted as one and the same, allowing the ego to float in an attitude of play. This kind of liminality is much less confusing to the analyst, because it is what one looks for and expects in analysis. For the analyst at least, this is a comfortable sort of liminality. What Rosemary Gordon calls "the symbolic process" and William Goodheart "the secured symbolic field" are transitional spaces in which the as-if attitude has been reached (Gordon 1977, Goodheart 1980). The as-if attitude, Gordon says, "enables men to relate to unobservable realities in terms of observable phenomena" (1977, p. 336). This is what the analyst hopes will happen, for, as Witenberg points out, if the analysand "does not ultimately see the transference as an 'as-if' experience the analysis cannot work" (1979, p. 52).

In fact, the whole analytic enterprise hangs on the attainment of the as-if attitude because it is this that allows a relation between the ego and the unconscious to become a psychological reality. This attitude is a necessary condition for the transcendent function to operate. Without it, one is limited in range to ego consciousness, and there is thus no penetration into depth, no emergent feeling for the Self, no sense of the levels of psyche and their harmonic resonances, and little integration of unconscious material.

The muddle is therefore usually seen by analysts as far from ideal, at best as a transitional state from concrete to symbolic process. It is akin to Goodheart's complex-discharging field. It introduces liminality of a sort different from the liminality of the symbolic process, a kind much less comfortable for the analyst.

## Struggles with Muddles

I would like to explore the muddle for more promising potential than has generally been noted. This type of liminality in analysis may generate an opportunity for a kind of consciousness and integration not offered by either concrete or symbolic experience. The muddle is uncomfortable, threatening, and anxiety provoking for both analysand and analyst, but this anxiety may allow them to bring to the surface hidden assumptions and to sort out transference and countertransference contents and dynamics. The muddle calls ingrained assumptions ("projections") into question and may break *participation mystique* by forcing awareness of differences of agenda, inner processes, and archetypal patterns. When a muddle thickens the analytic interaction, it leads to an awareness of "otherness" and to the sense that analyst and analysand are not what they first appeared to be. They live in different psychological universes. This awareness, in turn, may move the analytic relationship toward the "achievement of a satisfactory therapeutic partnership . . . an environment in which therapeutic transformations occur" (Redfearn 1980, p. 3).

This outcome, much to be desired, depends however upon the ability of both partners, but especially of the analyst, to sort out the confusion, to recognize projections and interpret them, and to accept the differences or adjust to them until they can, perhaps, be dissolved. The muddle creates a crisis of confidence and understanding, and it can just as well lead to an impasse and to premature termination as to a more workable partnership.

EXAMPLES

#1. An analyst tells her analysand, Mr. A, that she is taking an extended holiday of six weeks. Mr. A, who has been in analysis only briefly, reacts by saying he's had enough analysis for now and feels satisfied not to continue when she, the analyst, returns. The analyst accepts this and the analysis ends. Here the muddle is that the analyst is communicating concretely while the analysand hears the message as symbolic: "I'll be out of my practice for six weeks" is muddled into: "You're rejecting me, and before you can do so explicitly, I will reject you." The analyst makes the mistake of accepting the response on the same concrete level at which she delivered her vacation announcement, thereby most likely acting out a negative countertransference of her own. This muddle destroyed the analytic container.

#2: Mr. B comes to the analyst asking concretely for psychological help in overcoming a negative transference to his previous analyst after that analysis had ended in mutual acrimony and misunderstanding (itself a muddle). The analyst accepts this and begins sessions. As things progress, the analyst begins sensing an unconscious request for a magical cure to a deeply disturbed condition and some concomitant rage for not delivering it quickly enough. The analysand will not confess to this wish or engage the transference symbolically, so the analyst abruptly terminates the analysis with the explanation that they cannot communicate and therefore cannot possibly work together. The muddle here derives from the wide discrepancy between the analysand's conscious and unconscious expectations. The negative transference, unacknowledged or dealt with in an as-if manner, causes the analyst to feel battered and helpless. The analyst, in turn, cannot sort out the muddle, and he retaliates by communicating his rage in the form of a concrete termination. Again, the muddle destroys the analytic relationship.

The negative outcome of muddles is usually brought about by the refusal, on one or both parts, to enter the anxiety of its liminality and to experience it until the latent message can be deciphered. In the first example, the analyst might have confessed to being confused—"I'm only going away for six weeks; how does it follow that you're going to stop analysis?" The analysand might have replied, "Doesn't this mean that you're trying to get rid of me?" But this was too risky for both, and so the muddle, so rich in transference and countertransference allusions, was not used to create consciousness. In the second case, where the relationship was fraught with mutual hostility, the analyst was not willing to endure further the heat of an unacknowledged virulent negative transference. Perhaps, too, the analyst's grandiosity was offended when he could not help the analysand more expeditiously achieve the concrete aim set out at the beginning. Because the muddle was ignored in both instances, an impasse developed and neither party quite understood what happened. Premature termination affords few pleasures.

A successful passage through a muddle, however, can yield analytic gold.

**#3:** The analysis began with high expectations on the young man's part. He came to his analyst initially as to one wise, learned, and experienced. After a brief first phase of idealization, he entered a long middle period of analysis in which he mostly complained that the analyst was not close enough, did not give useful advice, said little, taught little, and was not stimulating. This was not what he had expected, and he was confused because he was coming, concretely, for help. He felt that he was being left to do all of the work by himself. The analyst, for his part, had realized early on that his interpretations were consistently ignored or bettered, so in his frustration he chose to remain mostly silent and passive and to wait for the transference to clarify itself. He, too, was confused by the contradiction between concrete demands for help and the consistent refusal to be symbolically helped. After a long period of intense disappointment and much complaint on the analysand's part, he began to uncover all the ways in which the analyst resembled his father: silent, remote, passive, helpless, inarticulate, unempathic, and generally useless. Gradually he became able to use the analyst consciously as a negative transference (symbolic) object to sort out his massive father complex and its pervasive influence in his emotional life.

Here the muddle occurred and reoccurred many times, when the analysand would concretely ask for advice and help in gaining insight and would then find that no matter what the analyst said or did, it was unhelpful and insufficient. The analyst, for his part, felt trapped between the concrete demand for advice and helpful interpretations on the one hand and the young man's inability to accept them on the other. The analyst's sense of frustration lay in his inability to negotiate the distance between concrete demand for help and the as-if symbolic attitude that is needed to make use of his psychological services. He simply had to wait until the analysand could make this crossing for himself, which in this case worked out successfully. The muddle actually became the door through which the analysis of the father complex could take place, and only later, after the passage had been made under extremely trying circumstances while the negative transference was largely unconscious, could the analysis enter anything that approached the as-if symbolic space. Shortly after that space had been achieved this particular analysis actually came to an end.

## Tracking the Muddle Maker

Muddles great and small are nearly inevitable in Jungian analysis because it is a multilevel field of operations. There are, however, various strategies available for avoiding them. One is to stay concretely goal oriented: you came to work on your unconscious, and all we will therefore consider are your fantasies and dreams; we will not deal with transference and will interpret resistance as only obstructionistic. Another strategy is to stay adamantly symbolic: all of your communications ("I have a cold today"; "my mother died yesterday"; "my car broke down and I couldn't get here on time") are symbolic, and that is the only level on which we will deal with them. Both of these are ego-dominated positions in that the analyst determines at the outset the appropriate, or the only, level on which communication and interaction will be considered. But if the ego-dominated attitude is put aside and the analyst remains open to every level of possible communication and interaction, muddles are inevitable.

The muddle may first crop up in the initial session (in one case it even occurred on the telephone when, in setting up the first appointment, the analyst became confused and could not give clear directions for getting to his office!). More likely, it occurs in subsequent sessions as the initial clarity of the case and the presenting issues and history became more complicated and opaque, and the outline of an ideal individuation process and line of development become submerged in the immediacy of a complex relationship. The dream series, often transparent and sharply delineated in theory and in retrospect, becomes protean and illusive. Life experiences happen to analyst and analysand—deaths, births, divorces, weddings, graduations, crises—and the pure and clean treatment situation is inevitably affected. Jung's account of the transference/countertransference process as an alchemical combination of psyches is accurately descriptive.

The mixture of conscious and unconscious elements from both sides creates a myriad of opportunities for falling into a muddle. And every analysis that goes at all deep, i.e., into the unconscious, will have to struggle with the muddle maker. The muddle maker is the unconscious itself, Mercurius. And both partners in analysis have one of these spirits.

Muddles occur at those points where it is not clear whether concrete or symbolic communication is taking place (as in the examples above). The concrete then feels symbolic, overdetermined, driven by a complex; but a symbolic apprehension of its as-if quality has not been established. Mercurius is present but invisible. This is the liminality of the muddle.

**#4:** The analysand opens a session by pointing out that a mistake had been made on her monthly bill. The analyst receives this as a concrete communication and offers to check the records and confirm later. This does not end the discussion, however, for the analysand goes on to show in detail, using her calendar and a pencil and paper, how the bill was incorrect. The analyst feels a good deal of affect and pressure but does not know quite where it is coming from. He asks: "Are you angry? You sound like it." She replies: "No, I just wanted to point this out." He: "But there seems to be something more behind it." She: "No, I just don't want the confusion to continue, and I'd like to get it straightened out now rather than let it go into the next month when it will be harder to track down." This scenario has the potential for turning into a full-scale muddle if the analyst pursues it by trying to probe for the underlying symbolic content. The muddle would form when the analysand clings tenaciously to the concrete level while the analyst tries to elicit some vaguely intuited transference content. Before long, neither would understand what the other was trying to say. The analyst could, on the other hand, see the problem coming and duck it altogether by accepting the concrete level and placating the analysand: "OK, I'll be sure to take care of it." But the feeling tone in the session by this time is such that this option seems unpalatable, if not irresponsible. Mercurius has struck and will not be denied. Is there some way to catch a glimpse of this "fugitive stag" (an alchemical image for this the elusive spirit) more clearly?

The analyst would ideally like to use this moment to enter the symbolic process, so that he and the analysand together could explore the various psychological levels of this interaction: all the reverberations of being overcharged by a transference object; the feelings of confusion, guilt, and anger that derive from this; the archetypal dimension of human-divine reciprocity and its breakdown; the need for retribution and justice, for being seen and acknowledged. This would be rich material for exploration in true analysis. But what the analyst actually confronts is anxiety and a compulsive defense aimed at reducing the anxiety. It is this anxiety that prevents them from moving to the symbolic level, and the muddle comes about because the analyst does not recognize the anxiety itself before probing for deeper reasons. The anxiety is committed to maintaining the concrete level because this is where the analysand feels safe and where the problem seems to lie. The muddle maker, Mercurius, cannot be caught at work here because the anxiety produced in the transference will not allow it. Because of the anxiety the muddle cannot be excavated for psychological gold.

There might be a chance to move this interaction to the symbolic process level, where Mercurius could be glimpsed, if the anxiety were first recognized and dealt with, and then deeper explorations were encouraged: "You feel anxious this won't be taken care of, that I will let it get out of hand, that you will be overcharged or have to continue struggling to get things straight in the future. I can assure you that I'll take care of it and we'll discuss it next time. But it might also be worthwhile to explore your associations to this kind of an experience just to see what might be behind the anxiety." This might, of course also go nowhere, but now the anxiety has been acknowledged and a way cleared to move into as-if territory. The analyst has actually addressed two levels: the concrete level of the bill, and the defensive level of the compulsiveness and anxiety. He has also introduced the possibility for yet another level, the as-if symbolic level, where the analyst is seen by the unconscious through the lens of the transference.

There is still another way to move in this scenario. The analyst may gain some consciousness about the psychological universe inhabited by this analysand just because this particular muddle developed. In the analyst's mental universe, this mistaken bill is no great cause for alarm. The more important matters are the psychological dynamics underlying such a concern. This (more or less standard analytical) attitude may truly misread the needs and concerns of this particular analysand. The analysand's insistence on holding to the concrete level may be as real and genuine as this person can possibly be. Such an analysand would be faking it should she begin taking everything on the symbolic process level. It would be disingenuous and simply adaptive to the analytic context and to the wishes and attitudes of the analyst to play the symbolic process game about the bill. The muddle might therefore rebound another way. Instead of trying to open the way to a symbolic as-if attitude, the analyst might adopt the concrete approach. This need not be seen as a mere capitulation to the analysand's anxiety and compulsiveness. It could be a clearer recognition of the psychological world in which she lives and out of which she operates. This kind of clarification of the analyst's view of the analysand—where and who she actually is, as different from him—can also move the therapeutic partnership to a more effective level "where ego boundaries are dissolved and transcended" (Redfearn 1980, p. 3). They may decide to meet on the concrete level to work out problems, such as the billing problem, and in working out something together, they may experience the "healing factor that we encounter in the good womb and the good mothering experience" (ibid.). The anxiety that drove the compulsion to solve the problem concretely would, of course, be allayed, but more importantly, the muddle would have led to a clearer understanding, on the analyst's part, of how this person must be treated. For this person, the as-if experience may come only through the concrete and never apart from it.

In making this latter adjustment in his attitude, the analyst is not actually giving up on attaining the symbolic process level with this person, but is rather changing the strategy for getting there. Rather than achieving symbolic process by reflecting upon events and persons as symbols or experiencing the many dimensions of an event or person, one narrows the doorway leading to the symbol to concrete events, objects, and tasks. The feeling of being in a symbolic field may not be present, or only minimally so, in the consciousness of the analyst, although it should always be there theoretically. And while it does not feel or seem like this is an as-if experience, it is! Working out the muddled bill in concrete terms resonates on the symbolic level—what has been divided comes together; there is a unity of focus and purpose; the outcome is mutually arrived at and defined. The *coniunctio* is actually experienced, but not as-if, not as a symbol, but as a concrete event that has symbolic overtones. For this particular analysand, this is a more effective experience of the *coniunctio* than a more self-consciously symbolic as-if experience would, or could, be. Here Mercurius is trapped in the concrete.

Muddles are of course meant to be resolved in one way or another, otherwise they harden into impasses and stalemates. But it is a mistake to escape the liminality of the muddle too cheaply or too quickly. Mercurius is behind the muddle and may be glimpsed at work behind the scenes. Muddles can therefore be one of our most effective teachers leading the way to a more conscious therapeutic partnership, if dealt with creatively and courageously.

### REFERENCES

Goodheart, W. B. 1980. Theory of the Analytical Interaction. *San Francisco Jung Institute Library Journal* 1/4:2–39.

Gordon, R. 1977. The Symbolic Experience as Bridge between the Personal and the Collective. *Journal of Analytical Psychology* 22/4:331–42.

Jung, C. G. 1946. On the Psychology of the Transference. In *Collected Works*, vol. 16. New York: Pantheon Books, second edition, 1966.

———. 1948. The Spirit Mercurius. In *Collected Works*, vol. 13. Princeton: Princeton University Press, 1967.

Redfearn, J. W. T. 1980. Romantic and Classical Views of Analysis. *Journal of Analytical Psychology* 25/1: 1–16.

Turner, V. W. 1969. *The Ritual Process*. Chicago: Aldine.

Winnicott, D. W. 1971. *Playing and Reality*. London: Tavistock Publications Ltd.

Witenberg, E. G. 1979. The Inner Experience of the Psychoanalyst. In *Countertransference*, L. Epstein and A. H. Feiner, eds. New York: Jason Aronson.

# *eleven*

. . . . . . . . . . . . . . . . . . . . . . . .

# In the Grip of Sleep

Now see the god, his bough
A-drip with Lethe's dew, and slumberous
With Stygian power, giving it a shake
Over the pilot's temples, to unfix,
Although he fought it, both his swimming eyes.
                                                        *Aeneid*, Bk. V

### *The Case of William*

There is a psychic field over which the god Somnus reigns. Occasionally it is constellated in analysis. Then the air becomes heavy with "Lethe's dew," and a "Stygian power" draws the eyelids forcefully downward. Like Palinurus, the unlucky pilot of Aeneas's ship who is the target of Somnus's interest and ends up dropping from his vessel into the water at the touch of the god's hypnotic bough, the analyst may fight valiantly but perhaps unsuccessfully to resist the compelling force of drowsiness. Occasionally one will drop overboard into sleep for a moment and perhaps wake with a start, hoping the moment was short and unnoticed.

When William first entered my office, he looked like a big sleepy child. He stated his age as twenty-something, but my thought was that he was more like an overgrown seven-year-old. He was of average height and overweight to the point of having little definite shape. An ill-defined pear might describe his form best. His round face revealed none of the contours of adulthood. With his hair closely cropped, he had the appearance of an angelic child of latency age.

He smiled readily, could appear thoughtful and reflective, but mostly he seemed to be absent, gazing into the far distance and absorbed in his own inner world. His dress was casual, as befit the life of a student, and during the year that I saw him in analysis he wore only thin tennis shoes, even in the depths of a brutal Chicago winter.

From the beginning, it was a struggle for me to stay awake during sessions with William. It must be confessed that this can happen to me in individual sessions with almost anyone. (I have spoken to many other analysts about the problem of sleepiness in sessions, and all confirm having such a problem occasionally.) For me, sleepiness is generally a function of how well I slept the night before, or of the time of day it might be (after lunch and early afternoon are the most trying), or of the degree to which a patient is present emotionally or stimulating in a particular session or is blocked or resistant to the pain of analytical uncovering. An analyst friend has told me that he gets sleepy when there is unclaimed anger in the room, and I have found that to be the case too sometimes. But it is rare that an individual is able to cast a strong hypnotic spell over me on a regular basis no matter what the time of day or what else of interest might be happening. William had this sort of hypnotic force about him, and from the first session onward I had to struggle to keep my eyes open and my hands on the helm of the analytic vessel. Often I prayed for strength to stay awake.

Typically William would enter the office with a floating, ambling sort of gait, take his place on the couch, gather himself together a bit, and proceed to stare off dreamily into empty space. As I sat across from him and observed his face, I would wait quietly and seek to enter the vacant silence with him. Eventually he would begin to speak. It might be about his chronic struggle with food and overeating (he had always been overweight and at times in his life was obese), or his difficulties with school work (self-discipline eluded him and deadlines always caught him unawares) or with school mates. He had come to me originally because of depression and a lack of motivation at school, and this might occupy us for a while. Whatever the topic might be, though, the hypnotic aura was always present. An initial surge of energy that produced some verbalization would be followed by long silences during which William's eyes would glaze over, his face would assume an expression of soft vacancy, and several minutes would pass before another momentary burst of energy brought him back into the room with me.

Sometimes I would respond to one of these verbalizations with a comment or a question, or even with an attempt to interpret (there might be a link to something else from a previous session or to earlier history). Generally these would produce an acknowledgment (he was not rude) or even a response that would elaborate the theme with further associations, but soon this energy would have run its course and we would return to silence.

There are many kinds of silence in analysis: the pregnant pause that brings a new thought or perspective; the angry silence that seeks to punish; the painful silence of conflict and mental paralysis; the desperate silence of despair. To me William's silence felt like a void, but one that drew me to it. There seemed to be no content to it. It was not unpleasant at first but simply empty and vacant but also extremely hypnotic. Is this what snakes do to birds? I wondered. Sometimes I asked him where he had been during such a silence. Usually he could not tell me much about the content of his thoughts during that period, and he would drift back to his somnolent state. If I interrupted a silence, he would shake himself and gaze at me in surprise, as though I had just awakened him from sleep and was asking him to recount a dream. Again, he could not give a very satisfactory account of mental contents during the silence. This was blank mindlessness.

Upon the islands of consciousness that were gradually built up during the course of our fifty-some sessions, we did erect quite a bit of structured material—a detailed personal history, a sense of the psychodynamics in various important relationships, a fairly careful definition of several key conflicts—but the overarching impression of this analytic encounter, in retrospect, is of vast stretches of empty sea divided up by several pieces of solid land and the presence of Somnus throughout the voyage. Over and over it was as though

> Now dewy Night had touched her midway mark
> Or nearly, and the crews, relaxed in peace
> On their hard rowing benches, took their rest,
> When Somnus, gliding softly from the stars
> Put the night air aside, parted the darkness,
> Palinurus, in quest of you.
> *Aeneid,* V:839–44

And I was the hapless Palinurus. But so was William.

For me the struggle with Somnus began the moment William ambled into the office. Eventually it became so severe that his physical presence alone was a cue for me to want to nod off. I never did actually fall asleep completely, but many times my head touched the waters and I would pull myself up from them with a start. The fantasy that came to me occasionally was of being mesmerized by a snake or by a snake charmer. The air would get thick, my eyes heavy, my mind utterly blank, and only by the greatest effort of will was I able to hang on to the slightest shred of consciousness. It is not that William was *boring* (see M. Khan for a discussion of the "boring patient"), because the sessions were not painful in the way that boredom "bores" and irritates. William was hypnotic.

I wondered if he had this same effect on other people. The opportunity to find out came about when he moved to another city and began working with an analyst there to whom I had referred him. At a professional meeting, this analyst thanked me for the referral, and I asked him in a general way about how things were going with William. "Oh wonderfully! He's such an interesting case!" I could honestly agree, William was interesting all right, but I fished a little further to see if this analyst had also felt the mesmerizing force I had found so prominent. It seemed he had not! I was astounded. This is still a puzzle to me. Was William completely different with him? Or was this other analyst so completely different from me that he was not affected by Somnus or did not constellate the Somnus factor with William? Perhaps Somnus was not interested in him. Or perhaps he was not telling me the whole truth about his experience of William for fear that I would think poorly of him; I, too, had not told him about William's mesmerizing effect on me. (The communications among analyst colleagues are usually heavily disguised, not only for reasons of confidentiality but as much for reasons of self-esteem and persona preservation.)

## The Interactive Field

The case of William has become for me one of the most graphic and convincing experiences of an interactive field in analysis. The idea of a field in analysis is borrowed from physics, where fields of force, like magnetic fields, are described and analyzed. A field is a pattern of energy flow that affects objects in its domain. In a psychic field, psychodynamic forces are at work, usually at a mostly unconscious level, and these produce particular states of consciousness in both analyst and analysand. "Projection," "projective identification," "participation mystique," "transference/countertransference processes," "fusion" are all terms used, in various contexts and literatures, to think about such interactive fields. We may be at the place now in the development of analytic thought where we can use myth and image to name and define *kinds of field* that are constellated in analysis, and thus obtain a more differentiated map of analytic territory than we have had by being limited to one or another of these abstract terms.

One kind of field often spoken of in the literature of analytical psychology is the erotic field. Eros launched psychoanalysis and has been central for discussions of the analytic relationship for the last nine decades. Eros defines the classic interactional field. Ares, the god of aggression and conflict, defines another well-known and much studied field. What I am proposing is that there are many other fields as well, each of which deserves scrutiny, discussion, investigation, and a name. The field of sleep, the realm of Somnus, is the one under consideration here.

This field, which might also be called a field of poppies, is soporific. In it both analyst and analysand want to nod off and drop into a state of more or less complete unconsciousness.

There is a spectrum of conditions in this field. At the extreme there is a pull toward sleep that is practically irresistible; at the other end, there is only a mild, barely perceptible, gentle, lulling, numbing seduction, a slight drift in the direction of nodding off or passively daydreaming, a gradual slippage away from tracking what is going on. How strong the magnetic force of Somnus happens to be in a particular case will depend on the size and power of the complex that supports it.

## Diagnosing the Field

To obtain a grip on the psychological nature of this field, diagnostic categories and developmental perspectives can be helpful. While the danger of freezing a human being in the icy box of a diagnosis is always a hazard and to be avoided, a diagnosis, along with a developmental understanding of the genesis of psychological structure, can guide the way as we try to penetrate more deeply and empathically into subtle layers of the unconscious psyche surrounding the symptomatic surface and to discern possibilities for further analytic insight.

So, how would William be diagnosed? Among the pre-Oedipal possibilities (for he was clearly pre-Oedipal and existed almost entirely in the world of the Mother), both of the two standard ones, Narcissistic Personality Disorder and Borderline Personality Disorder, fit to a degree. He did show some evidence of the "extreme self-absorption, lack of empathy, inability to accept criticism, and grandiose and exhibitionistic needs" (Schwartz-Salant, p. 55) of the narcissistic personality. Also there were features characteristic of impenetrable narcissistic defenses. Aspects of the Borderline Disorder were evident as well. He did demonstrate the typical kind of "environmental enmeshment" (ibid., p. 56) that borderlines show, although the rage and abuse that therapists so frequently experience with borderline patients were absent. He was also somewhat avoidant, somewhat dependent, and somewhat autistic.

William lived on the margin, socially speaking, and often he felt himself to be an outsider and even an outcast, and he had a bone to pick with those who represented the establishment. He would quietly

at first idealize and then denigrate important persons in his surroundings, the way borderline personalities typically do, and yet he seemed
more than borderline. In a sense he was over the border. Yet he was
not manifestly psychotic, and he did not routinely confuse fantasy and
reality. His was a type of consciousness that goes into and out of
autisticlike states, which alternate with normal interpersonal awareness. These could be thought of as fugue states, but momentary ones
and quite easily interrupted. To capture William diagnostically I have
found Thomas Ogden's description of the autistic-contiguous position
a good fit.

Ogden writes of a "mode of generating experience" that is "the most
primitive," in which "psychic organization is derived in large part
from sensory contiguity, that is, connections are established through
the experiences of sensory surfaces 'touching' one another" (p. 31, n.
6). The autistic-contiguous position is an extension of the Kleinian
depressive and paranoid-schizoid positions into an earlier and, in
adults, a more regressed and primitive type of mental organization.
The autistic-contiguous mode of experience is characteristic of early
infancy and is "built upon the rhythm of sensation (Tustin), particularly the sensations at the skin surface (Bick)" (ibid., p. 31). The ego's
experience is nonreflective here, and the major features of experiencing are rhythm and surface contiguity with objects (p. 32). A regression
to this mode of experiencing in analysis looks not only preverbal but
presymbolic (there are no clear images or thoughts present), and while
this state is not autistic in the strict definition of childhood pathology,
it is profoundly diffuse.

Ogden lists a number of typical countertransference reactions to the
patient who is in the autistic-contiguous position, among which is
the following:

> At times, the space between the patient and myself has felt as if
> it were filled with a warm soothing substance. Frequently, this is
> associated with a dreamy countertransference state that has nothing
> to do with boredom. It is a rather pleasant feeling of being suspended
> between sleep and wakefulness.
>
> (ibid., p. 44)

This is a reference to a state that Bion calls reverie, an ideal state of
the nurturing mother when she is emotionally in intimate contact
with her infant and laying the groundwork for "alpha function" in the
infant's incipient mind.

There is, however, also a typical kind of anxiety associated with the
autistic-contiguous position. According to Ogden, there is "an unspeakable terror of the dissolution of boundedness resulting in feelings

of leaking, falling, or dissolving into endless, shapeless space" (ibid., p. 81). This terror can also be experienced in the countertransference. In my work with William, this was felt as a terror of falling into the clutches of Somnus, of drowning in sleepiness. This was not the pleasant feeling of reverie, but rather a fear of being drawn by a forceful undertow toward a dark void of empty blankness. In Bion's terminology, we were threatened by a pull into mental territory that contained no alpha function and could therefore be exposed to beta elements lurking in the hidden recesses of the unconscious. I sensed at times the dim shape of a sinister presence. Later I would learn that this was the shape of a psychotic mother, who presented a threat of death by suffocation.

## Staying Awake in the Countertransference

How much one can learn from a single case? This is an open question. It is possible to overgeneralize, to leap from a single instance to an assumption that this describes a whole class of clinical phenomena. But it is also true that the field that I experienced with William in such extreme and sustained form is one that I have registered momentarily and less intensively with many analysands. There is a strong probability, I believe, that the unconscious dynamic forces and complexes that were operative in this case are active in many other cases, perhaps more subtly, but identically for all that. I do believe there is a field of sleep in which Somnus reigns, just as there is a field of love in which Eros holds sway. Many analysts and students have confirmed this in private discussions.

One could perhaps conceptualize this type of induced paralysis of mental alertness as an analysand's ego defense that works through creating a state of dissociation within and a wall of somnolence without. It could be seen as a defensive function whose purpose is to ward off the unwanted and intolerable intrusions of a disturbed mother. And the narcotic field may as well function as a defense against psychic pain within: It is better to go to sleep than to feel despair, unconnectedness, and depression. For such a person to enter analysis and then proceed to fall asleep and to drag the analyst along into the poppy field is like going to the dentist's office because one is suffering from a toothache but then refusing to open one's mouth because of the knowledge that drilling will hurt. And yet the tooth, rotten and decayed, hurts too. This was certainly in part William's dilemma.

This type of analysis of sleepiness as a defense seems accurate as far as it goes, but it does not tell the whole story, or even the most essential parts of the story. I do not completely subscribe to the notion that the field of sleep is only an ego defense because I sense a much darker purpose behind the threat of Somnus. A defense, like denial for instance, pretends to protect and sustain the individual's life, to have an adaptive function. But Somnus does not come upon the scene with such benign intent. He wants Palinurus to drown; he wants death. There is a sinister design that cannot be written off to defense completely.

The major effect of this hypnotic force is to produce a stagnant surface of consciousness, where, as in the fairy tales of bewitchment, everyone is asleep. This spell is cast not to protect the sleepers but to halt life, growth, development. All movement towards individuation is stopped dead in its tracks. And anyone else who wanders into this field goes to sleep there, too.

Meanwhile, far beneath the surface of consciousness, there exists an intense but vague fantasy realm that is alive with activity. But the only way to enter this territory is to pass the morphic test, to avoid the final effects of the drowsiness induced by (what I believe to be) the dark side of the mother complex. This seemed clearly to be the case with William. In his psyche the mother complex generated a field of paralyzing bewitchment in which William's ego was trapped, and the main purpose of this was not to protect William but to hold him.

There are many fairy tales in which bewitchment takes the form of sleepiness and in this manner halts further development. Sleep freezes growth. "Snow White" and "Sleeping Beauty" are famous examples. "The Shoes That Were Danced to Pieces" (Grimm) is a less well-known tale in which the theme of being put to sleep plays a key role and one that for my purposes here identifies the key elements needed by the analyst in order to survive and penetrate into a psyche like William's.

The story runs like this.

A king had twelve daughters whose shoes were worn out with dancing each morning, despite his locking the door to their rooms and posting guards. The proclamation went out that whoever could discover how this happened could marry the princess of his choice. Death was the reward for failure. It happened that many princes accepted the challenge, but all failed because they would fall asleep at the post. No one, it seemed, could stay awake through the night. While this powerful field of sleep held sway, the mystery continued and the princesses remained unwed.

The hero of the story receives some advice from an old woman who knows how the status quo is maintained. She tells him not to drink the wine the princesses will offer, and then to dress in the invisible cloak she will give him and to follow the princesses wherever they go. In this way he will discover their secrets. He does as he has been advised, and what he discovers is the secret life of the princesses. After dark, they go down into the earth through a trap-door, walk through a magical garden, are each rowed across a great lake by a corresponding prince, and spend the night dancing wildly in a beautiful palace. At dawn they return, close the trap door, and act as if they had been sleeping all night. The hero is able to accompany them, silently and invisibly, and the next day he reports to the king what he has found. This breaks the spell. He marries the eldest daughter and inherits the kingdom. The princes, on the other hand, "were bewitched for as many days as they had danced nights with the twelve" (p. 600).

At the beginning of analytic sessions with William, I often felt like the would-be hero of this fairy tale. There would be a period of blank silence, and I would immediately feel the threat of Somnus in the atmosphere. I might make a comment, ask a question, refer to our last session—or not. Whatever I did or he did, the first minutes were spent by me trying to get used to the space. Gradually I acquired the ability to stay alert and to wait quietly (invisibly) until an opening appeared. William would seem to drop down into himself, and from there he might speak and reveal something of his inner life. Through many dark passages in the months we spent together, I was able to glimpse his childhood history with a psychotic mother, to witness the psychological incest that occurred between them, to understand the damage that was done to his sister (who was by his account psychotic intermittently and severely obese), and to acknowledge the valiant but vain efforts he had made to separate psychologically from his mother.

He also led me into the territory of his sexual fantasies and occasional activities. This was terrain that he protected to a great extent from everyone else. It was a secret and dangerous part of his life. Even his own ego would remain more or less asleep when he went there. This is where the princesses would dance the night away while his ego and his parental complexes slept. Here his secret life ran on while all was quiet and asleep on the surface. In the morning he would rise exhausted and not know quite why.

It took considerable time and patient effort to establish any clarity about what took place in this hidden fantasy territory, so vague at first were the stories and images that appeared. The scene, as it emerged into view, appeared to me childlike, paradisal, innocent. While sexuality was a prominent feature, it was not yet genital for the most part. There were scenes with boys and young men holding hands or dancing, being tender and intimate with one another, caring for each other. Nothing obscene or raw entered these pictures. They revealed great intensity and longing, feelings of deep communion in the gestures of holding and fondling. In these scenarios, vast amounts of time could be spent talking quietly and intently. There might be a momentary burst of Dionysian frenzy in the fantasies, but mostly they resembled a long, slow summer's day or a late evening at a club.

In the course of the year during which this brief analysis took place, William gained considerable capacity to put into words what was going on at this inarticulate level of fantasy activity. Some of the material was made up of memories, some of wish fulfillments in the present. There was at least one great mother fantasy in which William was being fed by a goddess directly through a tube.

As all of this material, especially the sexual images, became more integrated into his ego complex and William could accept his liminal wishes and thoughts into consciousness with less conflict and fear, the fantasy scenes also gained in precision and lost some of their dark vagueness. At this point we were less subterranean in our psychic explorations. Our sessions were also somewhat less soporific, although this element never vanished altogether.

In the single most important dream of the analysis, William finds himself trapped on his grandmother's farm. He comes upon his father's truck, however, and steals it to make an escape. He is on the way out, having overcome the greatest barriers, when he awakens. This dream preceded a good deal of later ego consolidation and conscious strides towards individuation; it marked the initiation of a new stage in his development. We both immediately recognized the importance of this dream and referred to it often during the remainder of the analysis. It was the equivalent in the fairy tale of the hero's winning a bride from among the twelve princesses who nightly danced their shoes to pieces. The emergence from the unconscious brought with it new energy and a stronger commitment to life and to real relationships.

## Two Kinds of Sleep

What happened in the course of this analysis can be further amplified by another story about being put to sleep. According to the Yahwist writer, God created Adam and then the animals and birds to be his helpers. After Adam is asked to name the animals, God realizes that none is an adequate helper,

> So the Lord God caused a deep sleep to fall upon the man, and he slept, then he took one of his ribs and closed up its place with flesh. And the rib that the Lord God had taken from the man he made into a woman and brought her to the man. Then the man said, "This at last is bone of my bones and flesh of my flesh; this one shall be

called Woman, for out of Man this one was taken." Therefore a man
leaves his father and his mother and clings to his wife, and they
become one flesh.

(Gen. 2:21–24)

There is considerable and surprising isomorphism between this
story from the Bible and the Grimms' fairy tale of "The Shoes That
Were Danced to Pieces," and also between these two tales and the case
of William. The deepest points of contact have to do with two themes:
(a) the theme of separation from an identification with childhood images and figures, and (b) the theme of creating a single anima figure
with whom the ego complex (Adam in the Bible, the hero in the fairy
tale, and William in my case) can relate.

In the Biblical story, these themes are vividly presented. This passage from Genesis is classically recited at weddings, which is an initiation ceremony with a rite of exit (giving the bride away), rites of
liminality (the vows), and a rite of reincorporation (the return to society as a new couple). The note of leave-taking from the parental figures
is unmistakable. This is clearly paralleled in the fairy tale, which also
ends with a wedding and a child's consequent separation from the
paternal home.

Similar to the fairy tale, too, there is in the Biblical story a movement from the "many" (i.e., the twelve princesses; *all* the animals
and birds as helpers) to the "one" (i.e., the eldest princess only as
bride; one Woman, Eve). In both cases this represents a consolidation
of the anima into a single psychic entity.

In the case of William, too, there was a gradual emergence (separa-
tion/individuation) from identification with the complexes of childhood (imaged dramatically in the dream of escape from his
grandmother's farm in his father's truck) to a more conscious recognition of self/other distinctions and the beginnings, at least, of an integration of sexuality in his consciousness. He was gradually making his
way out of the autistic-contiguous position.

Both fairy tale and Biblical story end at the moment when explicit
sexuality is constellated and immanent, and William's case also concluded at a point where his sexuality was being accepted consciously.
The consolidation of a single anima heralds the end of the smothering
mother phase and the beginning of the dynamic anima phase of inner
development. In a sense, the ego is born here for a second time, this
time out of the psychological (as opposed to the physical) mother.

One crucial point of difference between the fairy tale and the Biblical story, however, is the function of sleep in each. In the fairy tale,
falling asleep while watching the princesses is a lethal failure, and

wakefulness is rewarded with the grand prize. Sleep supports the continuance of the pathological status quo. This was the state of affairs with William, too. Sleepiness prevented movement and development in his life at all levels. In the Biblical story, on the contrary, sleep is the necessary condition for beginning individuation; it is a creative womb out of which the anima-mate is born.

There are obviously therefore different kinds of sleep or different functions and meanings to be assigned to the experience of falling asleep. The one is defensive and prevents individuation; the other is creative and facilitates individuation.

In William's life, too, there were two kinds of sleep: the one was the narcotic field that was constellated in our sessions, which was a defensive screen thrown up by the mother complex to stifle development, to prevent separation, and to block fantasies from being registered by the ego; the other was the sleep of dreaming, which gave birth to the invaluable dream of stealing father's truck and escaping from grandmother's farm, a psychic event that was of great use to us in the analytic effort to free him from his mother-bound condition.

Perhaps this difference between two kinds of sleep rests upon the fact that one is induced by a Father God who apparently wants the ego complex to solidify, unify, and individuate, at least to a certain degree, while the other is induced by an amorphous (in the fairy tale no mother is mentioned) and highly disturbed (in William's case) mother complex. With William, it was important that analysis valued nocturnal dreams and used them to further individuation.

## The Analyst's Interpretive Function in the Field of Sleep

"The Shoes That Were Danced to Pieces" indicates some hazards in trying to make analytic interpretations in this "field of sleep." The old wise woman who meets the hero on his way into town gives him two things: a piece of advice and an object. The advice is: "You must not drink the wine which will be brought to you at night, and must pretend to be sound asleep" (p. 597). The object is a little cloak: "If you wear this, you will be invisible, and then you can steal after the twelve" (ibid.). By following these instructions, the hero is able to achieve his goal. This would suggest a prohibition on making sounds (i.e., giving conscious interpretations) in a case like this. An interpretation that would venture into the meaning of what is going on in this interactive field prematurely would disrupt the process.

Interventions from the side of consciousness, based as they usually are on theory and clinical experience, are dangerous. In fact, interpretations based on even the most specific material from a single case can have a disruptive effect when the field is constituted by strong features of an autistic-contiguous position. The premature presentation of edges, boundaries, conceptual formulations, subject-object differentiations, such as might be made in transference interpretations for instance, have a startling effect and break the spell. The hero must go with the princesses into the underground caverns and simply observe what is there before reporting it to any part of the personality in treatment.

At one point in the story, the hero breaks a twig from a tree, to take back with him as a token of where he has been. The tree "cracked with a loud report. The youngest cried out again: 'Something is wrong.'" (p. 598). This field is easily disturbed, like the surface of a quiet pond in the forest. The challenge is to stay alert in it, to observe what is going on, to bring back a report to the ego complex (the befuddled king, in our story) later, but at the moment of observation it is necessary to remain quiet and invisible.

In William's case, I of course made many "sounds." I observed, labeled, interpreted, educated, and even gave advice from time to time, but these sounds usually did not take place while we were in the narcotic field. At some point during the hour, or at the end of it, there would often be a brief time to offer some clarifications and to hold ego-to-ego discussion and to make some observations. At no time did I comment directly on the nature of the field itself. I did this out of instinct rather than theory or foresight. It seemed correct to go as far into the dissociated state with William as I could and to fetch back from it the bits of fantasy that gradually could be pieced together, later, into what would eventually become a fairly clear image of his fantasies and desires, as well as his recollections from childhood.

## On the Nature and Origin of Interactive Fields

Analytical cases eventually settle down into a particular pattern or image of interaction between the two persons involved in it. This image pattern, which characterizes the relationship and defines its deepest essence, lies at the heart of the interactive field. In chapter 10 I write about "the muddle," which was the core image of an interactive field in a particular analysis; it was a pattern of confusion and misunderstanding that endured throughout a rather lengthy analytic relationship. The pattern I am describing here, which typified my much shorter working relationship with William, was chiefly characterized by a kind of hypnotic stupor, by a strong pull toward deep unconsciousness.

How do these fields come into being? They may take form almost instantly, as was the case with William, or they may take a period of time to show their face. They are the product of the psychic alchemy that transpires in analysis, as described by Jung in "The Psychology of the Transference." These fields seem to constellate as a result of a particular mixture of specific psychic ingredients that are placed into the analytic container by both analysand and analyst.

Typically the analyst will begin an analysis by quietly observing and taking in the spoken and unspoken communications of the new analysand (cf. Dieckmann, 1991, chapter 2 for an excellent discussion of the initial session). This receptivity on the analyst's part in the initial session and the subsequent several sessions allows a kind of psychic infection to take place in the analyst (cf. Stein, 1984). It is as though a psychic virus enters the field and finds a host body in the form of the analyst whom it can probe for entry. The virus fixes onto a psychic complex of the analyst's and once it slips in, begins to do its work of self-replication.

This penetration into the analyst's psyche of contents that are projected there by the analysand's psyche ( through "projective identification"—cf. Grotstein) produces a state of psychic awareness in the analyst that is akin to that in the unconscious of the analysand. Generally it is dark, opaque, and confused at first. Jung spoke of this as "influence" and "psychic infection," and he referred frequently to the shamanic model of healing to discuss the analytic process. This transfer of psychic contents makes possible the almost miraculous "mindreading" that analysts can often perform to the amazement of their analysands.

According to the shamanic model (see chapter above), the "illness" that the analysand suffers from is transferred to the analyst (a quite literal form of transference), and the analyst begins suffering from the same problem. Within the psyche of the analyst, there occurs a quasi identification with the projection (a form of countertransference that is due to the response to the projection, called by Fordham syntonic countertransference), whereby the analyst makes the alien illness his own. Now the analyst not only can empathize in a highly precise way with the analysand but also can actually observe the analysand's psychic unconscious process at first hand, both for its destructive aspects and for the healing, restorative efforts that the presence of the virus constellates within the wider range of the psyche. One hopes that the analyst's psychic constitution is healthy and strong enough to withstand the illness and to counteract it with sufficient force to produce an antidote, though this is not always the case.

Some analysts succumb to the stronger personality and the virulent toxins of certain analysands and are badly injured or destroyed by them (for an excellent example of this, cf. chapter 1 of Irwin Yalom's *Love's Executioner*, in which a young and gifted psychotherapist falls victim to an elderly female former patient and as a result finds it necessary to abandon his profession). These are the would-be heroes who take the wine offered by the princesses, become drugged, fall asleep, and then wake up to the sound of the executioner's blade sharpening. Usually one thinks of this happening in instances of sexual acting-out by analysts with analysands, but the field of sleep also has its considerable hazards, not the least of which is feeding an already enlarged mother complex in the analyst with all its attendant symptoms of grandiosity and inflation.

To be honest, however, one must also admit that analysts can infect their analysands with psychic viruses as well. These seemly charismatic but actually dangerous analysts often actually consider it to be a "cure" when they see their analysands becoming more and more like themselves. What is happening usually is that their influence is creating a false persona without touching the underlying structures of the analysand's psyche. It would be wise to question this, at least, to avoid the inevitable disaster of a "transference cure."

When considering the phenomena of projection, of which transference is one type, the analyst must keep in mind that while the psychic virus with which infection begins is a foreign element and belongs to the analysand, every projection requires a "hook" to fasten upon (cf. von Franz) and every projective identification needs a suitable and rich "container" to house it (Grotstein). So completely one-sided accounts in which either analyst or analysand is labeled as the "carrier" are clearly erroneous. In the analogy of the virus seeking entry into a host cell, there is the recognition that virus and host have something in common structurally—there must be a "fit"—in order for the infection to take place. The virus must search out a suitable host cell (i.e., complex) in the analyst's psychic body to fix upon and to enter.

In the case of William, the virus was clearly located within the mother complex. In his early history, he had been infected by his mother through their umbilical union. They never had come truly apart at the unconscious level of their union. William was still symbiotic with a psychotic mother. What this had done to him was to block his individuation into masculine maturity. His psychic structures had remained amorphous and vague, and his ego complex could not extricate itself from the mother via identification with an available father.

Hence William had remained chronically stuck in the mother, not consciously identified with her but not separated from her either. The enlarged mother complex had so filled his psychic system that there was no room to grow an individuated ego complex. Most of his psychic life therefore took place underground within the unconscious. And one of the chief observable symptoms indicating this state of affairs was the narcoticlike field that William's own ego was trapped in, i.e., his fuguelike dissociations. It was this that also communicated itself to me as analyst and infected me. I became nearly as sleepy and unmotivated as William was.

When William first met with me, he almost immediately infected me with this hypnotic, deadening force. His physical and psychological presence had a soporific effect on me. I hypothesize that the pathogenic virus entered my psyche via my mother complex, through a similarity in structure. (Although my own actual mother was quite different from his in many respects, she shared the trait of unconsciously undermining my separation from herself and my identifying with my father.) Through this complex, the virus could enter and in it reproduce itself. Once inside my psychic body, this virus exaggerated those similar aspects in my mother complex, and as a consequence my ego very quickly felt the same stifling, smothering, hypnotic effect as William lived with chronically. Thus the shamanic contact was made, and the circuit was closed.

In the course of the analysis, I became familiar with William's psychic structures through this infection, and I was able to observe his struggles to stay alive and sane directly from my own experience when in his presence. It was not the case that the hypnotic force was chiefly a defense on his ego's part against my intrusions or against his own psychic pain, but rather that we both fell into the same condition, both of us struggling to keep ourselves from falling into a state of possession and losing our minds by what could now be considered a mutual mother complex. At the core of this interactional field lay the Great Mother archetype in her containing, smothering, potentially castrating and devouring form. When our struggles to stay awake and to become conscious began to succeed, there was also support from another quarter: the dream of escaping from the grandmother's farm in the father's truck. This mobilization of individuation energy in a Hermes—the—thief trickster form, sufficient to escape the realm of the Great Mother, appeared in our work as a sort of divine intervention. The act of theft was transformational, as trickster is meant to be (cf. Henderson). And the paternal, spiritual aspect of the psyche was making itself available to William's fledgling ego in the image of a pickup truck. Perhaps this reflected the result of an incipient father transference to me.

The crisis that led to the conclusion of our analytical relationship was created by a source opposed to the Great Mother as well, namely by William's sexuality. William had been drawn to the Church, largely by his Great Mother projection, and while I saw him he was studying for a career in Her sanctuary. After our analytic work had reached the point of escaping from the Great Mother's realm (in the dream), William acted out sexually in such a way that he was banished from the Church: he was required to drop his studies and to remove himself from the Church's precincts. In other words, the Mother kicked him out. As a result, he was obliged to move to another part of the country for employment, and our analytic work came to a rather abrupt end. We were unprepared for this consciously, since it all took place within the course of one week, and yet the work that had been done to this point could sustain the break and use it for William's further growth and benefit.

Symbolically, the timing was good. William's ejection from Mother Church into the world of independent living, of work, and of freer interpersonal relationships would thrust him out of Paradise and require him to develop his autonomy and masculine standpoint in relation to the rest of the world. After he left the city, he telephoned me for a referral in his new location. I gave him the name of a male analyst friend of mine, and he followed up on the referral by continuing analysis. It was this colleague who later reported to me that the work was going well and who showed no signs of experiencing the hypnotic field that I had found to be so potent. Perhaps William had truly escaped the hypnotic force field of the Great Mother; perhaps the virus was no longer active; perhaps the new analyst did not have a suitable receptor site.

After several months, I received a card from William thanking me for the help he had received in analysis and giving me some news of his present activities. I remember feeling pleased with the outcome, but I also noted to myself that William had not returned a book he once borrowed from a bookshelf in my office: Erich Neumann's *The Origins and History of Consciousness*. It is a book about the development of consciousness in Western culture through a release from the Great Mother cultures of the past into the presently waning but still dominant patriarchal form. I wondered if this book represented William's father's truck, which he used to escape his grandmother's farm, as well as an extension of me and of our work. To myself I hoped that this vigorous statement by a keen and manly spirit would continue to release an effective antidote against William's Great Mother virus and keep him on the path of psychological development towards maturity.

## REFERENCES

Bion, W. 1962. Learning from Experience. In *Seven Servants*. New York: Jason Aronson.

Dieckmann, H. 1991. *Methods in Analytical Psychology*. Wilmette, IL.: Chiron Publications.

Grotstein, J. S. 1981. *Splitting and Projective Identification*. New York, London: Jason Aronson.

*Grimms' Fairy Tales*. 1972. New York: Random House.

Henderson, J. 1967. *Thresholds of Initiation*. Middletown: Wesleyan University Press.

*Holy Bible* (New Revised Standard Version). 1989. Oxford: Oxford University Press.

Jung, C. G. 1946. On the Psychology of the Transference. In *Collected Works*, vol. 16. New York: Pantheon Books, second edition, 1966.

Khan, M. 1986. Introduction to *Holding and Interpretation* by D. W. Winnicott. Grove Press, 1987.

Ogden, T. H. 1989. *The Primitive Edge of Experience*. Northvale and London: Jason Aronson.

Schwartz-Salant, N. 1989. *The Borderline Personality*. Wilmette, IL.: Chiron Publications.

Stein, M. 1984. Power, Shamanism, and Maieutics in the Countertransference, in *Transference/Countertransference* (ed. by N. Schwartz-Salant and M. Stein), Wilmette, IL.: Chiron Publications.

———. 1991. The Muddle in Analysis, in *Liminality and Transitional Phenomena* (ed. by N. Schwartz-Salant and M. Stein), Wilmette, IL.: Chiron Publications.

Von Franz, M.-L. 1980. *Projection and Re—Collection in Jungian Psychology*. LaSalle and London: Open Court.

Yalom, I. 1989. *Love's Executioner*. New York: HarperCollins.

# *twelve*

. . . . . . . . . . . . . . . . . . . . . . . . .

# On the State of Soul in
# the Narcissistic Personality

During the decade of the 1980s, a significant number of Jungian authors (for example, Asper, Corbett, Gordon, Jacoby, Kalsched, Klaif, Satinover, Schwartz-Salant) drew up comparisons between Heinz Kohut's revisions of psychoanalytic theory and similar ideas in analytical psychology. The energy for this work was generated by the excitement around Kohut's discoveries concerning the narcissistic personality disorder and by certain obvious similarities between his concepts and Jung's.

These often elaborate exercises in comparative psychoanalytic thinking have greatly clarified the similarities and differences between Jung and Kohut, particularly regarding the meaning of the key term in both Kohutian and Jungian systems, notably the self. Whether the Kohutian self is identical to the Jungian Self, and if so in what precise ways this is and is not the case, has been a crucial theoretical question addressed in these studies, of which the most complete and detailed is Mario Jacoby's *Individuation and Narcissism* (1990). In general, there now seems to be agreement that the Kohutian self is not the Self of analytical psychology and to try to use these terms interchangeably results in more confusion than utility on both sides.

Beyond this point of theoretical clarification, the issue remains as to whether analytical psychology can be useful, either theoretically or clinically, for deeper understanding and more effective treatment of narcissistic personality disorders and borderline states. Certainly a number of Jungian authors among those cited above have thought this to be the case and have made significant contributions.

It seems to me that if there is indeed a way in which Jung's theory can be useful for shedding more light upon the structural and clinical problems presented by patients with narcissistic to borderline character disorders, the route may have to be directed through the territory of anima/animus development rather than by immediately evoking the concept of the Self. It is here that closer parallels can be actually seen between the Kohutian self, the detailing of which has been of such great clinical usefulness in understanding and treating the problems presented in the narcissistic personality disorders, and the personality structures described by Jung and employed clinically in analytical psychology. On the other side, Kohut's insights can be of use to analytical psychology, particularly for understanding the development of anima/animus structures and certain pathological outcomes of their misdevelopment.

In utilizing Jung's anima/animus theory for the purpose of exploring the psychology of narcissism and borderline states, I will limit myself to two extended passages in the *Collected Works*. The first passage occurs in the "Definitions" chapter of *Psychological Types* (1921), and the second comprises the third chapter of *Aion* (1951), "The Syzygy: Anima and Animus." Between these two texts, I believe it is possible to garner enough theoretical material to link up the theory of anima/animus with some major issues of the narcissistic personality, as delineated by Kohut, and also to offer some reflections on borderline states as well as some possibilities for individuation that lie beyond narcissistic object relations.

It will be my contention that the narcissistic personality disorders and borderline states rest upon a misdevelopment of anima/animus structures.

## Narcissism and the Soul

In the last chapter of his monumental work, *Psychological Types*, Jung provides extensive definitions of the terms he uses throughout the book. He includes a long passage, itself a small essay, on the term *soul*. Here he defines the earliest version of his concept anima/animus. From a structural point of view, it is a single concept, although it has two main variants corresponding to the genders. In other words, the term *anima* is supposed to apply to men, and the term *animus* is supposed to apply to women. But Jung deals with this concept only after first defining the term *persona*. These two terms represent complimentary psychological structures. By posing them as contrasting structures, he clarifies the definition of both.

Jung opens his definition of soul by speaking of the "functional complex" as a "personality" and distinguishing complexes from the ego (par. 797). Everyone, he argues, has a sort of multiple personality. This is not the same as MPD (multiple personality disorder), but it means that everyone contains more than one singular personality within the whole of the psyche. The wholeness of the personality is a complexity of many aspects, multiple attitudes, numerous tendencies, many of them often in conflict with others. A man's personality at his place of work, Jung writes, is typically businesslike, aggressive, and decisive, while is domestic personality at home around the family and in the household may be compliant, passive, and easygoing. What this reveals is that we possess—or are possessed by—a variety of "functional complexes," each of which can be thought of as a separate personality (par. 798).

The ego complex is in turn colored by these other functional complexes, or personalities, through "identification" (ibid.). When the executive at work adopts his typical commanding tone, for example, his ego is identifying with a functional complex of a certain collective sort and enacting its attitude. This is not necessarily his "true," or his only, personality (ibid.). The functional complexes with which an ego identifies in order to deal with the outer social environment make up the persona structure. The persona may itself be quite multisided and plural, not always the same in every environment. Jung is impressed by how chameleonlike the human person is, changing situationally to adapt to the needs and expectations of a surrounding milieu. Personality, then, and to some extent even character are highly milieu sensitive. Samuels has picked up on this side of Jung's thought and extended these notions in his book *The Plural Psyche.*

It is quite easy to grasp and to use the concept of the persona. It is a mask, or a set of masks, worn to adapt to situations as they arise in one's social world. It is harder though, to grasp the complementary concept of the anima/animus. This is the functional complex that faces the inner world. Like the persona, it often is colored by a typical and collective attitude. And it is usually—Jung appeals here not to theory but to experience—quite different from and complementary to the persona. If the persona is hard, aggressive, and businesslike, then the anima is typically soft, sentimental, and emotional.

It is crucial to recognize that Jung does not at this point link anima/animus structures to gender, at least not as the essential definition of this psychological structure. The anima/animus structure is simply the face turned inward, the attitude one takes toward oneself, toward one's own subjectivity, toward moods, emotional reactions, dreams, impulses, thoughts, and fantasies. The anima/animus is the structure a person uses to adapt to the inner world, to states of mind. If one is soft and open and tender with oneself, this is the face of the anima/animus; if one is hard, aggressive, attacking to oneself on the other hand, then this is the anima/animus's attitude. In analysis one is sometimes asked to paint the face of the anima or the animus, to give it form. This will tell patients how they treat themselves. Generally, the complementary face will be turned outward. It is psychological truism for many that they are their own worst critics, usually much more empathic toward others than toward themselves. Theirs is a harsh and scolding animus/anima attitude. And the reverse may be true as well. One spoils oneself and punishes others.

I have sometimes suggested using an ungendered, neutral term like *anime* to refer to this psychological structure of interiority. Anima and animus are strongly gender-linked in the minds of those who read, study, and employ Jung's writings, for the good reason that Jung himself usually speaks of these structures in that way. In fact, the gender of the terms follows from their Latin differences: anima has a feminine ending and animus a masculine. When Jung writes about the anima and leaves abstraction for experience and psychic image, he invariably refers to its feminine features. And, conversely, with the animus he refers to the masculine element in a woman's personality.

Jung's own account of how he first came to speak of the anima in this way is instructive. In *Analytical Psychology: Notes of the Seminar* (1989), he confesses that his first realization of the anima in himself occurred during his work on Miss Miller's fantasies, which eventually resulted in his seminal book *Psychology of the Unconscious*. It was while he was writing this book that he first became fascinated with mythology and mythological thinking. This kind of thinking, which he found so pronounced in the Miller materials, actually began to overtake him too, he says, and as a scientist he was horrified:

> As a form of thinking I held it to be altogether impure, a sort of incestuous intercourse, thoroughly immoral from an intellectual standpoint. Permitting fantasy in myself had the same effect on me as would be produced on a man if he came into his workshop and found all the tools flying about doing things independently of his will. It shocked me, in other words, to think of the possibility of a fantasy life in my own mind ... and so great was my resistance to it, that I could only admit the fact in myself through the process of projecting my material into Miss Miller's. ... I had to realize then that in Miss Miller I was analyzing my own fantasy function ... and thus in this book the question of the inferior function and the anima comes up.
>
> (Jung 1989, pp. 27–28)

These associations among a man's fantasy life (usually inferior compared to his more conscious and rational functioning), the image of woman, and the inferior function would remain constant throughout Jung's writings on the anima.

The place of the feminine in this set, however, is arbitrary and more accidental than essential. One can use the terms anima and animus to refer to the mind's fantasy function and interiority without linking them to gender and still retain their conceptual value for analytical psychology. It was only by historical circumstance and cultural influence that anima became linked with the feminine in the first place. It happened that in Jung's own psychology the anima has this particular form. In another person, whose cultural and personal associations are different, who lives in a different age with different collective images of masculine and feminine, the psychological structure that we name anima may well have an entirely different cast, including a different gender. This is to say that the contents of the structure are constructed by society, culture, and history, while the structure itself is stable through time and cultures. The anima/animus is an archetype structurally, therefore universal and innate, while its contents and coloration is constructed by culture and individual life experience.

In *Psychological Types* (1921), which was incubated during the decade following the analysis of Miss Miller's fantasies and the break with Freud, Jung points out that the ego can identify with anima/animus structures as well as with persona complexes. When this happens, the ego becomes, as it commonly said, anima (or animus) possessed. For the ego, we can see, this notion presents a Scylla and Charybdis problem: on the one side lies persona identification, on the other anima/animus possession. Either way, the ego loses its neutrality and freedom and becomes unduly influenced by the values and styles embedded in the functional complexes. Only the supremely conscious person can, Odysseuslike, chart a course between them.

When the ego tends toward persona identification, Jung points out, the anima/animus complexes are projected onto a suitable external object, typically a person of the other sex and certainly someone who embodies in his/her character style the strongest features of the anima/animus attitudes. This seems to be the normal state of affairs, developmentally speaking. A person relates first to mother and father, to the family members, and then later to the peer group. The functional complexes that get built up to carry out this adaptation (the persona) are based principally on the models offered. A little girl will relate adaptively to her mother, and then will relate to others as she did to her mother and as she saw her mother relate to herself and to others. One says casually that she "takes after her mother," more technically that she has introjected her mother and identified with her. What has actually happened, according to Jung's theory, is that a functional complex has been created out of the interaction between the daughter's latent personality and the mother object, and that the ego tends to identify with this complex when relating to others. This is especially the case when the mother is seen to be successful in her adaptations. If mother is admired for the way she handles herself in the world, then daughter sees this as a promising strategy for doing the same thing. Kohut speaks of the transmuting internalization of idealized objects, while Jung speaks of complex formation and identification. Other theorists might speak here of imitation, of "modeling," or of learning.

For men traditionally, it is the father or a father figure who plays the role of persona model. Through the interaction between the little boy's unconscious and his father's character, he builds up a functional complex with which he can identify in relating and adapting to the world. The father's imago (an inner psychic image) thus helps the son to "bridge to the world" by way of this functional complex, a persona, through the son's identification with it.

The anima/animus functional complexes come into being alongside this persona development and seem to be somewhat dependent upon what happens there. While the persona "is strongly influenced by environmental conditions," Jung writes, "the anima is shaped by the unconscious and its qualities" (par. 806). But, when the external environment is "primitive," he continues, the persona will necessarily also reflect this, and "the anima similarly takes on the archaic features of the unconscious" (ibid.). These processes of persona and anima/ animus formation are seen, therefore, as correlated: what happens in one sector has a strong effect on what happens in the other. The anima/ animus complexes reflect something of the outer environment even if only by compensating for the persona complexes. They are, however, principally shaped by the unconscious and its qualities. The anima/ animus complexes are, in a manner of speaking, the individual's unconscious answer to the environment—to the mother on the daughter's part, to the father on the son's, to the predominant family attitude, and even to society and contemporary culture as a whole.

As indicated, the usual picture of a personality's development shows the ego identifying increasingly with the persona complexes, which reflect the environment and are shaped by important figures in it, like mother and father and other significant people. Meanwhile, the anima/ animus complexes remain distant and other, on the whole not being identified with in the sense of forming a person's conscious identity. Typically they are projected onto suitable other people. This projection creates intense bonds ("soul-mating"), as the other person represents the inward-turned "other" within. Later in life, a person may gradually gain consciousness of the anima/animus complexes as inner attitudes and draw them into the structures of consciousness and ego identity.

Then they cease being projected upon figures in the environment, at least to some extent. This is the expected course of maturation and individuation, the gradual approximation to psychological wholeness. Anima and animus integration are a second-half-of-life developmental achievement.

Jung mentions another possible line of development, however. This occurs when the ego does not identify primarily with the persona complexes but rather with the anima/animus complexes:

> If the soul-image is projected, the result is an absolute affective tie to the object. If it is not projected, a relatively unadapted state develops, which Freud has described as narcissism. . . . If the soul image is not projected, a thoroughly morbid relation to the unconscious gradually develops. The subject is increasingly overwhelmed by unconscious contents, which his inadequate relations to the object makes him powerless to assimilate or put to any kind of use, so that the whole subject-object relation only deteriorates further.
>
> (pars. 810–11)

It is noteworthy that Jung refers to Freud's term *narcissism* here. This term is rare in Jung's *Collected Works,* occurring only a half dozen times. Occasionally Jung uses narcissism as the disparaging way in which people often regard introversion. But in the kind of narcissism Jung is considering in this passage, which is the classic psychoanalytic kind introduced by Freud himself and later picked up and elaborated by Kohut, he sees a developmental deficit owing to the ego's lack of identification with the persona complexes. It is a case of the individual's ego not identifying with the available persona complexes, which means, practically speaking, that the complexes associated with the same-sex parent are more negative than positive. The negative valence produces aversion on the part of the ego. Of a son, one would say that he does not, or cannot, identify with his father. For a daughter, this would be true of her relation to her mother. The persona complexes formed around the interaction with these figures do not attract the ego sufficiently to form a positive identification. There is a gap. The girl may admire and even idolize her mother, but she cannot identify with her because the persona complex needed to do so has not formed or because the one that has formed is repellant. The boy may look up to his father but from a distance and from a position of inferiority and fear; his persona complexes do not draw his ego into a bond of identification.

If we ask why this is the case, we need to look deeply into the intricacies of development in infancy and early childhood. The object around which the persona complex forms (the mother for a girl, the father for a boy) may communicate a subtle, or blatant, rejection of the infant or young child. This element of rejection gets built into the complex in such a way that the ego cannot get close to it without feeling rejection, low self-esteem, or criticism. If this parental object is envious or rivalrous, then hatred is built into the complex and creates self-hate. The persona complex hates the ego, so to speak. It is a negative image from the ego's point of view. Thus, bad outer objects become bad inner ones. The function of therapy for this person is to cure this by providing a caring and empathic new object around which to form a new persona complex that can be identified with.

However this pathological early development takes place, it throws the ego into a state of social alienation and isolation, such that the result is a profound lack of adaptation to the outer world and a state of absorption in the inner world.

It might seem that the unconscious would, under these circumstances, compensate the bad persona complex with a positive and attractive anima/animus complex. To some extent, this is what happens, but it turns into a seduction and becomes an escape from reality. The anima acts as a siren, the animus as a demon lover. When this incestuous self-involved development takes place, the ego withdraws into a secluded inner world of fantasy, hides increasingly from the outer world and from its demands, and the psychological state that Jung calls "morbid" comes about. This resembles the schizoid withdrawal classically described by Fairbairn (1952).

Unfortunately, the anima/animus complexes, when unhitched this much from the outer world, deepen into their archaic and highly charged, intensely conflicted archetypal polarities. Beside the seductive, sirenlike anima lurks the death-dealing witch; beside the ghostly lover animus stands the dark magician. Typically, the people who enter into this psychological condition become fascinated with magic, esoteric religion, and occultism. They are highly vulnerable to archetypal influences and symbols and easily fall under the influence of persons who employ such things to gain power and to manipulate. Others simply retreat into a world of their own personal fantasies and obsessions, becoming confused and delusional in their identifications with these inner figures. The anima/animus functional complexes do not, it seems, become structured particularly well, in the sense of providing protection and suitable adaption to the inner world of unconscious forces and figures, if the persona complexes are poorly or negatively structured or are defective. This is most likely due to the practical reason that if one parent is defective, the other probably is as well. The persona complexes are usually structured in and through the interaction between the subject's personality and the same-sex parent. Girls use their mothers to bridge to the world, and boys their fathers. This forms the functional complex that the ego can use to deal with the outer, social world. In parallel, the anima/animus functional complexes are formed and structured typically through the interaction between the subject's personality and the other-sex parent. Sons use their mothers, daughters their fathers, to face inward and deal with the inner world, to meet its demands and face its pressures from instincts and archetypes. If the anima/animus complexes are inadequate, the person's ego will be insufficiently adapted to the unconscious and will tend to be overwhelmed by the unconscious.

In cases where only one parent is available for both persona and anima/animus constellation and structuring, or where one parent is so inadequate as to be useless for this purpose, there is likely to be confusion of identification and consequently of identity. Persona and anima/animus structures will be similar and used for purposes of adaptation to both the outer and inner worlds. A man will come across socially as effeminate, a woman as masculine, and each may feel ashamed and self-conscious about this. Similarly, this person may have a difficult time facing inward if the single parent was of the same sex. Such is a typical picture of the narcissistic personality disorder: a sense of shame and low self-esteem combined with inner shallowness.

If the problem is even more severe, we come upon the borderline personality disorder. Consider the person, not an uncommon candidate for psychotherapy today, who has had a more or less distant same-sex parent with whom he or she could not easily identify. This means that the persona ends up being inadequate, defective, or generally unavailable. This person also has a negative other-sex parental complex, due to a domineering and controlling attitude in that parent, and this means that the anima/animus structures are defective and cannot be relied upon to face up to inner life and the unconscious. Here we see that we have a person who is poorly adapted to the outer world and extremely vulnerable to onslaughts from the unconscious. It is not that this person has identified with the anima/animus complexes—this would yield the picture of extreme introversion or schizoid withdrawal—but he or she has neither persona nor anima/animus structures to identify with and rely on. This, it seems to me, lies in the background of the borderline personality—there is an ego that is fragile in the outer world and excessively vulnerable to being taken over by the unconscious, by affect, ideation, imagination, from within. This person may appear to be creative but is also extremely vulnerable to the world without and the world within.

## A Case

Godfrey is the oldest of seven children. Born to a young woman slightly more educated and cultured than her handsome but unambitious husband, Godfrey was only two when his next sibling came along, and then in rapid succession five more appeared. The house was small and quickly overcrowded. Godfrey's father was a traveling salesman and out of the house most of the time on his routes. His mother was overwhelmed with all the children and looked to Godfrey, the oldest to help with the others. Early on, he realized that he would not much enjoy the other neighborhood children, especially the rough and rowdy boys. Godfrey was intelligent, sensitive, and artistically gifted, not especially athletic. He often longed for solitude, for order, for beautiful things. There was little money to go around, and the father was not available both because he was gone much of the time and also because he was narcissistic and favored his own hobbies and interests over his son. So Godfrey grew up more or less by himself, despite a crowd of family members.

In adolescence, Godfrey suffered from acute social unease and developed severe skin problems, usually a sign of persona inadequacies. He did not feel accepted by his peers and tended to be a loner. He discovered escapes in drugs and sexual fantasy. In college, he was courted by an older male student whom he admired, and he entered a homosexual relationship. At the same time, he had a girlfriend, whom eventually he married. Gender confusion and identity problems run through his history from that point on.

Godfrey came into analysis when he was in his midthirties. By then he had several young children and managed to support himself and his family in a family business. He suffered from severe mood swings, depression, uncontrollable rages, and feelings of hopelessness and emptiness. He was highly vigilant and anxious in groups, and frequently woke up from nightmares. His preferred form of sexual activity was masturbation with homosexual fantasies. He had once attempted suicide ten years earlier, using drugs, and had narrowly escaped death. Presently he did not abuse drugs except for an occasional puff of marijuana.

Suffering from acute abandonment anxiety as a result of a threat of divorce, analysis quickly revealed severe structural problems. The absence of a good enough father figure resulted in inadequate persona complexes, hence his extreme anxiety in social situations, especially with men. His fear was that they would laugh at him and consider him inadequate as a man. He could not speak with them on their level. With women, he felt more comfortable but he did not usually like them or respect them. The anima complexes were colored by his largely negative mother complex. His mother had been extremely intrusive and domineering, and she had been too close to her son for his comfort. The anima, therefore, as she appeared in dreams, was usually threatening. Godfrey lived in terror of his inner life—his moods were unpredictable and extreme, veering from euphoria to painful depression. The slightest emotional event in his world could trigger massive inner upheavals and panic attacks; his imagination came up with fiendish Satanic figures, and his dreams contained similar images. His conflicted relations with the outside world were matched by his conflicted relations with the inner world. He tended to berate himself on all counts, and he felt he could not trust himself in any way.

The point to be made with the brief clinical description has to do with the anima problem. Godfrey's anima complexes were structured in such a way that they did not protect him from his unconscious. This is the normal (or ideal) role of the anima structure in the psyche. Probably this was due historically the lack of an empathic mother and a failure of mirroring. This inner structural defect in the anima left Godfrey severely at risk with respect to his inner states and emotional reactions, highly charged as they were with affect, and left him vulnerable as well to inner attacks and sudden losses of self-esteem, all of which has been classically described by Kohut. This is a narcissistic character disorder with some borderline features.

A clinical incident illustrates how this psychic structure is experienced. At one point in the analysis, Godfrey had begun to admire an older man who was a teacher. Godfrey had been invited to lunch by this man, but at the last moment the teacher canceled the lunch with what seemed to be a lame excuse. Godfrey took it in stride at first, but by the time he saw me for analysis a few hours later he was in an inexplicable funk. We traced his black mood to that event. Then in the days following, this mood actually deepened to the extreme and lasted for about two weeks. Dreams reflected this injury to self-esteem, and all of our analytic work during this period was taken up examining this incredible reaction. No amount of insight or empathy on my part, or understanding on his, had much effect on his mood and feelings. This sort of acute sensitivity to slights from idealized others is a hallmark of narcissistic disorder, and it indicates the failure of the inner structures, the anima, to protect the ego from severe attacks from within. The whole sense of self-worth is blasted, and there is no inner resiliency. There is no compensating sense of being loved from within when one is not loved by an admired person without. The psyche lets him down and he falls into a bottomless hole.

Godfrey had a sort of pasted-together exterior shell that functioned defensively as a persona, seeming to provide a mask or armor against the slings and arrows of reality. But this protection is only apparent. At a deeper level there is acute suffering and extreme vulnerability to these rebuffs, and the attacks from within—the self-criticism, the slings and arrows of self-abusive thoughts—hit their mark with drop-dead accuracy.

After several years of analysis there was some amelioration. We could see in dreams the emergence of a helpful, praising, masculine dream figure who can show the way on his quest into the depths; also some female figures appeared who were responsive and friendly. The persona complexes, meanwhile, were being slowly modified and formed around his interaction with me, and his relations with the outer world improved markedly both in effectiveness and in reduction of anxiety. There was also some evidence in dreams of the constellation of a Self figure.

From cases such as this, it has become clear that in narcissistic to borderline character disorders there are inadequate developments in both the persona and the anima/animus sets of functional complexes. The possibility for achieving some degree of psychological wholeness depends upon repair of both of these structures.

## *Anima/Animus as the Projection-Making Factor*

There is another and more subtle kind of narcissistic problem, however, one in which there seems to be a normal and good enough development in both persona and anima/animus functional complexes. This type of problem has to do with a developmental issue that is usually only encountered in adulthood and often only in the second half of life. The challenge here has to do with becoming conscious of the anima/animus complexes and the psyche's projection of them. This kind of narcissism—not the obviously pathological kind discussed above (the Freudian kind, in Jung's words), but a subtle and insidious narcissism—results in object relations that are highly determined by projection of the anima/animus complexes.

In *Psychological Types*, Jung points out that normally a person's ego becomes identified with the persona complexes and the anima/animus attitudes are found only in projection onto others: "In all cases where there is an identity with the persona, and the soul accordingly is unconscious, the soul-image is transferred to a real person. This person is the object of intense love or equally intense hate (or fear)" (1921, par. 808). (An implication of this, incidentally, is that when the ego is not identified with the persona complexes, the person also does not project the anima/animus complexes. That this person does not fall in love, or hate, is a diagnostic indicator that helps differentiate between primary and secondary narcissism. The primary narcissist cannot fall in love, the secondary narcissist falls in love regularly and compulsively.)

There is a feature of the narcissistic personality that has to do with the projection of the anima/animus functional complexes and with the object relations consequent to this dynamic. Kohut speaks of "selfobjects" in this connection. A selfobject is an object so interlaced with projected psychic material that it stands as much for an inner content as for itself, so that the ego's relation to it is to a piece of its own unconscious psyche. When we conceive of an individuation process— a maturational process—as moving past this type of object relating, we must think of it as an *opus contra naturam*, for to relate affectively to the world-as-projection seems to be the more or less natural human state of affairs, in that it is "natural" to remain unconscious, particularly of the projections of the anima/animus complexes.

By the 1940s, when Jung was writing *Aion*, which includes a chapter entitled "The Syzygy: Anima and Animus," he had extended his understanding of anima/animus projection from the magical love relationship to include a much wider range of object relations, indeed perhaps in the case of a narcissistic personality the entire gamut:

> It is often tragic to see how blatantly a man bungles his own life and the lives of others yet remains totally incapable of seeing how much the whole tragedy originates in himself, and how he continually feeds it and keeps it going. Not consciously of course—for consciously he is engaged in bewailing and cursing a fruitless world that recedes further and further into the distance. Rather it is an unconscious factor which spins the illusions that veil his world. And what is being spun is a cocoon, which in the end will completely envelop him.
>
> (1951, par. 18)

Women, Jung adds, are similarly subject to this cocoon-spinning activity (of the animus): "The woman, like the man, becomes wrapped in a veil of illusions by her demon-familiar, and, as the daughter who alone understands her father (that is, is eternally right in everything), she is translated to the land of sheep, where she is put to graze by the shepherd of her soul, the animus" (par. 32). Anima and animus are parallel structures and dynamic archetypal factors in men and women, and in both sexes they are responsible for spinning illusions, creating projections, and disturbing the ego's object relations.

For Jung, as for Melanie Klein (1959) in her later theorizing, projection and introjection begin in earliest infancy. An internal picture of the world is built up by a combination of these processes. For Jung, the personal mother is the first carrier of the son's anima projection and the father is the first carrier for the daughter's animus projection (1951, par. 28). These figures (i.e., mother and father) are, of course, also introjected, and so the anima/animus complexes develop their particular lineaments and features. But behind these anima/animus complexes, which are used by the ego to relate to and govern the expression of the unconscious and of instincts in daily life, there lie the archetypes of anima and animus. And the archetype extends far beyond the personal mother/father figures and continues to function as projection maker throughout later life. It is this factor that is, in Jung's view, responsible for turning objects into selfobjects.

## A Case

A clinical example illustrates the kind of problem that appears in a man when there is strong ego identification with the persona functional complexes, almost total unconsciousness of the anima functional complexes and archetype, and consequent narcissistic object relations.

Jason, in his early forties, was "sent into therapy" by his wife with the ultimatum: either learn to relate to me or learn to live without me. He himself did not understand her problem, only knowing that she was extremely unhappy and serious about divorce. He was happy and successful in his profession, came into therapy well-dressed and groomed, and had a charming and pleasant demeanor.

Since it was his wife who had the complaint, I asked to see her for a session to hear her side of the story. She told me that her spouse had pursued her ardently in courtship and had insisted on marriage. She had been ambivalent and would have preferred to wait, but his intense pressure was too much for her, and she made a premature decision to marry him. She quickly regretted this, but went ahead with the wedding anyway, not wanting to rock the boat once launched. During courtship and the early years of marriage, her husband was, she said, passionately sexual, but this diminished and after a few years became almost nonexistent, largely by his choice. He remained extremely jealous of her, however, and would often check on her whereabouts during the day. There was never any doubt of his loyalty to her, and she never had the sense that he wanted another woman or wanted to change anything about their relationship. He was most content when she stayed home and was there for him on weekends. When they were together, however, he rarely spoke or listened to her, and this was the major problem. She had the feeling that he was completely unaware of who she was or what she thought or felt. He was not interested in her actually, although he wanted her to be around all the time. When they did have sex now, he closed his eyes and seemed to be in his own world. He was totally preoccupied with his own thoughts, which focused on work and his hobbies. He made unilateral decisions about expenditures but resented her doing the same. She felt completely controlled by him and unseen. All of their friends found him charming and few could understand her problem with him. Only the ones who knew him more intimately could see what she saw.

As his story came out in therapy, it turned out that he was the oldest child in a tightly structured, traditional, patriarchal family. His mother served his father, who was largely silent at home and preoccupied. As a boy he admired his father but had no personal relationship with him, and he grew up to be much like him in appearance and demeanor. Many people commented on this. After his father's death, he continued to have a close but largely nonverbal and unconscious relationship with his mother.

When he met the woman he was to marry, he fell in love with her instantly. To have her was his greatest desire, and he could not believe his luck when she responded positively to him. He viewed their marriage as basically a success and was completely content with it and with her, except for her bitter complaints, which he could not understand and which made him increasingly uncomfortable. He felt devoted to his family and wanted nothing to change in it. His work gave him great satisfaction, and he was making steady progress up the corporate ladder. His bosses and coworkers all liked him. He could not understand what he was doing here with me. Perhaps his wife was the one who needed help, he suggested. But he was willing to come. He would do anything to save the marriage.

This is the picture of a man wrapped in an anima cocoon. His Eros has reached out, claimed a soul-mate, and now is trying to preserve her in amber. He is unreflective, "objective," without interest in self-knowledge, and has never considered his own inner processes. He accepts the world as it is, and it is as he sees it. Jung would say he had identified with his persona complex and was projecting his unconscious anima into the world. The real world, meanwhile, is receding from him. Witness his wife.

## Object Relations Beyond Narcissism

Jung acknowledges the difficulty of making the anima/animus factors conscious: "whereas the shadow can be seen through and recognized fairly easily, the anima and animus are much further away from consciousness and in normal circumstances are seldom if ever realized" (1951, par. 19). This type of narcissism would seem to be the normal human psychological state, and only in abnormal circumstances would one be forced or drawn to an analysis of the very foundational concepts and attitudes and perceptions by which consciousness operates and from which the psyche has made up a world.

Fortunately, therapy usually begins with such abnormal circumstances. Persons come to therapy in crisis, in inner and outer upheaval, and their deepest and dearest assumptions about life, about themselves, and about their grasp on reality are exposed for conscious examination. When the psyche is opened up in this way and a person is painfully suspended in psychological liminality, the necessary readiness for a thoroughgoing analysis is available. Until then, transformation of consciousness and release of the occluded or ensnared Self cannot take place, and wholeness is not even a theoretical possibility.

Jung claims (1951, par. 42) that when the anima/animus factors are made conscious, through crisis and confrontation and analytic introspection with a suitable "other," a "triad" emerges: there is the ego (the subject), the other (the object), and the "transcendent" element (the anima/animus). Object relations have therefore been radically altered: no longer is the other an anima/animus projection carrier, a selfobject. Rather, a conscious distinction can now be made between the soul-image (as inner other, transcendent, i.e., belonging to the unconscious) and the actual other. The relation to the other, now freed from projection, can take entirely new forms. There is a new kind of freedom in this for both ego and other, to be themselves more fully vis-à-vis the other, with no need to enact the projection of anima or animus.

Winnicott, in a late paper entitled "The Use of an Object and Relating through Identifications" (1969), writes about this as the difference between projection-based "object relating" and projection-free "object use." In the latter, the subject is much freer to be creative with the object because it is now known that thought and fantasy cannot destroy the other, as it can be if related to through identifications. For Winnicott, the passage from the one type of object relation to the other is not automatic and "natural" (as it is also not for Jung, where making the anima/animus conscious is an extremely rare and difficult *opus contra naturam*), but is achieved through the experience that destructive fantasy and expression do not kill the other or drive him or her away. I believe Jung would also subscribe to this, although he does not emphasize this explicitly. Both would agree that through patient and caring analytic work, this result may be achieved and that this is also the way to the experience of the (true) Self.

### REFERENCES

Asper, K. 1987. *Verlassenheit und Selbstentfremdung.* Olten: Walter.

Corbett, L. 1989. Kohut and Jung: a Comparison of Theory and Therapy. In *Self Psychology, Comparisons and Contrasts,* Detrick and Detrick, eds. Hillsdale: Analytic Press, pp. 23–47.

Corbett, L. and Kugler, P. 1989. The Self in Jung and Kohut. In *Dimensions of Self Experience: Progress in Self Psychology,* vol. 5, A. Goldberg, ed. Hillsdale: Analytic Press, pp. 189–208.

Fairbairn, W. R. D. 1952. *Psycho-analytic Studies of the Personality.* London: Tavistock.

Gordon, R. 1980. Narcissism and the Self. *Journal of Analytical Psychology* 25:247–64.

Jacoby, M. 1981. Reflections on Heinz Kohut's Concepts of Narcissism. *Journal of Analytical Psychology* 26:107–10.

———. 1990. *Individuation and Narcissism: The Psychology of the Self in Jung and Kohut.* London: Routledge.

Jung, C. G. 1912a. *Wandlungen und Symbole der Libido.* Vienna: Franz Deuticke.

———. 1921. *Psychological Types. Collected Works,* vol. 6. Princeton: Princeton University Press, 1971.

———. 1951a. *Aion: Researches into the Phenomenology of the Self. CW,* vol. 9ii. Princeton: Princeton University Press, 1959.

———. 1989. *Analytical Psychology: Notes on the Seminar Given in 1925.* Princeton: Princeton University Press.

Kalsched, D. 1980. Narcissism and the Search for Interiority. Quadrant 13(2):46–74.

Klaif, C. 1987. Emerging Concepts of the Self: Clinical Considerations. In *Archetypal Processes in Psychotherapy,* Schwartz-Salant and Stein, eds. Wilmette, IL.: Chiron Publications, pp. 75–92.

Klein, M. 1959. Our Adult World and Its Roots in Infancy. In *Envy and Gratitude.* New York: Dell, 1975, pp. 247–63.

Kohut, M. 1977. *The Restoration of the Self.* New York: International Universities Press.

Samuels, A. 1989. *The Plural Psyche.* New York and London: Routledge.

Satinover, J. 1980. Puer Aeternus: The Narcissistic Relation to the Self. Quadrant 13(2):75108.

———. 1984. Jung's Contribution to the Dilemma of Narcissism. *Journal of the American Psychoanalytic Association* 34(2):401–38.

Schwartz-Salant, N. 1982. *Narcissism and Character Transformation.* Toronto: Inner City Books.

Winnicott, D. W. 1969. The Use of an Object and Relating through Identifications. In *Playing and Reality.* New York: Basic Books, 1971, pp. 86–94.

## thirteen

. . . . . . . . . . . . . . . . . . . . . . . . . .

# Envy and Sibling Rivalry
# as Blocks to Wholeness

### Conceptualizing Envy

In a searching and vividly written work entitled *Mal Occhio*, Lawrence DiStasi recalls the tactics used by his Italian grandparents to guard against the influence of the "evil eye." He notes especially their avoidance of boasting to strangers about their children, for fear of stimulating envy. Children were so highly prized that they became the chief targets for envy attacks. Should a child become suddenly and unaccountably ill, the workings of *mal occhio* were instantly suspected, and a countersorcerer would be enlisted to speak some healing incantations to overcome the sickening effects of the evil eye's attack.

DiStasi does not comment on how envy attacks were avoided within the family among siblings. Some of the nastiest envy attacks take place within the supposedly cozy sanctuaries of immediate and extended family networks. For it is not only the stranger whom one envies, but the brother, the sister, and the cousin. Envy is the root of the most malignant and chronic forms of sibling rivalry, and in the long run envy hurts both the caster of it and the recipient equally. Both can become blocked from moving toward wholeness.

When considering the psychology of envy, it is important to note that as in DiStasi's account, where children were the most frequent targets of envy within his culture, it is the object or quality of highest worth that draws the evil eye of envy to itself. A child will draw the attention of an evil eye in a particular setting, for example, because children symbolize the highest value there: They are the "treasure hard to attain." With this realization we can understand that envy is fundamentally based on a person's frustrated desire for direct access to the fountainhead of value, which in Jungian psychology is known as the Self.

It may seem puzzling at first to conceive of envy as being driven by the ego's deprivation of and longing for the Self, since both ego and Self are lodged in the same person and make up a single psychological unit. Yet it does seem to be the case that this is what envy most essentially is. The English word "envy," which is a derivative of the Latin *invidere*, means at root "to look into" something with intense hostility. The eye becomes hostile in this fashion when it rests upon an object that enjoys the grace of selfhood if that same blessing is not felt inwardly as one's own inheritance too.

The envious person casts a hostile glance in the direction of a favored one and feels, at the same time, that an impassible distance lies between here and that circle of privilege and fortune. What the envious eye sees is a selfobject (Kohut) that cannot be brought close or enjoyed in relationship, but rather one that unrelentingly deprives oneself of grace and worth simply by virtue of its continuing existence. The graced person appears to be withholding this treasure and to want to hoard all the glory. The inner void that is hewn out and maintained by envy, which Fordham calls a "no-breast" state (p. 199), is the breeding ground for the hatred and destructiveness that are so central to envy's energy. It is the ego's alienation from a self perceived externally in projected form that creates the profound despair and deadly malevolence found in classic examples of envy's ravages such as Shakespeare's Iago. Envy is the alarm signal of a deep rupture in the ego-self axis.

Envy's corrosiveness "denudes"' (Bion's phrase, p. 47) the inner world by destroying the site of an inwardly felt self-center. Self-energies and selfobjects, which constitute a wellspring of self-esteem and resilience when they are internally available to a person, are, in the condition of envy, perceived as being located outside of oneself, withdrawn and withholding. Thus envy is fueled by an overinvestment of value in others and by a concomitant underinvestment in oneself. In this state a person becomes emptied of value and resource, and the ego's total charge of energy comes to be concentrated and aggressively dispatched through *mal occhio*, the evil eye.

## The Literature on Envy

In researching this chapter, I embarrassed myself by falling personally into considerable envy of those who have written previously on this subject. At times this nearly paralyzed me by generating the very states articulated in the literature: emptiness, inadequacy, and excitement in the presence of the envied object. Gradually this reaction became transformed, fortunately, and I can now feel admiration and gratitude for the painstaking and insightful work done by those who

have previously ventured into this rich but tortured emotional territory before me.

The thread of envy in the psychoanalytic literature was picked up,
after its remarkable introduction by Freud in his frequent discussions
of penis envy, by Melanie Klein, who shifted the focus of envy from
the penis to the breast. But beyond merely changing the focus of envy,
Klein argued that primary envy is innate in humans, and she linked
it to *thanatos*, the death instinct. Both females and males are born
with a specific amount of primary envy, based on the strength of the
death instinct in them. How the impulses of the death instinct are
handled and deployed is the story of later development, but at the
point of birth each of us inherits, like original sin, the capacity and
the proclivity to fall into envy.

This even-handed approach with regard to gender continues in
Klein's account of infancy. Since both little males and little females
are nursed by a female mother, who blesses or denies them with her
breast, the breast becomes the first and remains the primary object
around which the emotions of love and hate swirl.

Klein's account of how envy operates in infancy and later in life is
seminal to later writings by Freudians and some Jungians as well,
whether these authors agree with, reject, or ignore her premise of a
death instinct.

In her paper "Envy and Gratitude," which has become a classic
in the field, Klein makes an analytical distinction between envy and
jealousy. This distinction is important to keep in mind when thinking
about sibling rivalry, because sibling rivalry long outlives childhood
and parents and often has nothing to do with winning or losing the
love of a third person. Envy has its proper location, according to Klein's
analysis, in a two-person relationship, primordially within the mother-
infant dyad, whereas jealousy is a phenomenon of three-person trian-
gles, classically constellated within the Oedipal relationship. Envy is
therefore "pre-Oedipal" and based on the feeling that the other person
(originally the mother) has something good to give (a breast) but is
withholding it for her own enjoyment. Her withholding of the good
object is what generates envy and then also hatred of the mother.
When mother is seen as reserving her goodness for herself, this perception generates the wish to harm and spoil the mother's withheld breast.

Jealousy, on the other hand, erupts when it is discovered that someone else (the father or a sibling) is enjoying the desired object instead
of oneself. Jealousy drives a person to destroy the rival so that one can
have the loved object for oneself but not to destroy the object itself.
In some instances of sibling rivalry it is clearly jealousy that motivates

the conflict, but in the most virulent forms the issue has little to do with satisfying oneself by gaining the ownership of someone or something but rather revolves around the wish to harm or destroy the envied other as an end in itself. The existence of a fought-over object, a family business for example, only forms the excuse to face off against the envied sibling. The real wish is to destroy the envied person.

Greed, the third Fury in this shadow Trinity analyzed by Klein, is closely linked to envy: It is the urgent desire to have more than one can possibly use and enjoy, to have it all (to devour the whole breast), to control and possess it completely. Both envy and greed aim for the destruction of the desired object: envy by spoiling the goodness of the loved object with one's own badness through projecting the bad parts of the self into the other (projective identification); greed by introjecting all of the other into oneself.

In Klein's view, the mother's breast is the original love object around which all of these dark emotions swirl. The breast is the source of life and therefore also symbolizes creativity itself. Klein believes that the ultimate issue encountered wherever envy appears is creativity. Having access to creativity and to the wellspring of creative energy is what envy is finally all about. From the beginning, the infant's own potential creativity is projected onto the mother's breast, creativity which the ego will need for its own growth and future integrity. Because the first vision of creativity is thus located outside of oneself, one feels dependent upon it for growth and life itself. Thus the nascent ego is alienated at the very outset from its own source of psychic creativity and growth. This must eventually be recovered by the individual psyche through reintrojection, for as Klein conceives of development, "the mother's breast forms the core of the ego and vitally contributes to its growth and integration" (p. 215). Ego development is made up, then, of these two movements: projection of the Self into the other followed by introjection of it back into the ego.

In her discussion of the centrality of the breast for creativity, integrity, and ego development, Klein is clearly referring to the same entity that Jung called the Self, the principal organizing archetype of the psyche, even if their descriptions and conceptualizations are very different. While Klein's discussion is object oriented, however, Jung's is intrapsychic. For Jung, the Kleinian breast would be taken as a symbol of the Self, a mandala with a clearly defined center. An object or image becomes a symbol when it mediates energy between the ego and an archetype, and the breast is such an object/image. The archetype that the breast mediates is the Self, which, according to Jung's later work, constitutes the core of the ego and promotes its growth and integration throughout life. The Jungian critique of Klein is that she locates the inside outside: the reason the breast has such centrality and power is that it carries a projection of the Self.

It is the absent Self, therefore, that is fundamentally at issue in the projective and introjective fantasies of the envious and greedy. Jung could easily join Klein in saying that the issue of envy is the location of creativity, but they would disagree on where psychic creativity originates and is sourced.

In a Jungian theory of envy, we would think of it as a psychic symptom rather than as an expression of primary destructiveness, death wish, or evil. The arousal of envy is a signal of something being wrong, but it grows out of an otherwise benign hunger for full selfhood. Once constellated, however, envy can become chronic, and it can then ally itself with the shadow side of the Self. At that point envy has the capacity to channel the energy of individuation (the drive toward wholeness) into destructiveness. This is the tragedy of envy. It is the story of Iago destroying Othello not to gain Desdemona for himself or to take Othello's place in the kingdom but as an end in itself.

The insight that creativity is the fundamental issue in the problem of envy, while admitted by Klein, is not developed by her to any great extent, due perhaps to her linking envy with *thanatos*. The Jungian authors who follow after her, on the other hand, tend to take this other path. The connection between envy and creativity was picked up and elaborated by the London Jungian, Michael Rosenthall. Rosenthall held that the envied object is not the breast but rather "a primitive image of a phallic nature. It is an object capable of excitement, orgasm, hatred, and omnipotence. It is bisexual. This image is primarily derived from the archetype of the mother" (p. 73). In Rosenthall's view, envy has the corrosive effect of blocking the constellation of the contrasexual opposite (the anima/animus) and thereby prevents the full experience of love. With Rosenthall, the imagery has shifted from breast back to phallus, but both are symbolic of creativity. Both are rooted ultimately in the Great Mother archetype. Both are symbols of the Self. For the chronically envious person, creativity remains in and with the Great Mother, and so the development of the individual is arrested. This person has not or cannot extract him/herself from the unconscious enough to develop individuality and separateness. Envy, according to Rosenthall, is symptomatic of an arrest in psychological development, and it functions to maintain that state of psychic stagnation by blocking the constellation of the anima/us. It is precisely the latter that is needed to lead the individual out of bondage by constellating love.

In connection with Rosenthall's observation about the object of envy, one recalls Jung's famous childhood dream of the underground phallus, which Aniela Jaffe interpreted as the earliest symbolic representation of Jung's creativity. In Jung's case, the numinous phallus did not remain locked in the realm of the Great Mother, but became available to his conscious personality and accounted for the awesome potency (and anima availability) of his mature life. Had it not been so, he could have turned into an Iago, a genius of envy due to thwarted creativity and blocked contact with the Self.

Mary Williams, another London Jungian, followed Rosenthall's ideas in an important paper on "primary envy," and developed a list of traits that characterize chronically envious patients. Chief among these are severe borderline features, the inability to accept analytic interpretations from the analytic "mother" (a rejection based on envy), and a strong tendency to attempt to reverse the relationship with the analyst so that analyst becomes the patient and vice versa. Williams focuses on the transference features of the envious person, noting the disturbance in relationship capacities. The chronically, constitutionally envious person cannot relate to another in an appropriate object-related way.

Following on these fundamental contributions, Judith Hubback related envy to Jung's shadow concept. Her work cleanly detaches envy from *thanatos* and extends the discussion to unconscious envy, highlighting the importance for analysis, in uncovering transference and countertransference dynamics, of making envy conscious. Both Hubback and Schwartz-Salant point out the crucial need to uncover the envy component in the shadow in order for further development and experience of the Self to take place. According to these two authors— and also to the Ulanovs in their extensive and impressive study of envy in *Cinderella and Her Sisters*—the road to the Self paradoxically passes through the narrow gateway of unconscious envy, and unless this difficult passage is opened the ego may not be able to come into genuine inner contact with the Self. These authors would seem to support the Kleinian notion that all of us have some amount of envy and are perhaps born with it.

Envy may not be the most royal of roads to the Self, but it does seem to offer some possibility for arriving there nevertheless. The implication is that to live creatively one must become aware of the Iago personality within, otherwise the envy that is lodged in the unconscious will block the flow of energy. This line of thought provides a point of reference for problems such as "writer's block"; they may be due to the effects of unconscious envy.

## The Pattern of Envy and Sibling Rivalry in Myth and Religion

The eruption of envy in sibling rivalry occurs when a sibling gains privileged access to the Self (usually via a parent's special love and attentions) and becomes so identified with it—as the favorite child, the golden boy, the chosen one—in the mind of the rival that jealousy and the usual amount of normal sibling rivalry turn into envy. The heir to the Self (whether imaged as breast or phallus) can become its owner in such a way, or to such an extent, that its blessings and nourishment and enjoyment can be withheld from others. When the threesome of jealousy collapses into the twosome of envy, we come upon sibling rivalry in its most destructive form.

A myth that lies at the core of our cultural and religious heritage depicts and clarifies the pattern I am discussing. The classic rendition of this story is found in John Milton's epic poem *Paradise Lost.*

God the Father had a son who was his radiant companion, Lucifer, a leader of the hosts of heaven. But this son was ambitious, and he sought unseemly power and self-aggrandizement. Eventually he led a rebellion against the Father and was crushed by superior force. This son fell from grace. The Father had a second son, Christ. This son was obedient and willing to do exactly what his father commanded. He made himself into a servant and offered himself as a perfect sacrifice to his Father's will. Through perfect obedience the second son received the full blessing of the Father and became enthroned at the Father's right hand. In fact, he and the Father became one, and what this son commands to be blessed is blessed, and where he withholds his blessing the Father's is also withheld.

These two brothers are now eternal enemies. The elder brother's feelings toward the younger turned to envy as he saw him become fully identified with the Father and the Father with him. This deepened his destructiveness to the point of absolute evil: Lucifer became Satan and Antichrist. The Father supports and maintains their split-apart condition. The elder brother goes about seeking those whom he may devour; he is agonized by greed and can never be filled. He can only destroy; he cannot create.

In this myth, there is no resolution of the problem of the envious sibling, Satan. He who once was Lucifer, the lightbringer, became the Antichrist and is essentially defined by hostility and negativity. He is a representation of the Western ego's shadow. This is the image that native peoples describe when they observe the look upon the face of the rapacious, driven European.

When Milton, a Puritan Protestant and Cromwellian anti-Monarchist, retold this myth in *Paradise Lost*, however, he conjured an image of Satan that shows great vitality and even considerable emotional appeal. One does not shudder in his presence as one would in the presence of absolute evil. In fact, William Blake later commented that Milton was secretly on the side of Satan. This preference certainly reflected Blake's own psychology and his personal hatred toward the favored religious establishment in England. Both of these poets, it might be argued, felt a need to redeem the Luciferean shadow from its identification with absolute evil.

Jung, too, in many ways took up the part of the elder son, arguing for example that the task of modern man is to integrate, consciously, the shadow of Christianity and its lofty ideals. It is clear from Jung's writings that he was trying to bridge the split between good and evil, between the ego ideal and the ego-as-real, in himself and in his patients as well as in culture at large. This would require facing up to the problem of envy in the personal and collective shadows.

Jung discusses the problem of the Father and his two hostile sons in his essay, "A Psychological Approach to the Dogma of the Trinity." There he places this myth into the perspective of a developmental process. First there is the stage of only the Father, which is characterized by pleromatic oneness. This is the idyll of infancy, a state of primordial oneness and unity in the mother's womb and then at her breast. As this state of unconscious wholeness breaks up and begins to differentiate, the ego emerges and the second stage begins. As the initial stage of wholeness and unity with the world (*participation mystique*) becomes disturbed and the stage of duality sets in, the ego begins to make distinctions. The distinction between mother's breast and infant occurs to consciousness—the "I" and the "not-I"—and then comes the distinction between the mother as a whole, who is in charge of the breast, and the infant. In this stage, too, the discrimination is made between good and bad (as parts of the mother initially, perhaps; her "good breast" and "bad breast," in Klein's terms), and soon follows the distinction between good and bad parts of the self. This begins the formation of shadow images.

This second stage is inevitable, as consciousness will develop and the discrimination of elements in the world and of disparate parts of the Self must take place. But this also inaugurates tension and conflict between the opposing parts. Now there is a good child and a bad child, a good mother and a bad one. These parts conflict with one another in the child's mind. In later development this is the conflict that rages between the persona-ego personality on the one hand and the shadow personality on the other. At the level of religious ideation and imagery, this stage of development underlies the Christ—anti-Christ conflict.

Normal development of consciousness leads inevitably to the stage of duality, because in order to function adaptively human consciousness must be able to make distinctions. But this does not necessarily lead to the kind of permanent alienation that we see in the Biblical myth, which breeds chronic enmity between the two parts, the brothers, and chronic envy in the less favored one. An alternative outcome can be seen in the Greek myth of Hermes' birth as recounted in the Homeric Hymn to Hermes, for example, where there is sibling rivalry between the upstart Hermes and his elder brother Apollo, but the brothers work out a relationship under the instruction of Father Zeus, and this results in an exchange of gifts and in friendship between them. Envy becomes the issue only when the rival is perceived as totally controlling and permanently preventing access to the source of creativity and value, when one is permanently "chosen" and the other is permanently disowned.

In the third phase of development as outlined by Jung (the Trinitarian stage), the duality of the second stage is transcended and harmony is restored. (This is imaged in the myth of Hermes and Apollo: They experience gratitude and they share gifts.) Now ego consciousness is consolidated and integrity is achieved. The hostile parts are brought back together and integrated.

Here the problem with our collective Judeo-Christian mythology becomes evident. Unlike the Greek myth of Hermes and Apollo who achieve reconciliation and brotherhood, the Biblical myth retains the image of the "bad son" (Lucifer-turned-Satan), who is never brought back and included in the heavenly realm, alongside the image of the "good son" (Christ), who sits at the right hand of the Father. According to Jung, the Holy Trinity of Christian doctrine represents only the first stage of a possible solution to the problem of duality (and envy) and can therefore be considered only a partial representation of the integrated Self. It remains ideal and spiritual but lacks shadow integration.

Since the good-bad split remains so incorrigibly entrenched in our mythology, a similar structure in our personal psychology is strongly encouraged. The shadowy, envious Luciferean shadow of the Western ego, which has been constellated in our cultural history and is revealed in this myth, has yet to overcome its estrangement and be included in the self.

With this myth of an eternal split between good son and bad son and with the identification of the good son with the father/Self as our common psychological background, it is not hard to understand why it is such a struggle for many of us to feel good enough without being perfect. In Christendom, the bond to the Self passes through the image of Christ, beside whom our egos look much more Luciferean than otherwise. The very perfection of Christ's goodness casts a dark shadow on ourselves by contrast. Since Christ occupies the privileged position of the self-image and controls access to the Self—the heavenly food, the water of life, the divine nourishment for our daily lives—we are necessarily drawn to him for our creativity, hope and self-maintenance, but then we are equally estranged from ourselves because of our imperfection. The psychological problem is that only part of our ego can identify with Christ, and the other part—the Luciferean shadow side—remains excluded and unredeemable. In this position it inevitably becomes projected outward upon others, typically upon those who threaten our access to creativity and value. Shadow carriers are simultaneously the generators of envy reactions, and envy breeds absolute hatred and contempt. For this reason we find it so easy to destroy our enemies with a good conscience: they are evil. But our envy, as Judith Hubback points out, is in the shadow and therefore unconscious.

The Bible, in which this myth is housed, repeats with great frequency the theme of two brothers who become locked in bitter rivalry and enmity. As we know from analytic experience, recurrent themes are critically important. Something wants to become conscious and has not been able to do so. This is the envy dynamic that is constellated by the pivotal act of God when he chooses a favorite and makes a covenant that excludes the rest.

At one level of reading, the Bible is a family saga (like Thomas Mann's *Buddenbrooks*, for example) extending over many generations. Cain and Abel set the stage. The offerings of the younger brother, a shepherd, are preferred over the offerings of his elder brother, a farmer (Genesis 4:3—5). Cain endures this humiliation until sibling rivalry turns into envy and rage overcomes him. He kills his brother. Later in the family saga, Joseph, again a younger brother, is singled out by his father for special favors. Joseph flaunts his specialness and stimulates envy in his brothers, who want to kill him but at the last minute sell him into slavery instead. Once again sibling rivalry congeals into envy and leads to murderous rage. Then David, the youngest of twelve children, is singled out to be king of Israel, being elevated not only above his brothers but also over King Saul, who flies into envy-induced rages and attempts repeatedly to kill David.

Finally, there is the instance of Jesus as the "chosen," replacing Israel in this position of privilege and entitlement. In the wider context of Western history, Israel itself now becomes the displaced elder brother. As the risen Christ, Jesus offers entry by adoption into the

Father's family, and those who enter in through this means occupy the same position of privilege that Christ enjoys. This leaves Israel in the position of making rival claims to this place of honor as the "chosen," and so Judaism and Christianity fall into a sort of collective sibling rivalry. Each brother claims priority of relation to the Father/ Self. In certain instances this rivalry has transmuted into envy and led to the wish to destroy the other.

At the heart of this family story is the image of a Father who first created all earthly peoples and then picked favorites from among his many children. The presence of this willful Parent haunts the entire family chronicle.

Chosenness is perhaps the Bible's most crucial theme. God makes a covenant with his chosen ones. Everything else hinges on this fateful decision. When the Father chooses a favorite for some irrational, inexplicable reason, he sets in motion a dynamic that in turn generates jealousy, sibling rivalry, and ultimately envy and murderous attacks both upon the chosen and the unchosen. The duality that is created by this act of discrimination becomes fixed and generates in turn a severe splitting process within history. The "chosen" form a target for envy attacks because they hold a privileged position in relation to the source of creation and sustenance; the unchosen are attacked because they carry the shadow of the chosen and are seen as evil and worthless.

Sibling rivalry and envy are embedded in the fiber of our cultural and religious traditions.

## Envy and Sibling Rivalry in Analytical Practice

Among those who seek psychotherapy, there is a significant group of persons who suffer from chronic envy. Often this is more unconscious than conscious at first, in the shadow rather than openly acknowledged and consciously suffered. These people are subtly identified as rejected children, as the "bad" sons or daughters. Often these are older children who were displaced in the affections of parents by younger, perhaps more talented or presentable, siblings, the "chosen" or special ones. What may have begun as sibling rivalry of the jealous variety has hardened into sibling hatred of the envy type. These people live with envy as a daily psychic reality, and consequently they have great difficulty in forming and maintaining relationships.

Sometimes the severity of their disturbance places them in the diagnostic category of borderline personality disorder, as Mary Williams already implied. Sometimes, though, the chronic envy is so well disguised and deftly managed by ego defenses that the person does not show the typical traits of the borderline personality. This person may be well adapted with strong and capable ego functioning, yet be continually vulnerable to subtly debilitating attacks of envy. These undermine self-confidence and self-worth and create a chronic state of tension and anxiety. This person may not explode with rage, as is so typical of borderline personalities, but rather contain and compensate for the anger and hatred by overeating, heavy drinking, smoking, or overworking. In work, there is little enjoyment of success, however, because the result is always seen as second best. As one patient put it to me many times, "I am often almost it, but never quite *the one."*

When these persons are faced with their seemingly more successful counterparts, they suffer intensely. The envied ones are those in whom everyone delights, who enjoy success and a place of privilege, upon whom the sunshine of honor and attention beams unceasingly. The envious subject is then required to contain powerful charges of hatred and destructive impulse, and these are generally channeled into some form of self-destructive behavior.

It must be stated, too, that everyone experiences occasions of envy. Envy is a universally human emotional reaction. Patients may well feel envy toward their analysts from time to time, and analysts will also feel envy towards certain patients on occasion (cf. Hubback, p. 111). The people I am specifically referring to here, however, are chronically envious. They live in a psychic world of continuous vulnerability to envy reactions, and it becomes their central psychological task in analysis to resolve this. The project of making chronic envy conscious is the necessary precursor to working through whatever may be its causes.

Analytic observation of the chronically envious reveals a characteristic disturbance in the relation between ego and Self. It is as though the myth cited above plays itself out in their inner world. The ego has its position and its role, but it is a Luciferean one, alienated from the Self. For this ego, even if intact, there is no comfortable inner center. In going inward, this person typically enters a void or a world of tormenting self-accusations. These persons cannot effectively soothe themselves, they cannot find comfort in meditation or active imagination, and mostly they experience anxiety, low self-esteem, emptiness, and critical inner voices. If another type of figure does appear in this person's active imagination or fantasy, it becomes the object of envy; it is the preferred one, the favored, the chosen, and the ego is thrown back into feelings of rejection and worthlessness. Fantasy in this respect follows the pattern of life experience, whose origins lie in early childhood experiences of sibling rivalry. This person lives with a constant feeling of being abused and shamed. At its extreme in the borderline personality, this is a soul in hell, consigned to everlasting torment by an indifferent or hostile parent/God.

Soothing analytic words can exacerbate the pain for this type of patient, and this creates a problem for the therapist who is trained to empathize. The patient "knows" that the analyst prefers the other patients, and certainly when the analyst's world of family and friends are taken into account the patient comes in at the end of a long line of preferred others. The transference is heavily loaded with expectations of rejection and humiliation. The analyst can of course become the object of envy as well as the rejecting parent. Always the Self-bearer prefers another figure, and always the ego is second (at best) or scorned and humiliated.

Here we have the psychology of someone whose shadow may well be ideal rather than repulsive in quality. The shadow consists of the repudiated parts (traits, qualities, impulses, desires) of oneself towards which one feels aversion. In these cases of chronically envious persons, paradoxically, the aversion is felt toward the qualities (and the persons who embody them) that are usually valued by society and even as well by the envious person (though secretly). The psychological function of idealization, which is usually found to be either a defense against intimacy or a lure forward to greater integration of the Self, is here turned instead into the occasion for an excruciating envy reaction. What is projected and idealized as a valuable quality is an aspect of oneself, but because of the internal structuring of the relation between ego and Self in these persons, this turns into the meaning that someone else has it more or better and is therefore to be envied and hated, not that it is something to which one may aspire or even admire. The projection of these idealized features of the Self onto others drives the ego away, alienates it even further, and creates the painful repetition of humiliation and isolation. The selfobject is a shadow figure to be avoided or destroyed. For this reason, these persons form relationships with idealized analysts and others that are deeply conflicted: on the one hand there is admiration, on the other hatred and a wish to destroy.

It is tragic when these persons end up feeling evil. They become identified with the outcast child who has been condemned and driven into isolation. In their isolation, they feel worthless. Then, filled with envy toward the favored ones and consequently charged up with hatred and the desire to destroy them, they come to feel that they themselves embody evil. So complete can this distortion become that it is actually a gesture of goodness and generosity on their part when they offer to commit suicide: they would be diminishing the presence of evil on earth by at least that much!

It is this person's difficult psychological task to allow the envy-driven rage and destructiveness to enter fully into consciousness and to transform its energy into the quest and the demand for self-affirmation. In making this much envy conscious there is at the one extreme the danger of suicide or homicide; at the other there is the possibility of redeeming the Luciferian envy-ego and forging a home for it within the order of the chosen and the acceptable. There is also the demand and the opportunity for healing the relationships with significant others that were conflicted and broken by envy attacks.

In taking this kind of person into analysis, the analyst faces the unenviable challenge of enduring the inevitable envy attacks as transference takes hold. Understandably, the analyst comes to be seen as a person who has access to an abundant supply of good things such as nurturance, love, warmth, and admiration. The analyst also has the power to give or to withhold such things from patients. Typically in these cases the analysand will complain of feeling deprived by the analyst who could give so much more if only s/he were more open, more willing, more "there," more generous. The silent, receptive, empathic analyst will be seen as slyly holding back and enjoying his own rich feelings and thoughts, unwilling to share this wealth of psychic gold with the starving patient. Furthermore, the analyst could share her/his body but withholds that, too. Soothing interpretative words of empathy spoken from this position can irritate and further humiliate the patient. Attempts at self-disclosure, to show that the analyst too is human and suffers similar blows and pains of living, will paradoxically stimulate envy even further: the analyst is someone who can surmount such problems and is not dragged into the mire by them. Counseling admonitions or words of consolation are taken as insults, as subtle attacks that make invidious comparisons between patient and analyst. The helplessness and diminished self-confidence felt by the analyst in response to sessions with such patients serve exquisitely well the destructive purpose of the envious analysand.

The challenge for the analyst is to survive these attacks and to contain all this hostility while waiting for the Self to show its hand from another direction. The analytic relationship can become an inky alchemical bath that may remain in the *nigredo* phase for a seemingly endless period of time. Analysis is the container for this corrosive affect, and its strength will be powerfully tested by the potent discharges of envy as the inner life of pain, bitterness, and humiliation fills the sessions. But as the alchemists said, one is to rejoice when the *nigredo* state is achieved: This is when the chronic unconscious envy can come fully into the open and be experienced consciously and directly. Only now can it become subject to possible transformation.

What needs to be transformed is the patient's hostile attitude toward his/her own hungry Luciferean ego, so that the ego-Self axis can be repaired. Greed can then be returned to its normal proportion of hunger for good things and for the Self, and envy can be reduced to a dynamic search for the Self. The "hungry, wanting, and emulating ingredient in envy" (Hubback, p. 115) is necessary for ego growth, not only in infancy but also in later development. Thus envy takes on a prospective function by showing the way to the Self. What the envious person envies is also symbolically what he/she desires, and needs for full personhood. These needs and desires are not in themselves evil; it is the despair in the hopelessness of ever obtaining them that creates hatred and destructiveness.

A woman in her early fifties, widowed, struggling with problems of being overweight and a smoker, but more deeply with lifelong issues of greed and envy that arose and were solidified in her original family and the sibling rivalry between her and her sister, had been in analysis for several years when she dreamed that she came to my home to go to the toilet. She entered the house but came upon my teenage son in the bathroom and so was unable to use the facilities herself. The teenager then pulled a hospital curtain around himself and withdrew behind it. This dream was interpreted in light of her attempt, reflected in the previous session, to place her "bad stuff" into me and my disinclination to let her do so. She restrained herself and did not let herself go completely. She was also angry and envious of my son who could do as he wanted in my house. Her envy attack was not fully unleashed, however, and she was able to maintain her composure and contain the affect. She commented that my distance created an atmosphere in which it was not possible to become "closer," and while this was a long-standing complaint she also recognized by now how destructive her envy could become.

In a subsequent dream she was presented with two babies by a nun. They are twins. She smiles at them, and they return the smile. She awakens happy and gratified. It was the first time she could recall that such a strong positive response had come from other dream figures. This dream, we came to realize, was an indication that a new development was under way in her ego's relation to the Self. In this dream she felt satisfied and joyful; she felt full, loved, seen, valued. In this session when she recounted this dream, she went on to tell me how much she appreciated me and our years of work together. Her eyes welled up with tears, the evidence of gratitude. She was working through her envy of me and was able to feel gratitude because she had something of her own, a smiling infant who responded to her and promised her love.

In Klein's view, the solution to envy comes about when one feels restored to the breast and can feel gratitude for being filled rather than hatred for being deprived. The experience of love becomes possible as envy diminishes. Hubback supports this clinical observation. I would only add that envy is overcome as the Self is experienced within and lived. In the dreams just mentioned, envy is being worked on. When the infants, who represent the Self, smile and give the dreamer a feeling of acceptance, the stage of duality between good and evil is transcended and a movement toward reconciliation and integration is shown to be under way.

The acid test of this reconciliation came about in the following months and years as this courageous patient worked on healing the deeply conflicted relationships with her mother and sister. Sibling rivalry from early childhood had spoiled the relationship between the sisters, and the hardening of it into chronic envy had its motive in the mother's perceived preference for the sister. This patient was able to transform her relationship with her mother to the point where she no longer felt rejected and pushed away. It was on her initiative and repeated efforts that this healing took place. Once the mother connection was improved, she was able to take up the relationship to her envied sister. Some two or three years after she had terminated her therapy with me, while all of this was still in the early stages of process, she came in once more to tell me of the work that she had done since we stopped meeting. She reported remarkable improvement in relationships generally, but most particularly those within her immediate family. She was now in steady contact with her sister and was able to enjoy her sister's children as never before. The envy of her sister's motherhood had dissolved enough so that it no longer interfered in her relationship to her nieces and nephews.

A second example of envy resolution is indicated in the dream of a man in his forties. Envy was a life theme with him as well, and it had recently been constellated in relation to his professionally successful wife and in the transference to me. In a sense both of us were sibling rivals. He dreamed of being placed in the humiliating position of having to become the student of a much younger man. This young teacher, though less experienced than himself, enjoyed the special favor of a senior mentor. At a critical point in the dream he makes eye contact with a senior supervisor in the audience, who indicates with a nod and a smile that he recognizes the dreamer's superiority to the young teacher. An unspoken but genuine alliance is established between the senior (father) figure and the dreamer over against the younger (positive shadow) figure. This dream shows the psyche's attempt to create an alliance between the Self and the envy-prone Luciferean ego, and to shift the burden of shadow and inferiority off the ego's shoulders. Here we see an elegant statement of the self-regulation of the psyche, as it attempts to overcome envy by creating a more positive relation between ego and Self. In tandem with this, a process of establishing a strong working relationship with me in the transference was under way. The idealization of the analyst became manageable and eventually could function as a guiding thread forward to important individuation tasks: improving his professional standing by acquiring an advanced academic degree, becoming involved himself in teaching and mentoring, and increasing his earning capacity. As envy was transformed, it became the signal for individuation needs and directions.

## Conclusion

The only genuine, nondefensive solution to the problem of envy is an improved ego-Self relation, in which the ego feels that it has at least equal access to the Self vis-à-vis other (and especially shadow, e.g., fraternal) elements. This then makes further shadow integration possible. Until this point is reached, the shadow, much too positive and idealized, cannot be approached without envy. The ego needs to feel that "I am the embodiment, the incarnation, of the Self" in this particular space-time continuum that is my body and my life. In short, we need to feel loved.

Culturally we are heirs of a rather hostile and critical father collective complex. This may be passed on through a mother's animus or through such a father directly. But as cultural heirs of the myth of Adam and Eve, we are in the position of the disinherited and displaced, and therefore we are especially vulnerable to envy and sibling rivalry. We do not have cultural support for feeling held and contained in the generous spirit of a loving and accepting parent who adores us. Rather we are subject to judgment and criticism and often to the intuition that others are preferred over us. We wonder if we are among the favored, the "elect."

Many of us, too, have been raised by critical fathers, and so we raise our children with more blame than praise. It is easier and more natural for us to find fault with ourselves, with our children, with our colleagues, and with our world than to feel cause to bless and praise them and to feel gratitude. Our spirit is ridden with judgment, self-doubt, and criticism, and consequently with the potential for envy toward those upon whom we project a more positive ego-Self relation.

Perhaps on the collective level the emergence of the goddess myth is an attempt to ameliorate and to rectify this problem. The goddess may be less harsh and less preferential in her treatment of siblings.

Of course, there is also a danger of regression to the predualistic stage here. But for women at any rate, who find in the goddess a representation of the Self to which their egos can look for positive identity and strength, this may well be a movement toward the postdualistic stage of development. For men, who cannot find a Self image in the goddess, this image may represent some softening of the harsh father's critique and of his preference for one over the others of his children. Ultimately, the Self image for both sexes must mirror the ego, and the ego must feel that it is embodying the Self. "I and the Father (or the Mother) are one" is a statement of the resolution that must take place in everyone. In this sense, we need all to become Christ-like. Each must feel the ego to be the proper place for incarnation of the divine. All this, while not giving up the ego's independence, self-assertion, and energetic expansion into the inner and outer cosmos.

### REFERENCES

Bion, W. 1962. Learning from Experience. In *Seven Servants*. New York: Jason Aronson, 1977.

DiStasi, L. 1981. *Mal Occhio*. Berkeley: North Point Press.

Fordham, M. 1985. *Explorations into the Self*. London: Karnac.

Hubback, J. 1988. Envy and the Shadow. In *People Who Do Things to Each Other*. Wilmette, IL.: Chiron Publications.

Jaffe, A. 1972. The Creative Phases in Jung's Life. *Spring, 1972*.

Jung, C. G. 1942b. A Psychological Approach to the Dogma of the Trinity. In *Collected Works*, vol. 11. Princeton: Princeton University Press, 1969.

———. 1961a. *Memories, Dreams, Reflections*. New York: Random House.

Klein, M. 1956. A Study of Envy and Gratitude, in *Selected Papers of Melanie Klein*, ed. J. Mitchell. London: Penguin Books.

Rosenthall, M. 1963. Notes on Envy and the Contrasexual Archetype. *Journal of Analytical Psychology*, 8, 1.

Schwartz-Salant, N. 1982. *Narcissism and Character Transformation*. Toronto: Inner City Books.

Ulanov, A., Ulanov, B. 1983. *Cinderella and her Sisters*. Philadelphia: Westminster Press.

Williams, M. 1974. Success and Failure in Analysis: Primary Envy and the Fate of the Good. In *Success and Failure in Analysis*, ed. G. Adler. New York: Putnam's Sons, 1974.

# Bibliography

Adler, G. 1961. *The Living Symbol*. New York: Pantheon Books.
Asper, K., 1987. *Verlassenheit und Selbstentfremdung*. Olten: Walter.
Bion, W. R. 1977. Learning from Experience. In *Seven Servants*, New York: Jason Aronson.
Buber, M. 1957. *Eclipse of God*. New York: Harper and Brothers.
Burnham, J. S. and McGuire, W., eds. 1983. *Jeliffe: American Psychoanalyst and Physician*. Chicago and London: University of Chicago Press.
*Cassell's New Latin Dictionary*. 1969. New York: Funk and Wagnall's.
Corbett, L. 1987. "Transformation of the Image of God Leading to Self Initiation into Old Age." In *Betwixt and Between*, ed. L. Mahdi, S. Foster, and M. Little, pp. 371–88. LaSalle, IL: Open Court.
———. 1989. Kohut and Jung: a Comparison of Theory and Therapy. In *Self Psychology, Comparisons and Contrasts*, Detrick and Detrick, eds. Hillsdale, NJ.: Analytic Press.
Corbett, L. and Kugler, P. 1989. The Self in Jung and Kohut. In *Dimensions of Self Experience: Progress in Self Psychology*, vol. 5, A. Goldberg, ed. Hillsdale, NJ: Analytic Press.
Csikszentmihalyi, M. 1990. *Flow*. New York: Harper & Row.
Dieckmann, H. 1976. Transference and Countertransference: Results of a Berlin Research Group. *Journal of Analytical Psychology* 21/1 :25–36.
———. 1986. Opening Address. In *Symbolic and Clinical Approaches in Theory and Practice*. Einsiedeln: Daimon Verlag.
———. 1991. *Methods in Analytical Psychology*. Wilmette, IL.: Chiron Publications.
DiStasi, L. 1981. *Mal Occhio*. Berkeley: North Point Press.
Dogen, and Kosho Uchiyama. 1983. *Refining Your Life*. New York: Weatherhill.
Edinger, E. 1972. *Ego and Archetype*. New York: Putnam.
———. 1979. "Depth Psychology as the New Dispensation," Quadrant 12/2:4–25.
Eliade, M. 1959. *Cosmos and History: The Myth of the Eternal Return*. New York and Evanston: Harper & Row.
Ellenberger, H. 1970. *The Discovery of the Unconscious*. New York: Basic Books.
Fairbairn, W. R. D. 1952. *Psycho-analytic Studies of the Personality*. London: Tavistock.
Fordham, M. 1957. *New Developments in Analytical Psychology*. London: Routledge.
———. 1969. *Children as Individuals*. New York: C. G. Jung Foundation.
———. 1978. *Jungian Psychotherapy*. New York: John Wiley & Sons.
———. 1985. *Explorations into the Self*. London: Karnac.
———. 1985. The Self in Jung's Works. In *Explorations into the Self*. London: Academic Press.
Franz, M.-L. von. 1972. *Creation Myths*. Dallas: Spring Publications.
———. 1974. *Number and Time*. Evanston: Northwestern University Press.
———. 1980. *Projection and Re-Collection in Jungian Psychology*. LaSalle, IL. and London: Open Court.
Frey-Rohn, L. 1974. *From Freud to Jung*. New York: Putnam.

Galimberti, U. 1989. Die Analytische Psychologie in Zeitalter der Technik [Analytical Psychology in a Technical Age]. In *Zeitschrift fuer Analytische Psychologie und ihre Grenzgebiete* 20:87–120. (Author's translation)

Goodheart, W. B. 1980. Theory of the Analytical Interaction. *San Francisco Jung Institute Library Journal* 1/4:2–39.

Gordon, R. 1977. The Symbolic Experience as Bridge between the Personal and the Collective. *Journal of Analytical Psychology* 22/4:331–42.

———. 1980. Narcissism and the Self. *Journal of Analytical Psychology* 25:247–64.

*Grimms' Fairy Tales.* 1972. New York: Random House.

Grotstein, J. S. 1981. *Splitting and Projective Identification.* New York, London: Jason Aronson.

Guggenbühl-Craig, A. 1971. *Power in the Helping Professions.* New York: Spring Publications.

Harding, E. 1956. *Journey into Self.* New York: Longmans, Green.

Harvey, Van A. 1966. *The Historian and the Believer.* New York: Macmillan.

Heisig, J. 1973. Jung and Theology: A Bibliographical Essay. *Spring* 1973: 204–55.

———. 1979. *Imago Dei: A Study of Jung's Psychology of Religion.* Lewisburg: Bucknell University Press.

Henderson, J. 1967. *Thresholds of Initiation.* Middletown, CT.: Wesleyan University Press.

Hillman, J. 1983. *Archetypal Psychology: A Brief Account.* Dallas: Spring Publications.

Hoganson, G. 1994. *Jung's Struggle with Freud.* Wilmette, IL.: Chiron Publications.

Holy Bible (New Revised Standard Version). 1989. Oxford: Oxford University Press.

Homans, P. 1970. *Theology after Freud.* New York: Bobbs-Merrill Co.

Hubback, J. 1988. Envy and the Shadow. In *People Who Do Things to Each Other.* Wilmette, IL.: Chiron Publications.

Humbert, E. 1988. The Wellsprings of Memory. *Journal of Analytical Psychology* 33:3–20.

Jacoby, M. 1981. Reflections on Heinz Kohut's Concepts of Narcissism. *Journal of Analytical Psychology* 26:107–10.

———. 1990. *Individuation and Narcissism: The Psychology of the Self in Jung and Kohut.* London: Routledge.

Jaffe, A. 1972. The Creative Phases in Jung's Life. In *Spring* 1972, pp.162–90.

Jung, C. G. 1907. *The Psychology of Dementia Praecox.* In *Collected Works* 3:1–151. Princeton: Princeton University Press, 1960.

———. 1912a. *Wandlungen und Symbole der Libido.* Vienna: Franz Deuticke.

———. 1912b. New Paths in Psychology. In *Collected Works*, vol. 7. Princeton: Princeton University Press, 1966.

———. 1913. The Theory of Psychoanalysis. In *Collected Works*, 4:83–226. Princeton: Princeton University Press, 1961.

———. 1916a. *Psychology of the Unconscious.* Supplementary Volume B of *Collected Works.* Princeton: Princeton University Press, 1991.

———. 1916b. The Transcendent Function. In *Collected Works*, vol. 8, pp. 67–90. Princeton: Princeton University Press.

———. 1917. *Collected Papers in Analytical Psychology.* New York: Moffat, Yard.

———. 1921. *Psychological Types.* In *Collected Works*, vol. 6. Princeton: Princeton University Press, 1971.

———. 1931. Problems of Modern Psychotherapy. In *Collected Works*, vol. 16, pp. 53–75. Princeton: Princeton University Press, 1966.

———. 1932. Psychological Commentary on Kundalini Yoga. Unpublished seminar notes.

———. 1935. The Tavistock Lectures. In *Collected Works*, 18:267–90. Princeton: Princeton University Press, 1976.

------. 1936a. Psychological Factors Determining Human Behavior. In *Collected Works*, vol. 8, pp. 114–25. Princeton: Princeton University Press, 1969.

------. 1936b. Wotan. In *Collected Works* 10:179–93. New York: Pantheon Books.

------. 1937. The Realities of Practical Psychotherapy. In *Collected Works*, 16:327–38. New York: Pantheon Books, second edition, 1966.

------. 1938. Foreword to the Second German Edition, Commentary on "The Secret of the Golden Flower." In *Collected Works*, vol. 13, Princeton: Princeton University Press, 1967.

------. 1939. The Symbolic Life. In *Collected Works*, 18:267–90. Princeton: Princeton University Press, 1976.

------. 1940. The Psychology of the Child Archetype. In *Collected Works*, 9/1:151–81. Princeton: Princeton University Press, second edition, 1969.

------. 1942a. On the Psychology of the Unconscious. In *Collected Works*, 7:3–119. New York: Random House, second edition, 1966.

------. 1942b. A Psychological Approach to the Dogma of the Trinity. In *Collected Works*, vol. 11. Princeton: Princeton University Press, 1969.

------. 1942c. Transformation Symbolism in the Mass. In *Collected Works*, vol. 11. Princeton: Princeton University Press, 1969.

------. 1944. *Psychology and Alchemy*. In *Collected Works*, vol. 12. Princeton: Princeton University Press, 1968.

------. 1946. On the Psychology of the Transference. In *Collected Works*, 16:163–324. New York: Pantheon Books, second edition, 1966.

------. 1948. The Spirit Mercurius. In *Collected Works*, vol. 13. Princeton: Princeton University Press, 1967.

------. 1950. Concerning Mandala Symbolism. In *Collected Works*, 9/1:355–84. Princeton: Princeton University Press, second edition, 1968.

------. 1951a. *Aion: Researches into the Phenomenology of the Self*. In *Collected Works*, vol. 9. Princeton: Princeton University Press, 1959.

------. 1951b. The Psychology of the Child Archetype. In *Collected Works*, vol. 9/1:151–81. Princeton: Princeton University Press, 1969.

------. 1952a. *Symbols of Transformation*. In *Collected Works*, vol. 5. Princeton: Princeton University Press, 1956.

------. 1952b. *Answer to Job*. In *Collected Works*, vol. 11:355–472. Princeton: Princeton University Press, second edition, 1969.

------. 1952c. *Psychology and Alchemy*. *Collected Works*, vol. 12. Princeton: Princeton University Press, 1968.

------. 1952d. Synchronicity: An Acausal Connecting Principle. In *Collected Works*, vol. 8. Princeton: Princeton University Press, 1960.

------. 1954. On the Nature of the Psyche. In *Collected Works*, 8:159–234. Princeton: Princeton University Press, second edition, 1969.

------. 1961a. *Memories, Dreams, Reflections*. New York: Random House.

------. 1961b. *Septem Sermones ad Mortuos*. In *Memories, Dreams, Reflections*, Appendix V, pp. 378–90.

------. 1966a. The Practice of Psychotherapy. In *Collected Works*, vol. 16. Princeton: Princeton University Press, 1966.

------. 1966b. *Two Essays on Analytical Psychology*. In *Collected Works*, vol. 7. Princeton: Princeton University Press.

------. 1970. *Mysterium Coniunctionis*. *Collected Works*, vol. 14. Princeton: Princeton University Press.

------. 1973. *Letters*, vol. 1. Princeton: Princeton University Press.

------. 1975. *Letters*, vol. 2. Princeton: Princeton University Press.

------. 1976. The Symbolic Life. In *Collected Works*, vol. 18. Princeton: Princeton University Press.

———. 1989. *Analytical Psychology: Notes on the Seminar Given in 1925.* Princeton: Princeton University Press.

———. 1991. *Psychology of the Unconscious.* Princeton: Princeton University Press.

———. 1995. *Jung on Evil* (ed. by Murray Stein). London and Boston: Routledge.

Kalff, D. 1981. *Sandplay.* Los Angeles: Sigo Press.

Kalsched, D. 1980. Narcissism and the Search for Interiority. Quadrant 13(2):46–74.

Kelsey, M. 1974. *Myth, History and Faith.* New York: Paulist Press.

Kerr, J. 1993. *A Most Dangerous Method.* New York: Knopf.

Khan, M. l986. Introduction to *Holding and Interpretation* by D. W. Winnicott. Grove Press, 1987.

Klaif, C. 1987. Emerging Concepts of the Self: Clinical Considerations. In *Archetypal Processes in Psychotherapy,* Schwartz-Salant and Stein, eds. Wilmette, IL.: Chiron Publications.

Klein, M. 1956. A Study of Envy and Gratitude. In *Selected Papers of Melanie Klein,* ed. J. Mitchell. London: Penguin Books.

———. 1959. Our Adult World and its Roots in Infancy. In *Envy and Gratitude.* New York: Dell, 1975, pp. 247–63.

Kluger, R. 1967. *Satan in the Old Testament.* Evanston: Northwestern University Press.

———. 1974. *Psyche and Bible.* New York: Spring Publications.

Kohut, M. 1977. *The Restoration of the Self.* New York: International Universities Press.

Lambert, K. 1981. *Analysis, Repair and Individuation.* London, New York, Toronto, Sydney, San Francisco: Academic Press.

Langs, R. 1978. *The Listening Process.* New York: Jason Aronson.

Machtiger, H. 1995. Countertransference/Transference. In *Jungian Analysis,* M. Stein, ed. LaSalle and London: Open Court.

McGuire, W. and Hull, R.F.C., eds. 1977. *C. G. Jung Speaking.* Princeton: Princeton University Press.

Meier, C. A. 1977. *Jung's Analytical Psychology and Religion.* Carbondale, IL.: Southern Illinois University Press.

Moore, B. E. and Fine, B. D. 1991. *Psychoanalytic Terms and Concepts.* New Haven and London: Yale University Press.

Neumann, E. 1955. *The Great Mother.* Princeton: Princeton University Press.

Niebuhr, H. R. 1960. *The Meaning of Revelation.* New York: Macmillan.

Ogden, T. H. 1989. *The Primitive Edge of Experience.* Northvale, NJ. and London: Jason Aronson Inc.

Otto, R. 1958. *The Idea of the Holy.* New York: Oxford University Press.

Partridge, E. 1966. *Origins.* New York: Macmillan.

Perry, J. 1976. *Roots of Renewal in Myth and Madness.* San Francisco: Jossey-Bass.

Plaut, A. 1994. *Analysis Analyzed.* New York and London: Routledge.

Progoff, I. 1973. *Jung, Synchronicity, and Human Destiny.* New York: Julian Press.

Racker, H. 1968. *Transference and Countertransference.* New York: International Universities Press.

Redfearn, J. W. T. 1980. Romantic and Classical Views of Analysis. *Journal of Analytical Psychology* 25/ 1: 1–16.

Ricoeur, P. 1970. *Freud and Philosophy.* New Haven and London: Yale University Press.

Robinson, J. M. (ed.) 1988. *The Nag Hammadi Library.* San Francisco: Harper & Row.

Rosenthall, M. 1963. Notes on Envy and the Contrasexual Archetype. *Journal of Analytical Psychology,* 8, 1.

Samuels, A. 1985. *Jung and the Post-Jungians.* London and Boston: Routledge.

———. 1989. *The Plural Psyche.* New York and London: Routledge.

———. 1993. *The Political Psyche.* London and Boston: Routledge.

Sanford, J. 1970. *The Kingdom Within: A Study of the Inner Meaning of Jesus' Sayings.* Philadelphia and New York: J. B. Lippincott Co.

Satinover, J. 1980. Puer Aeternus: The Narcissistic Relation to the Self. Quadrant 13(2):75–108.

——. 1984. Jung's Contribution to the Dilemma of Narcissism. *Journal of the American Psychoanalytic Association* 34(2):401–38.

——. 1985. At the Mercy of Another: Abandonment and Restitution in Psychosis and Psychotic Character. In *Abandonment*, N. Schwartz-Salant and M. Stein, eds., pp. 47–86. Wilmette, IL.: Chiron Publications.

Schwartz-Salant, N. 1982. *Narcissism and Character Transformation.* Toronto: Inner City Books.

——. 1986. On the Subtle-Body Concept in Clinical Practice. In *The Body in Analysis*, N. Schwartz-Salant and M. Stein, eds., pp. 19–58. Wilmette, IL.: Chiron Publications.

——. 1989. *The Borderline Personality: Vision and Healing.* Wilmette, IL.: Chiron Publications.

——, and M. Stein (eds.). 1984. *Transference and Countertransference Processes in Analysis.* Wilmette, IL.: Chiron Publications.

Searles, H. 1979. The Patient as Therapist to His Analyst. In *Countertransference and Related Subjects.* New York: International Universities Press.

Sedgwick, D. 1995. *The Wounded Healer.* New York and London: Routledge.

Singer, J. 1972. *Boundaries of the Soul.* Garden City, NY: Doubleday.

Stein, M. 1978. "Psychological Interpretation: A Language of Images." In *Dragonflies*, 1/1.

——. 1980. Hephaistos: A Pattern of Introversion. In *Facing the Gods*, J. Hillman, ed. Dallas: Spring Publications.

——. 1983. *In Midlife.* Dallas: Spring Publications.

——. 1984. Power, Shamanism, and Maieutics in the Countertransference, in *Transference/Countertransference* (ed. by N. Schwartz-Salant and M. Stein), Wilmette, IL.: Chiron Publications.

——. 1985. *Jung's Treatment of Christianity: The Psychotherapy of a Religious Tradition.* Wilmette, IL.: Chiron Publications.

——. 1991. The Muddle in Analysis. In *Liminality and Transitional Phenomena* (ed. by N. Schwartz-Salant and M. Stein), pp.1–12. Wilmette, IL.: Chiron Publications.

——. 1992a. Power, Shamanism, and Maieutics in the Countertransference. In *Transference/Countertransference* (eds. N. Schwartz-Salant and M. Stein), pp. 67–88. Wilmette, IL: Chiron Publications.

——. 1992b. The Role of Anima/Animus Structures and Archetypes in the Psychology of Narcissism and Some Borderline States. In *Gender and Soul in Psychotherapy* (eds. N. Schwartz-Salant and M. Stein), pp. 233–50. Wilmette, IL: Chiron Publications.

——. (ed.). 1995. *Jungian Analysis*, second edition. La Salle and London: Open Court.

Stern, P. 1976. *C. G. Jung: The Haunted Prophet.* New York: George Braziller.

Tillich, P. 1973. *Systematic Theology*, vol III. Chicago: University of Chicago Press.

Turner, V. 1967. *The Forest of Symbols.* Ithaca: Cornell University Press.

——. 1969. *The Ritual Process.* Chicago: Aldine Press.

Ulanov, A., Ulanov, B. 1983. *Cinderella and Her Sisters.* Philadelphia: Westminster Press.

Van Eenwyk, J. 1991. The Analysis of Defences. *Journal of Analytical Psychology* 36:2, pp. 141–63.

White, V. 1960. *Soul and Psyche: An Enquiry into the Relationship of Psychology and Religion.* London: Collins.

Whitmont, E. 1969. *The Symbolic Quest.* New York: G. P. Putnam.

Williams, M. 1974. Success and Failure in Analysis: Primary Envy and the Fate of the Good. In *Success and Failure in Analysis*, ed. G. Adler. New York: Putnam's Sons, 1974.

Winnicott, D. W. 1969. The Use of an Object and Relating through Identifications. In *Playing and Reality*. New York: Basic Books, 1971.

———. 1971. *Playing and Reality*. London: Tavistock Publications Ltd.

Witenberg, E. G. 1979. The Inner Experience of the Psychoanalyst. In *Countertransference*, L. Epstein and A. H. Feiner, eds. New York: Jason Aronson.

Yalom, I. 1989. *Love's Executioner*. New York: HarperCollins.

# Copyright Acknowledgments

# INDEX
. . . . . . . . . . . .

# Index

abandonment, 192
  sense of, 108, 155
active imagination, 31, 34–35, 211
  as pathway to healing, 91, 92–93
Adam and Eve, myth of, 174–75, 216
  interpretations of, 18–19, 23
addictive behavior: roots of, 43
Adler, Alfred, 114
  on power as motivating force, 48–49, 82–83, 142
  on psychic compensation, 86
aggression
  Freud's view of, 82–84
  Jung's view of, 83–84
  repression of, 83
*Aion* (Jung)
  anima/animus theory in, 184, 195
  model of self in, 17–18
alchemy, 68–72, 213
  Jung's interest in, 21–22, 65–66, 68–70, 114
alcoholism, treatment of, 45
alienation
  of the ego, 190, 201, 203, 211
  of siblings, 208
analysis
  as healing process, 79–80, 86–88, 92–94, 96, 104, 144
  interactive fields in, 168–71
  limitations of, 54–55
  and repression, 37–39, 57, 80–81, 83, 112, 130
  and a sense of destiny, 96, 100, 104, 108, 111
  silence during, 166–67, 176–77
  termination of, 181
  wholeness as goal of, 55–56, 79–80, 86, 88–91, 94
  *See also* Communication in analysis
analysts, 40, 179
  communication among, 168
  drowsiness of, 165–81 passim
  as objects of envy, 212

psychic infection of, 178–80
  as symbols, 155–56
  traditional versus scientific, 79
*Analytical Psychology: Notes of the Seminar* (Jung), 186
anger: envy as cause of, 211–12
anima/animus structures, 187
  defective, 190–91, 193–94
  gender connection of, 185–87
  Jung's concept of, 184–88, 196, 197–98
  projection of, 194–95, 197–98
  repair of, 194, 198
  unconsciousness of, 196
anima/animus theory, 91, 183–91
  Jung's view of, 184, 187, 189, 195
  in treatment of borderline states, 183–84, 187
  in treatment of narcissism, 183–84, 187
anxiety, 126–27
  abandonment as cause of, 192
  during countertransference, 170–71
  defenses against, 126, 162, 194
  and the ego, 89–90
  envy as source of, 211
  neurotic, 105, 120
  separation as cause of, 127, 129
  in social situations, 192
  transference as cause of, 162–63
*Apocalypse of Peter* (Gnostic text), 74
archetypes, 23, 54, 72–73
  as bases of complexes, 116, 118, 125, 196
  definition of, 44, 50, 107
  Jung's conception of, 23, 50, 54, 81–82, 84, 106–7
  in life-history reconstruction, 106–7, 110–11
  meaning of, 43, 96, 156
  in organizations, 68–73
  of savior-hero, 68, 69
  of scapegoat, 68–69, 73–75
  Self as, 203
  splitting of, 137–38, 144
  *See also* Great Mother archetype